BEING
JAMES BOND

VOLUME ONE • SECOND EDITION

Joseph W. Darlington

Being James Bond: Volume One - Second Edition

Joseph W. Darlington
headofsection@beingjamesbond.com

Darlington, Joseph W.
Being James Bond: Volume One - Second Edition / by Joseph W. Darlington
p. cm.
ISBN: 979-8-9988432-0-4
1. Bond, James (Fictitious character).
I. Darlington, Joseph W.
II. Title

For information contact:
Joseph Darlington
headofsection@beingjamesbond.com

To You

Because you and I already share an instant kinship.
We both see James Bond as more than just a fictional
character, but as an ideal that can, and should,
be realized.

I'm honored to meet you.

Stop dreaming and start doing! **Being James Bond** brings the excitement of the films and books to your real life in a well researched and approachable manner. Each chapter takes one Bond skill and explains how it can become one "you" skill, in such an entertaining fashion, it will be hard to resist "diving" or "flying" right into the subject matter!

Crawford K. McDonald, Statesboro, Georgia

I came across **Being James Bond** at a rough time in my life. I was getting over a bout of depression and searching for a way to improve my life, when a friend recommended it to me. I have always been a casual Bond fan, but listening to Head of Section's podcast, I saw beyond the cinematic thrills and into a world of sophistication, confidence, and skill. Being James Bond gave me the impetus and focus to change my life. Between the great, informative podcasts, and the helpful members on the forum, I've managed to slim down, gain a good sense of self-worth, and a bit of class. Being James Bond is one of the best things I've ever come across.

Nicholas Slayton, Los Angeles, CA

During my senior year, I stumbled onto **Being James Bond**. I quickly signed up for the forum and discovered that there was an entire community of people that shared my goal–to follow Bond's dictum of living life to its fullest. It's almost as if Head of Section gives you a mission in the form of the topic (be it mastering the Vesper martini or visiting Bond locales around the globe), and then the message board is there for support while you carry out that mission and for celebration after you accomplish it. I consider it such a great benefit to be able to surround myself with other people who are all after the same thing; being James Bond. **Being James Bond** works incredibly hard to give its listeners, of any age, all the tools they need to live like Bond.

Colby Smith, Cumberland, Maryland

Being James Bond is a community of men (and even a couple of women) who are working together to improve their lives in line with the motto, WWJBD? (What would James Bond do?) I am very glad it exists. I know that I can always go there and no one will judge me harshly or mock me for my failings in living up to our ideal. Oftentimes when you try to make changes for the better in your life, strangely, people often criticize and discourage you. These people are not real friends. However, on the Being James Bond forums, people are always welcomed with kind words and encouragement. As long as you're attempting to make progress, people will always respond positively. If you've ever watched a Bond film and thought, "I wish I lived more like Bond," you owe it to yourself to listen to the podcasts and frequent the forums.

Tyler Huff, Charleston, South Carolina

In my every day world, I am a husband, father, consultant, and the guy who mows the lawn. On **Being James Bond**, I am a student and ad-venturer, allowed to explore topics like 'High-speed Driving' or 'Drinks & Mixology.' I have taken high performance driving classes and made pitchers of mint juleps for friends. Head of Section has inspired a band of like minded folks to come together and share, not only their love of Bond related culture, but secrets/tips/tricks that make their lives richer. People have written in the forum on how to become more fit and posted success pictures a few months later–all while getting encouragement from friends along the way. It is this community and positive atmo-sphere that keeps me coming back looking forward to see what new topics are being discussed. Head of Section does a great job pulling these topics together. Each serves as a guide book. They are entertain-ing and packed with information, and presented by a normal guy with examples from every day life. If he can learn it and do it, then so can I. That's why I love **Being James Bond**.

Dominic, Summit NJ

What you have done with **Being James Bond** is to take one of history's greatest movie heroes and turn him on his head–making him less about babes, bullets, and bad guys, and much more about being a man who lives life to the fullest. The Bond of **Being James Bond** is not a womanizer or a killer, but rather someone who takes advantage of the finest things in life and enjoys them all. And most importantly, with a little bit of discipline, planning, and goal-setting, his lifestyle is not only accessible and imitable, but completely within our own reach. And perhaps that's the most valuable thing of all about **Being James Bond**: learning just how we really can have an exciting lifestyle that enriches us inside and out.

James Fellrath, Columbus, OH

Being James Bond is the best! Head of Section provides an outstanding opinion on James Bond movies. He's also very knowledgeable on who James Bond is, and who he should be. He knows what he talks about, and explains how to do what James Bond does very well. Head of Section inspired me to take up skiing. I look forward to the book, and I'm sure it will succeed. I am 13 years old, and I suggest any Bond fan, at any age, to listen to this amazing podcast.

'007 Bond,' via iTunes

Wow! I love **Being James Bond**. I've been a James Bond fan since I was eight, since my parents gave me a set of movies for my birthday. I thought they were awesome, and that I wanted to be a spy myself (until my parents explained what a real spy actually did, and the risks.) When I found this podcast, I was like, 'Yes finally!' I've learned many new things like about planes, bungee jumping, and some tips about Texas Hold'em. I also enjoyed the Drinks & Mixology episode, and while I'm too young yo drink, I will definitely try a Vesper when I'm old enough. Keep up the good work.

'Mr. Arlington Beech,' via iTunes

BEING
JAMES BOND

VOLUME ONE · SECOND EDITION

Joseph W. Darlington

Preface to
the Second Edition

"So when are we going to see Volume Two?"

I don't think any one question has ever delivered such a triumphant feeling of joy and accomplishment, while simultaneously stirring up a sense of dread. I owed a book.

It's hard to believe that *'Being James Bond: Volume One'* is already 15 years old. Looking back, that book was truly a labor of love — self-published in 2010, written by a younger, wide-eyed version of myself; an eager young man, driven by ambition and a deep passion for the world of James Bond, and hoping to contribute something meaningful to the conversation. I wanted to connect with fellow fans, but it went beyond that; I wanted to be part of the inner circle – the thinkers, the scholars, the respected writers and commentators who shaped the dialogue around James Bond. I wanted to be a sage; someone who could offer insight, perspective, and maybe even inspire others the way he had once been inspired.

So, after about four years of researching and podcasting on various Bond-related topics, *'Being James Bond: Volume One'* was born.

I can still recall grabbing my then-girlfriend and whisking her off to the local bistro to order cocktails and tear away the cardboard to reveal the very first printed copy of *'Being James Bond: Volume One'*. I mean let's face it – if this doesn't impress a girl, nothing will!

That moment was a true turning point in multiple ways. Not only was I on my way to becoming a full-blown 'influencer' in the world of James Bond, but simultaneously, the vast majority of my time became all about relationship, marriage, step-daughter, and grandchildren. That single guy who recorded podcasts in his spare time from the confines of a pretty damn cool bachelor's apartment one-floor above the local watering hole was long gone. Time always seemed to get away from me, consumed by the domestic developments of the day to day.

But even with all that going on, I did manage to keep on writing whenever I could; slowly chiseling away at what would eventually become *'Being James Bond: Volume Two.'* While it seemed to drag on forever, it eventually came together. What's the adage about a roomful of monkeys with typewriters and a significant length of time?

So, after many years of tapping away on the keyboard, I eventually found myself with a new book. But, what did the final product look like? A few things I noticed:

The final word-count was significantly larger than *'Volume One.'* I wasn't using my humble, time-sensitive podcasts as my source material. I was expanding on new ideas, exploring different concepts, and frankly, taking a little more delight in just wandering down interesting roads. At over 87,000 words, *'Volume Two'* was potentially looking to be well over 300 pages. This wasn't going to be another "pocket edition."

This realization also brought on a moment of self-reflection. I had to take a hard look back on *'Volume One.'* There were three basic takeaways:

First, I still stand by *'Being James Bond: Volume One'* as a fine piece of work by a fledgling, wannabe author, writing in his spare time, and without assistance from traditional publishers or editors; however, if I'm being honest with myself, I could have done better. *(The fact that one instance of "Piz Gloria" was spelled "Piz Gloris" has dogged me for years!)* I wanted to give the book a little more polish.

Additionally, there have also been three new James Bond films in the years since. So, both *'Volume Two'* and the second edition of *'Volume One'* would now have to reflect and incorporate Bond's movements and activities in *Skyfall, Spectre,* and *No Time to Die.* Not to mention, my experience or access to certain places or things isn't what it was fifteen years ago. *(My last trip to Switzerland alone warranted a massive expansion of the 'Skiing' chapter.)*

Lastly, I just wanted to set the stage a little better. For some of the chapters in *'Volume One,'* I was able to use excerpts from the original Ian Fleming novels to establish a backdrop and build some excitement for the material to come. For example, I used a thrilling passage of Bond escaping Piz Gloria in *'On Her Majesty's Secret Service'* for my chapter on Skiing. Other chapters didn't have that same luxury.

With that in mind, I tried my hand at fan-fiction – or more accurately, at writing 'novelization.' So if a chapter doesn't already open with a quote from Fleming, it may now open with a fictional account from one of the films where Bond is engaging in the activity covered in the chapter. I have to say, I thoroughly enjoyed this undertaking, and I hope you enjoy my humble attempts at writing fiction.

All in all, the expanded chapters really pushed the boundaries of what the original edition had set out to do. What began as a 60,000 word project has now grown to over 77,000 words, and the page count has climbed from 216 to approximately 260. It's still the same core mission – but with more depth, more insight, and a lot more of what we've come to understand James Bond to be.

This new edition has been a joy to revisit and expand. I hope it speaks to you, inspires you, and brings a bit of Bond-like confidence to your own adventures. Enjoy the journey.

And yes, 'Being James Bond, Volume Two' is just around the corner.

Joseph W. Darlington

FOREWARD

Welcome aboard! If this is your first introduction to **Being James Bond**, I am pleased to meet you.

If you've come this far, then you and I already share a few common 'bonds,' and being fans of 007 is just the beginning. More significantly, you and I have dreams of living a little more like Bond. And even more accurately, we have plans to live more like James Bond.

Here's what you should know before you dive in: The following is a series of how-to essays on seven areas in which James Bond shows expertise, confidence, and ability.

In this volume of **Being James Bond**, we zero in on some pretty powerful subjects that highlight the essential qualities of James Bond. I hope you will enjoy the following chapters on *Poker, Skiing, Drinks & Mixology, Flying an Airplane, Traveling to London, Bungee Jumping,* and *Horseback Riding.* You can read this book from beginning to end, or you can jump to the topic that interests you, but don't miss the *Conclusion.*

Also, as this is the second edition of '**Being James Bond: Volume One**,' it now includes nods to the three most recent James Bond films: *Skyfall, Spectre,* and *No Time To Die.* This edition includes significant reworks, additions, and expansions to several chapters.

I hope you will enjoy learning and exploring these topics as much as I have enjoyed exploring and putting them together for you.

Good luck, 007!

TABLE OF CONTENTS

Drinks & Mixology 99

TRAVEL

London ....

EXTREME 007

Bungee Jumping **213**

INTRODUCTION

Being James Bond

In 2004, I was sent on a business trip to Geneva, Switzerland.

I had done my share of traveling, but I'd never been to Switzerland, and knowing James Bond had been there many times, I was pretty excited. I'd also heard that the famous bungee jump stunt from *GoldenEye* was done somewhere in Switzerland, and if there was anything sitting high on my bucket list, that was it. So naturally, I started looking into it.

I confirmed that the *GoldenEye* bungee jump was, in fact, performed in Switzerland – and better yet, it was open to the public. According to the website, the famous dam was located in the southern part of the country, near the city of Locarno. This was back in the pre-GPS era, so I had to rely on MapQuest Europe, which told me the drive would take just over four hours. With that in mind, I put together a plan: I was scheduled to land in Geneva on Saturday morning, but I didn't have to be at work until Sunday, which gave me an entire day to myself. After another quick scan of MapQuest, I decided I'd land, rent a car at the airport, drive four hours to the dam, do the jump, and head back to my hotel with plenty of time to return the car and get a good night's sleep before work.

When the day finally arrived, I was feeling unstoppable. I rented the car and set off without a hitch. As the journey began, the views were exactly what you'd imagine James Bond was seeing as he left Geneva in the Aston Martin DB5, tailing Goldfinger's Rolls-Royce through the stunning Swiss countryside. Not a bad start to the trip.

A few hours in, though, I started to realize that my plan might have been a little... short-sighted.

One minor detail that MapQuest failed to mention – or maybe I just overlooked – is that driving across Switzerland means crossing over the Swiss Alps. The rolling green hills I had been admiring gradually turned into towering, snow-capped peaks. Before long, I was navigating a compact rental car through blustery alpine weather, wearing nothing but jeans and a short-sleeved shirt, inching along narrow roads with snow-covered cliffs just a few feet away.

Meanwhile, it had never occurred to me to tell any of my co-workers what I was up to. So here I was, driving along the rim of a snow-covered cliff, knowing that if I went over the edge and vanished, no one would even know where to start looking for me.

I came to Switzerland looking for an adventure, but now I'm thinking to myself, *"be careful what you wish for because you just might get it."*

MapQuest also failed to mention that I'd be passing through parts of Italy as I crossed Switzerland. Before the trip, I had studied just enough French to order a cup of coffee, but Italian was a different story entirely. No one at the Italian checkpoint spoke English, and when they asked where I was going, I had no real way of explaining – partly because of the language barrier, and partly because I wasn't entirely sure myself.

As my journey continued, this four-hour drive dragged on for much longer than I had expected, and I never had a handle on just how long the drive would end up being. I kept on trekking around long stretches of winding roads without any street signs. Each time I circled around another magnificent mountain, I envisioned the dam just around the other side, but endured a lot of disappointments. I pressed on and kept hoping for the best.

Seven-and-a-half hours after leaving the airport, I finally found civilization again, and eventually reached the dam.

The dam itself was every bit as awe-inspiring as you might imagine. Standing 220 meters high (around 770 feet) it was roughly the height of a New York City skyscraper. It wasn't hard to believe that this was the site of a world-record-breaking stunt; the highest stationary bungee jump ever performed. Even the big screen can barely do it justice.

I parked the car, stretched my legs, and made my way out toward the center of the dam, where the bungee company was supposed to be set up. But as I got closer, it became clear that my wildly off-schedule arrival had caught up with me; everything was closed, and the dam was completely deserted. The bungee crew had packed up and gone home.

On the bright side, the bungee crew had packed up and gone home. And honestly? That may have been for the best. Let's face it – I'd just been spared the very real possibility of backing out. My nerves were shot. After nearly eight hours of white-knuckle driving through the Alps, I was in no condition to jump off anything.

Still, I was pretty thrilled to be retracing Bond's footsteps as I walked out onto the dam. That was, until I looked out over the edge – my heart skipped a beat and I instantly felt a wave of pins and needles shooting through my feet. Yeah, this might be more of a challenge than I had originally thought. With that sobering realization in mind, I began the long trek back to Geneva.

Not long into the drive back, I realized I should probably stop and buy a map – especially before it got dark. While looking for a place to park, I turned down an incredibly narrow alley that seemed to shrink tighter and tighter with every foot I crept forward. With only inches to spare on either side, I decided the best move was to keep going and squeeze through to the other end… only to discover there was no other end.

Sure enough, as I tried to back out, I heard a loud crunch – and promptly tore the side mirror off the driver's side of the car.

And no, I never did find a map.

With the mirror now dangling pitifully off the side of the car, I continued my drive back over the Alps and toward Geneva, hoping for the best.

When I finally made it back to the airport, I went to return the rental car– only to discover the agency was closed. That's when it hit me: I had no idea how to get to my hotel. And, since I couldn't drop off the car, taking a taxi wasn't an option. I was exhausted and running out of ideas.

So, I wandered out to the taxi stand and approached one of the drivers. I showed him the address to my hotel and asked if he knew where it was. He nodded and said yes. I asked how much it would cost to take me there. Without hesitation, he replied, *"Thirty francs."*

I handed the driver 50 Swiss francs and said, *"I'll follow you. Don't lose me!"*

The whole fiasco finally wrapped up the next morning when I returned the rental car, followed by a few co-workers who'd kindly offered me a lift to the nearby air show. Still mentally wiped from the previous day's misadventure – and not wanting to hold anyone up – I parked the car and tried to conceal the evidence by carefully wedging the side mirror back into place. I dropped the keys into the return slot and quietly slipped into the other car, hoping for a clean getaway.

I was almost in the clear when I heard a loud crash, followed by some pretty clear French profanity. The rental attendant had opened the door, and the mirror had come crashing down in spectacular fashion. Too tired and fed-up to be properly embarrassed, I just yelled back, *"Yeah, had a little trouble with the mirror! Sorry!"* and I tried to hurry the group along.

Thankfully, one of my French-speaking colleagues had the presence of mind to walk with me to the rental office and smooth things over. Let's just say – I was very glad I sprung for the extra insurance.

When I arrived at the air show, one of my European colleagues summed up the logic of my little adventure perfectly; landing in Geneva and driving to Locarno just because you happen to be in Switzerland is like landing in New York City and deciding to drive four hours to Cape Cod for lunch – just because you happen to be in the U.S. And that was if everything had gone according to plan.

Needless to say, I would need to plan better next time if I actually hoped to scratch this one from my bucket list.

Bond, the Grown-up?

I was one of those kids who hated going to bed–always convinced that if I closed my eyes, something amazing would happen and I'd miss it. These days, they call that "FOMO," but back then, it was just me sneaking out of bed to peek around the corner and see what the grown-ups were up to.

Truth be told, I don't think I ever really outgrew it. Call it immaturity if you want, but even now, I have a hard time going to bed at a decent hour – still holding onto that feeling that something interesting might be happening, and I won't be there to catch it.

As a child, my heroes were usually comic book legends, like Superman. Come on, don't tell me you never tied a towel around your neck and ran around the living room with your arms outstretched, imagining you were soaring through the sky, cape flapping heroically behind you.

I was nine years old when the original *Superman* with Christopher Reeve hit theaters in 1979, and I was completely hooked. Watching the Man of Steel rocket across the sky, with that soaring John Williams score blasting in the background, never failed to get my heart racing.

I was approaching adolescence when I discovered my first James Bond film in the summer of 1982. I was spending most of my summer break stuck indoors when *For Your Eyes Only* premiered on cable for the first time. After catching just a few scenes, I knew right away I'd stumbled onto something a little different from what I was used to. James Bond was the embodiment of the cool, confident action hero – but he definitely wasn't the kind of guy who wore a cape.

The plot of the film was way too complicated for me to figure out. It had something to do with spies and politics and a bunch of countries scrambling to recover a device that looked suspiciously like a giant calculator. Honestly, how important could this thing really be? Whatever the actual significance of this MacGuffin; all I knew was that as long as the guys with the funny accents got to it before the guys with the funnier accents, everything would work out fine.

But in the mind of a 12-year-old, the fact that the plot was hard to follow was actually a good thing – it felt like proof that I had found something meant for adults. And there's nothing more appealing to an adolescent boy than getting a sneak peek into the world of adults.

It was the very fact that this was a grown-up movie that gave the film a little extra weight with me. That alone made it feel important; like I was being let in on something sophisticated. Sure, there were ski chases and rock climbing stunts and helicopters, but there was also a different kind of thrill – James Bond knew how to charm the women. And somewhere in the middle all of that, I started to get the idea that maybe being an adult could be pretty damn fun.

Maybe I had just discovered why I never really wanted to go to sleep at night?

The next summer, *Octopussy* hit theaters. It would be my second experience with a James Bond film – and the first I'd ever seen on the big screen. Unsurprisingly, I walked out of the theater with no real understanding of what I'd just watched. There was priceless art, a circus train, and a nuclear bomb, all crammed into one movie. But it didn't matter. Even with other big blockbusters out that summer, I knew there was something undeniably cool about saying, *"I just saw the new James Bond film."* It sounded more sophisticated than saying, *"I just saw Superman III."*

The following summer is when my Bond fascination really took hold. Back in the day, when a movie hit pay TV channels – the '80s equivalent of streaming services – you could count on it to air almost daily. And every time *Octopussy* came on, I dropped the remote. To this day, I still think it's one of the most underrated James Bond films out there.

Once again, I couldn't shake the feeling that there was something refined and cosmopolitan about this character and his world. James Bond dressed well, ate well, drank well, stayed in the finest hotels – and he had no problem attracting beautiful women. Obviously, he knew something I didn't.

Also, my father only helped validate the idea that James Bond was meant for grown-ups, because he was a fan too. When he saw me getting caught up in the 007 movies, he told me he'd read all the original Ian Fleming novels when he was younger. He even said he once owned the *Goldfinger* soundtrack album–the one with the nude Golden Girl sprawled across the cover – until my very-Catholic grandmother took one look at it, called it "pornography," and promptly tossed it in the trash. He also kept going on about some guy named Sean Connery.

"When I became a man, I put away childish things"

As the years went by, other childhood fascinations quietly faded into the background, pushed aside by the responsibilities of adult life. But the James Bond obsession never really went away. It remained one of those rare guilty pleasures you really didn't have to feel guilty about. Even with time and maturity, I still found myself drawn to that feeling of wide-eyed curiosity, still fascinated by the possibilities the future held.

By the time I reached my late twenties, I had seen all the James Bond films and read most of the Ian Fleming novels – along with many of the continuation books written by other authors. When the Internet really started to take off, I found myself diving into message boards, chatting with other Bond fans, and bookmarking every 007-related website I could find. I devoured every article, every update, every rumor.

One day, while browsing *ianfleming.org* – the official website of the Ian Fleming Foundation – I came across something that stopped me in my tracks. At that time, the site functioned as an online magazine called *Mr. Kiss Kiss Bang Bang,* and it was absolutely masterful. This was the go-to hub for all things James Bond. Back then, the fan community was buzzing with excitement over rumors about the upcoming Bond 20, the release of the Special Edition DVD box set, Raymond Benson's latest Bond novel, and the newest 007 video game. It was truly a golden time to be a Bond fan.

On that particular day, one article in particular spoke to me. It was written by David Morefield and titled *"Orchids and Butterflies: James Bond as a Mr. Know-it-all."* Morefield wrote:

"Obviously something happened between 1964 and 1977 to transform James Bond from a well-dressed killer, with little understanding of electrical and atomic engineering, into a cross between Thomas Edison and Robert Oppenheimer."

The article continued to say: *"By the mid-eighties, he demonstrated an encyclopedic knowledge on subjects ranging from deep-sea diving gear and electromagnetic pulses, to butterfly collecting and even the history of rare orchids."*

The article continued to explore how Bond had evolved over the years into a kind of charming, unstoppable savant; a man who seemed to know everything about everything. That idea absolutely fascinated me and it struck at the very heart of what made James Bond so captivating to me: he wasn't just cool or courageous – he was competent. Exceptionally, endlessly competent.

At the end of the article Morefield asked, *"Did I miss any examples of Bond's genius?"*

So I decided to write in, and I was absolutely thrilled when my letter was published on their website. I wrote, *"Missed examples of Bond genius? Yeah, you missed plenty. But, who could blame you! With each film, Bond's vast knowledge grows more and more expansive. Let's face it; he can beat anyone at their own game, no matter what that game is. He is an expert at most social sports, and lately, even extreme sports. And as we all know, he is an expert on every possible aspect of the good life. You name it, whether it is perfume, caviar, wine, brandy, whatever; Bond knows the year, the region, and even the century if need be, and he is never, ever wrong."*

The Actual Reality of Being a 'Grown-up'

As I approached my thirtieth birthday, my James Bond fascination had reached a fever pitch – and was beginning to evolve. I found myself trying to emulate certain aspects of Bond's lifestyle. If I needed to shop for a new suit, I'd pop *GoldenEye* into the DVD player and pick something that matched what Bond was wearing. It wasn't just about looking sharp – it was about channeling that cool confidence.

Around this time, I came across an audiobook by Paul Kyriazi called *"How to Live the James Bond Lifestyle."* Honestly, all I needed to hear was the title and I knew I had to have it. I bought the tape, listened to it, and to this day, I still revisit it. At last, I'd found someone who saw James Bond as more than just a fun, fictional action hero; he saw Bond as an ideal.

Paul Kyriazi is the Frank Sinatra of the Bond lifestyle; a true gentleman with old-school class and effortless style. And like Sinatra, he's generous with his time, his energy, and his wisdom. If I had to sum up Paul's philosophy in three words, they would be: organization, inspiration, and determination. According to Paul, these are the traits that can help you move closer to the life Bond leads; not in fantasy, but in reality.

After listening to his tape, I reached out to Paul Kyriazi to let him know how much I appreciated his approach. I told him his ideas were terrific and that he'd inspired me to try a few of them in my own life.

At the same time, my James Bond obsession was well in place, and I was starting to feel a bit restless in my work life. This was during the dotcom boom, when the Internet was exploding and new companies seemed to appear overnight. With a background in web design, my phone wouldn't stop ringing. No exaggeration – potential employers were leaving multiple messages a day, and job offers were coming in fast and furious.

Fueled by a renewed sense of ambition – and that restless itch that tends to come with turning thirty – I decided to leave a comfortable job with a solid company and accept a high-paying position with a larger corporation headquartered in the World Trade Center in New York City. The job description was vague at best, but at the salary they were offering, it felt too good to pass up. It felt like the beginning of something big – a bold new chapter in the heart of the city that never sleeps. Naturally, I sent an email to Paul Kyriazi to let him know about the success I was having. This was in late 2000.

Long story short, I breezed through the application form, and I very conveniently left out the fact that – despite nearly six years of college – I had joined the workforce just a few credits shy of graduating. One routine background check later and I was let go. Two bad decisions had come back to bite me: not finishing my degree, and not being honest about it.

Needless to say, I would soon be very glad that I had been let go.

I hesitate to even reference the horrific terror attacks on the Twin Towers in this humble chapter about self-reflection and self-improvement, but it bears mentioning for one important reason. Shortly after the attacks, one of the first people to reach out to me was Paul Kyriazi. His email was simple: *"Please tell me you're okay."*

I was stunned. I wasn't even sure he would remember our brief communications – but here he was checking in on me. He proved what I had already suspected: beneath the tuxedo-and-martini lifestyle philosophy, was a kind, decent human being, and a genuine friend.

Paul Kyriazi has since passed on, and with his loss, I felt as though I'd lost both a mentor and a friend. Over the years, I had the good fortune to interview Paul several times on my podcast, and his wisdom continues to stay with me. Even now, though I've essentially memorized his original audiobook, I still listen to it when I need a little boost or reminder of the mindset he championed.

As I once told him personally, his audiobook became the nucleus for much of my learning and growth. Paul was truly the Sinatra of the James Bond Lifestyle generation – a man of style, class, and substance – and he remains both a pioneer and a legend among Bond lifestylers.

His influence endures, not just in the techniques he taught, but in how he confirmed what you already suspected – that becoming your best self wasn't just possible; it was essential.

The economy would take years to recover – and so would I. Talk about going from feast to famine overnight. I spent the next two years scrambling for any work I could find, bouncing between freelance gigs and short-term jobs. In one instance, I was laid off just five weeks after being hired.

In short, I felt like I'd hit rock bottom. The only job I could hold onto was tending bar in a sketchy neighborhood. From a swanky office in the Twin Towers to pouring beers and breaking up bar fights – my life had flipped upside down in just over a year. It was time to take a hard look in the mirror and figure out what came next.

The Bad Times

Motivational speakers love to ask, *"What would you do if you knew you could not fail?"* But as I stood there, looking at myself in the mirror, the question that echoed in my head was very different: *"What are you going to do now that you have failed?"* I began to wrestle with – and eventually accept – the worst-case scenario. What if I never got another job? What if my biggest fears had already come true? What if I never again worked in my chosen field? What would I do then?

It is true what they say; it's only when you've lost everything that you become truly invincible.

For the first time in my life, I felt kinda fearless. I had nothing left to lose. And with that strange sense of freedom, life began to take on new meaning and shift in a slightly different direction. I started asking myself some tough questions: If I had to start all over again, what would I do?

If I couldn't go back to the work I did before, what path would I choose now? And if I couldn't be the same person I was… who would I become?

And that's when **Being James Bond** was born.

The Birth of 'Being James Bond'

After years of being fascinated by Bond as a man who could seemingly do anything, this project became the natural evolution of that idea. While I didn't yet know exactly what form this cross-platform concept would take, I knew I wanted it to focus on real knowledge and real skills. The goal was to give readers and listeners the tools they needed to step into Bond's world–not just to watch it, but to live it.

"It was on the tip of everyone's tongue. We just gave it a name."

The motto is simple: *"if James Bond can do it, we can do it."* Whether it's learning a new sport like golf or skiing, buying a bottle of wine, trying an extreme sport, traveling to an unfamiliar destination, or walking confidently into a casino, **Being James Bond** aims to provide the kind of insight and guidance that turns curiosity into confidence. By the time we're done, you won't feel like a novice – you'll be ready to relax, enjoy yourself, and fully embrace the experience. You'll be surprised how quickly a little guidance can turn the unfamiliar into second nature.

The Appeal of Podcasting

When I first began reflecting on **Being James Bond**, I made a long list of all the potential topics I could cover – after all, Bond seems to know just about everything about everything. The challenge was figuring out the right format. I initially envisioned a book, but if I wanted to dive into Bond's knowledge with any real depth, it would have made for a very hefty volume. I tried to think about ways to start small; offering bite-sized pieces of information that could be explored one at a time. At one point, I even toyed with the idea of launching a newsletter.

Around that same time, I was becoming fascinated with a new medium called podcasting. I'd always loved audiobooks, so discovering podcasts felt like a natural progression. Not too long after, a good friend invited me to contribute a review of the newly released *From Russia with Love* video game for a gaming podcast he was hosting. I jumped at the chance.

I used that opportunity to create my very first podcast episode. I recorded it, edited it, added music, and had an absolute blast putting it all together. Once it was done, I realized I was hooked. And just like that, I knew that a podcast would be the perfect vehicle for **Being James Bond**. Looking back, it was one of the best creative decisions I ever made.

Podcasting gave me the ability to share ideas and connect with others who shared my passion. It became a way to "write" essays out loud; and more importantly, to build a community. In the beginning, doing a podcast feels like writing a letter, putting it in a bottle, and tossing it out into sea, wondering if anyone will ever read your message. But before long, I had regular, loyal listeners who encouraged me to keep going, sent feedback on every episode, and helped shape the direction of the show. If you're a struggling young writer looking for a new way to share your voice – I can't recommend podcasting enough.

Podcasting is refreshingly easy in one sense: anyone with a computer and a microphone can get started. But, making a good podcast? That's a different story, and that's where it starts to get complicated. Personally, I don't consider myself to be a particularly polished speaker, and I often need time to collect my thoughts while recording. The downside of that is the editing – it can be incredibly time-consuming, but it's priceless to be able to trim out the "umms," pauses, and stumbles. The experience has given me a great respect for real broadcasters.

Of course, the best part of podcasting is the connection you form with your listeners. The shared subject matter brings podcaster and audience together, and from that, a natural kinship forms. Conversations turn into great exchanges, and sometimes into long-lasting friendships. I've been incredibly fortunate to meet like-minded individuals who share my passion for using James Bond not just as entertainment, but as inspiration for self-improvement and living life to the fullest. Honestly, most of my closest friends today are people I've met through James Bond.

Mission Briefing:

So let's get into it–what exactly are we going to explore? When you break down **Being James Bond** into smaller sub-sections, the categories fall neatly into place: The Good Life, Bond the Sportsman, Extreme 007, Man of Action, Travel, Gambling, and Rest & Recreation. Let's take a look at each one, starting with a favorite:

THE GOOD LIFE

"There are moments of great luxury in the life of a secret agent." What is The Good Life? I'd say that getting a massage at the Fontainebleau Hotel in Miami Beach – just like James Bond did in *Goldfinger* – is a perfect example. This section is all about the finer things; the tastes, the style, and the effortless class that Bond brings to every room he walks into.

We'll kick things off with **Drinks & Mixology**. We'll dive into the world of cocktails – exploring various types of liquor and spirits, basic bartending techniques, and the equipment and glassware that you should have on hand, so you'll be knowledgeable and prepared to craft a proper cocktail.

BOND THE SPORTSMAN

If you plan to live like James Bond, there are certain activities you'll want to master – sports and pastimes that James Bond seems to pursue with ease and elegance. In this edition, we'll explore one of Bond's most iconic pursuits: **Skiing**.

We'll cover everything from what to expect on your first trip to the slopes, to how to prepare with the right exercises, clothing, and equipment. You'll learn how to navigate a ski resort and pick up some basic skiing techniques. And of course, we'll take a detour to one of the most legendary Bond locations: Piz Gloria, perched high in the Bernese Alps above the village of Mürren, Switzerland. This unforgettable setting of *On Her Majesty's Secret Service* is a must-visit for any Bond fan with or without a taste for the slopes.

EXTREME 007

Over the last few decades, James Bond has taken his action credentials to the next level – diving headfirst into the world of extreme sports. In this section, we call on the thrill-seeking side of James Bond: welcome to the world of **Bungee Jumping**.

As you've already seen in the introduction, we'll be heading to the Verzasca Dam near Locarno, Switzerland – the unforgettable site of the record breaking bungee jump from *GoldenEye*. We'll explore what to expect from your first jump, how to prepare for it, and where to find some of the best bungee locations in the world.

MAN OF ACTION

Show James Bond any piece of machinery with a steering wheel, and he can operate it. From cars and boats to tanks and planes, Bond is always in control. In this first edition of Man of Action, we're going to start off strong – **Flying an Airplane**. We'll walk you through the basics: from taxiing and takeoff, to straight and level flight, to smooth landings. And for those ready to take the leap, we'll show you how to pursue and obtain your recreational or private pilot's license, and show you what it really takes to earn your wings.

TRAVEL

In my opinion, the most Bond-like thing anyone can do is travel. Nothing captures the spirit of adventure quite like walking in Bond's footsteps and embarking on adventures abroad. In this section, we'll explore the thrilling destinations and focus on classic Bond locations; from the most iconic, to the hidden gems off the beaten path.

We'll kick things off in the same place that Bond's begins his missions; **London**. From red buses to vintage black cabs, London is still bursting with old-world charm and modern flair. We'll guide you through key landmarks, recommend spots for drinks and dinner, and help you experience the city with just the right James Bond touch.

GAMBLING

Join us at the Salon Privé of Royale-les-Eaux, where the stakes are high and the tuxedos and the cocktails are impeccable. In this section, we'll explore the world of gambling – from cozy card tables at resort casinos to the legendary halls of Las Vegas and Monte Carlo.

To begin, we'll focus on **Texas Hold'em Poker** – a modern classic. We'll cover the basics of Poker, and the rules and gameplay of Texas Hold'em, the principles of dealing and betting, then we'll watch a typical hand of poker and discuss the essential strategies that go along with it, and of course, bluffing and tells, and a little poker etiquette.

Even secret agents need time to unwind. After your mission, it's time for some well-earned Rest & Recreation. In this edition, we'll grab the reins – figuratively and literally – and leap into the world of **Horseback Riding**.

We'll cover everything from proper attire and gear, to how to mount, dismount, and control your horse at a walk, trot, canter, and gallop. You'll also learn about different riding styles, basic tack and supplies, and how to find the right riding instructor. Whether you're exploring scenic trails or channeling your inner 007 in a steeplechase, this is your guide to riding with confidence and class.

Redemption

One year after my first trip to Switzerland, I was sent there again – and this time, I was determined to plan things out a little better. I researched the location of the dam, mapped out nearby areas, and made arrangements for a long weekend. I recruited a friend and we made plans to spend a few days in Lake Como, Italy. I wish I could say I chose this beautiful Italian town because my intuition told me it would become a prominent setting in *Casino Royale* only a year later – but in reality, it was simply an hour from the Verzasca Dam.

Rather than attempt that fateful drive through the Alps again, we took a train from Geneva to Milan. From there, we rented a car and drove up to Lake Como. The hotel was absolutely stunning, and my room overlooked the magnificent lake – peaceful, vast, and impossibly still.

On the morning of the jump, I woke up, had a solid breakfast, and set out toward the dam. It took just over an hour to cross the border into Switzerland (though in my memory, it felt like a short twenty-minute drive). No more pins and needles this time. During my time in Switzerland, I'd spent each night meditating and visualizing the jump – imagining the feeling of success, breathing into the fear, getting myself back into that fearless frame of mind. *(Thanks again, Paul Kyriazi.)*

When we arrived at the dam, I took in the view, psyched myself up, and walked over to the registration desk. After a short training session, it was time. With my instructor behind me, I climbed up onto the platform. I stepped to the edge, held my chin high, stared straight ahead, and didn't look down. Then, I felt a tap on my shoulder. That was the signal.

I took a deep breath, smiled wide – and jumped.

For about seven unforgettable seconds, I plummeted straight down. My eyes watered as the wind rushed past and I forced them to stay open – I was determined not to miss a second of the experience. My smile only grew as I taunted certain death, defying anything that once held me back.

Just as I hit maximum velocity, I caught a glimpse of the dam wall in my periphery. In that moment, a scene from my childhood flashed into my mind – The Man of Steel soaring upward along the face of the Hoover Dam, racing to save Jimmy Olsen. I could almost feel the cape behind me, as I stretched my arms forward, and for one fleeting moment, I believed I was flying – powered by nothing but sheer will and the pounding of the John Williams score in my head.

For a few moments, I was absolutely invincible. I wanted that feeling to last forever. But then, the cord caught, the slack tightened, and I began to slow down – and as I bounced back up, I started to laugh. Without a doubt, this was the most incredible sensation I'd ever felt – and it was worth every bit of the fear, planning, and preparation it took to get there. I'd do it again in a heartbeat.

Afterward, I did exactly what James Bond would do. I found a quiet outdoor café overlooking Lake Maggiore, ordered a gin and tonic, and took a long, satisfying sip. I sat back, breathing in the serenity of the lake, wearing a quiet, contented grin as I thought about everything that had led me to this moment.

It hadn't been that long ago that I felt like I'd hit rock bottom – convinced things couldn't possibly get worse. But now? That felt like a lifetime ago. Today, I was in another part of the world, and for seven glorious seconds, I felt like a god. The weight was gone. I had done something that few people ever do, and it happened because I followed a different path; followed in James Bond's footsteps.

That's when it hit me – I had come full circle. What began as a child's fascination with adulthood had now allowed the adult to feel like a child again. No burdens. No worries. Just wonder, excitement, and the thrill of conquering the moment. These are the things that make life worth living. (And for the record, I did go back and finish my degree.)

I smiled at the new realization that these are the moments when I'm truly living like James Bond. And I kept on smiling because I also knew...

This was just the beginning of **Being James Bond**.

Texas Hold'em Poker

"The scent and smoke and sweat of a casino are nauseating at three in the morning. Then the soul-erosion produced by high gambling – a compost of greed and fear and nervous tension – becomes unbearable and the senses awake and revolt from it."

– Chapter One, Casino Royale, 1953

But of course, in the novel, the game is baccarat.

When the film version of *Casino Royale* was finally headed to the big screen, I had mixed feelings when I heard they were changing the game from baccarat to poker. Since the early '70s, the James Bond movies have had a tendency to follow the trends rather than set them. Knowing that Texas Hold'em poker had become a sensation in the last few years, I worried that this was simply a continuation of that same pattern.

On the other hand, perhaps the switch to poker was a brilliant move. Unlike many card games, Texas Hold'em is a game of risk that forces players to rely on skill, strategy, and even patience, rather than mere blind luck, making this the perfect game for the modern version of a classic James Bond thriller.

In this chapter of **Being James Bond**, we'll explore the game of Texas Hold'em Poker. We'll start with the basics, covering the elements common to all variations of poker, then focus on the specific rules and gameplay of Texas Hold'em. From there, we'll dive into strategies, the art of bluffing and reading tells, and finish with a bit of poker etiquette.

So pull up a chair. Let's shuffle the cards and begin.

The Basics of Poker

Long before James Bond tackled the game of poker, it was almost impossible to miss at least one of the many TV shows or movies highlighting the game of poker. Maybe you've flipped past the World Series of Poker, or caught one of many films over the years that had a poker game in it somewhere. Maybe it was a scene featuring gangsters with thick accents, chomping fat cigars in smoke-filled rooms, invariably sitting under dim lights with cards gripped in their hands and greed filling their eyes as they stare at enormous piles of chips in the center of the table.

Even if you don't understand how the game is played, you can at least understand the scene. When a player wins, he greedily gathers up that pile of chips. That's the object of the game; get those chips! If you win the hand you win the chips, and if you win the chips you win the cash.

The Object of the Game

So if the object of the game is to win the chips, then how exactly do you accomplish that? Essentially there are two ways to win a hand of poker: have the best poker hand of every player, or the other players have folded their hands, leaving you as the last player standing.

So what are the "best hands," and what does it mean to "fold?" First thing's first.

Breaking down a hand of poker to its bare essence would look like this: Two players. They shuffle a deck of cards, and then deal out five cards for each of them. Of those five cards, each hopes to create a combination of cards, known as a 'hand,' that will outrank the hand of the other player.

So what constitutes a good poker hand?

What is a "**hand**?" This word has more than one meaning. When we talk about "a hand of poker," we're basically talking about one round of cards, from the time the cards are dealt and until there is a winner, and the cards are reshuffled. One game of poker will have many hands of cards. When we refer to "your poker hand," we're talking about the combination of cards you hold in your hand. You want to get a good poker hand. So what are the good hands? Starting from the lowest and working up to the best hands, goes like this:

Poker Hand Rankings

High card: The card with the highest rank (numerical value, 2 through Ace) in the hand wins. If neither of us has even a pair of anything, if my highest card is a Jack, and your highest card is a Queen, you win. If there are no other combinations, the highest card wins the hand.

One pair: A pair is two cards of the same rank (or numerical value). If you hold a **3♠**, **6♣**, **8♦**, **8♣**, **10♥**, then you hold a pair of 8s.

Two pair: Two cards of the same rank, plus two cards of another rank. If you have **3♣**, **3♦**, **5♠**, **5♥**, **7♣**, you have two pairs, 3s and 5s.

Three of a kind: Also called trips, this hand contains three cards of the same rank. If you have **7♠, J♦, J♥, J♣, K♦,** you have three Jacks, or "trip Jacks."

Straight: A straight is a poker hand that contains five cards of sequential rank. Five cards in numerical succession, such as **2♥, 3♣, 4♠, 5♦, 6♠,** or **10♣, J♥, Q♣, K♦, A♠** make a straight.

Flush: This is a poker hand that contains five cards of the same suit, in any sequence. (The four **suits** being **hearts ♥, diamonds ♦, clubs ♣,** and **spades ♠.**) So, if you have **3♣, 6♣, 7♣, 9♣, Q♣** and they're all clubs, that's a flush.

Full house: A full house, or a "full boat," is a hand that's made up of three of a kind and two of a kind. So **5♣, 5♥, 5♠, 2♣, 2♦** is a full house. If you have a hand of **A♠, A♦, A♣, J♦, J♥,** you are said to have "aces full of jacks," or simply, "aces full." The suits are irrelevant.

Four of a kind: Four of a kind, also known as "quads," is a poker hand that contains four cards of one rank. So a hand of **8♦, 8♠, 8♥, 8♣, 3♦** is four of a kind. Since there are only four cards of the same rank in a single deck, four of a kind is a tough hand to get. The suits are irrelevant.

Straight flush: You know what a straight is, and you know what a flush is. A straight flush is a poker hand that contains five cards in numerical succession, all of the same suit. So a **3♥, 4♥, 5♥, 6♥, 7♥,** all of hearts, is a straight flush.

Royal Flush: A royal straight flush is the ultimate hand in poker. It's made up of **10♠, J♠, Q♠, K♠, A♠,** all of the same suit. The odds of getting a Royal Flush are astronomical: 1 in about 649,739!

Remember, the highest numerical hand wins. When two players have the same hands, the higher hand (the hand that contains the higher numerical value) is the winning hand. For instance, a pair of 8s beats a pair of 7s; simple enough. For example, if two players have a straight, and one holds 3♥, 4♦, 5♠, 6♣, 7♦ and the other holds 6♣, 7♦, 8♥, 9♣, 10♥, then the hand ending with the 10 wins. If two players have a full house, A♣, A♦, A♥, K♠, K♥ beats K♠, K♥, K♣, A♦, A♣ (the term is, 'aces-full beats kings-full').

Also, let's say that two (or more) players have hands of equal value, but one player has a higher 'other' card in their hand, the player with the higher card wins. This is called having a "better kicker." The "**kickers**" are the leftover cards, the ones that don't contribute to your best combination. For example, let's say you are holding 3♠, 6♥, 7♣, 7♥, 9♥, and I'm holding 2♣, 4♥, 7♠, 7, 8♠; we both have a pair of 7s, so who wins? Well, your kickers are the 3, 6, 9, while my kickers are 2, 4, 8. Since we both have a pair of 7s, your 9 will outrank my 8, so you have the better kicker. You might hear the dealer say, "Nine plays."

That's the hand rankings for the game of poker. If you are new to poker, it's not a bad idea to write down these rankings and keep them nearby.

So we understand that the player with the best hand wins, but I also mentioned that the other way to win is: the other players might fold, and you can win just by being the last player still in the hand. So what is folding?

Folding

Consider that poker is a game of risk. **Folding** simply means that you can opt out of the hand when you've decided you don't wish to risk any more of your chips. In other words, to fold means to forfeit the hand. This sounds like defeat, but quite to the contrary, this is often your best strategy.

Now while you will not always win, consider that there are two successful ways to complete a hand of poker: you can win the hand, or you can opt out of the hand before you have risked very much, or any, of your chip stack.

You never need to fold until it's time to match, or "see," another player's bet. **Seeing** refers to when one of the players has made a bet, and you match that bet to continue playing. For example, if the player across from you raises the bet by ten dollars, you could respond by saying, "I'll see your ten." The point is, if another player bets $10, then must also risk $10 of your money to stay in the hand.

And remember, unless you are down to just two players, winning at poker is not a fifty-fifty proposition. Unlike a typical casino game like Blackjack, where you are playing against a dealer, to win at poker, you must out-match every player in the hand. So if you don't feel you have a strong enough hand to win (and assuming you aren't bluffing yet), you generally want to fold.

Players who consistently win are the ones who know when to fold. If you choose your battles wisely, and for the most part, only stay in when you feel you have a strong enough hand to win, you can survive in the game, and eventually seize upon good opportunities and start to amass a large chip stack. So when you're in a position where your hand is weak, and you reach the point when you have to choose to put more money in to stay in the hand, be careful: you'll generally want to fold. The key is choosing your battles carefully. Your motto should be, "live to die another day."

So we've covered what the winning hands are, and we've established that winning the game means you either have the best hand, or the other players have folded, leaving you the last man standing. We also said that the object of the game was winning the pot. So let's talk about the pot for a second. How does all that money get into the pot? Well, that happens when the players start to call and raise bets. Let's talk about the terminology that goes along with betting.

Betting

In a poker game you're going to hear someone say, "Ante up!" The term "**ante**" has sort of a dual meaning, as both a noun and a verb. The ante *(noun)* is the wager; the established minimum bet. Players will establish what the ante is for the game. You could be playing with nickels and dimes, or you could be in a high-stakes poker tournament in Montenegro with a $10 million buy-in. Ante *(verb)* means it's time for the players to put up the minimum bets to get the betting ball rolling. So if a player tells you to ante, he's asking you to place your bet.

In most poker variations, each of the players will start the game off by making an ante, so that there's already some money in the pot as you begin the hand, and before you begin to make bets, so that each player starts off with an equal stake. In Hold'em poker, the ante betting is a little different than other poker games. Here you have what's called a "**blind**," which is an ante, but the way a blind works is: only two players are required to place that primer bet before the start of each hand.

We'll discuss the blind in more depth as we get into actual game play, but essentially it means that instead of every player throwing in an ante at the beginning of each hand, just two players will be required to place bets; these are referred to as the "**small blind**" and the "**big blind**." Players take turns being responsible for the blind bets as the deal rotates around the table, and as the names suggest, the small blind is a smaller bet than the big blind, normally half the size. So, for example, if the big blind is $50, the small blind would be $25.

Once the blinds have been established and the game gets under way, there will be rounds of betting during each hand, and you'll be betting (or not) according to the strength of your hand (unless of course, you're bluffing, but we'll discuss that later).

There are four options when it's your turn to act; check, call, raise, or fold.

If you choose not to make a bet, and no one has bet before you, you can opt to "check." "**Checking**," means you're still playing the hand, but you weren't required to put any money in the pot, so you choose not to bet. If another player makes a bet, it leaves you with three options. You can "call" that bet; "**calling**" means you are matching what the player before you put into the pot. If a player bets $10, you can say "call," and slide your $10 forward to match him. Or, you can "**raise**" the bet, meaning you matched the amount your opponent bet, and you're now going raise the bet to a greater amount. If a player bets $10, you can match his $10, and then raise by another $10, making the bet $20, and the other player will now have to add another $10 to match your bet, or he can fold. This is also the time where you can choose to **fold**. If the bet is high and you don't want to stay in, you can simply say, "too rich for my blood," and surrender the hand.

One note about betting and raising; you must bet or raise by at least the minimum bet. Say the big blind is $10, when it's your turn to act, you can't bet just $5. You must bet or raise by at least $10.

Those are the basic elements of betting in poker, but of course there is a certain art to deciding when to call, when to raise (and by how much,) and when to fold. That's why Texas Hold'em poker has rapidly become one of the most popular games in the casino. There's plenty of skill and strategy involved, as opposed to other poker games which can often be dismissed as; as Vesper might say, "a game of luck." There's genuine action in Hold'em poker, but it's also a game of deception and bluffing.

The Rules of Texas Hold'em

Let's briefly describe a typical round of Texas Hold'em, and then go back and break it down to the specifics. An over-simplified round would look like this:

TEXAS HOLD'EM IN 30 SECONDS:

Each player at the table is dealt two cards. Players then make a round of bets based on the strength of those two cards. After the first round of betting, the dealer lays out three community cards in the middle of the table, face up. Players can now start sizing up the strength of their hands, based on the two cards in their hands, and the three community cards. Then, another round of betting takes place. Next, the dealer lays down a fourth card, followed by another round of betting. Finally, the dealer places the fifth card down on the table, and the last round of betting happens. Once the final round of betting is over, the players who have not yet folded will reveal their cards, and the player with the best hand wins.

Now let's go back and break down each step of the game play.

"High card for dealer position…"

Before the game can get underway, the player who happens to be holding the shuffled deck may say, "High card for dealer position," and will proceed to deal out one card to each player at the table. The player who was dealt the highest card will be the first dealer. Now the game can begin.

POSTING THE BLINDS

Before the cards are dealt, the initial bets are placed. The two players sitting to the left of the dealer are the blinds. The player to the immediate left of the dealer is the "small blind," and the player two seats left of the dealer is the "big blind."

The players will have established the limits before the start of the game. So let's say you're playing a friendly game and the minimum bet is $10. Therefore, the small blind will put up $5, which is half the minimum bet in this case. The big blind will put up $10, which is equal to a full minimum bet. Now that the blinds have been posted, the deal begins.

DEALING

As with every card game, you always deal to the player on your immediate left first, and then around the table clockwise, until you've dealt the final card to yourself. With each hand, the responsibility of dealing each hand rotates clockwise around the table, rotating the blinds along with it. In a typical home game, each player will get a chance to deal the cards.

However, at a poker table in a casino (as with any casino table game) a professional dealer will deal each hand, as seen in *Casino Royale.* You might notice a small disk sitting in front of one of the players with the word "DEALER" inscribed on it, despite the fact that this player isn't actually dealing the cards at all; this is referred to as the "**button**." Why do we need the button to identify the dealer position? Because, while the actual dealer deals every hand, the dealer position and blind positions rotate accordingly. So the players will rotate the button after each hand, and the dealer will send the first card to the player to the left of the button.

You probably won't see the button so much in a friendly, non-professional game, since players will actually take turns dealing the cards, making it fairly obvious who is dealing the hand. But, you'll definitely see it in the casino so that it's perfectly clear where the dealer position is at all times.

So we've established who the dealer is, and we know who the small blinds and the big blinds are. The bets are in, and everyone's got their drinks, so now it's time to deal the cards. The dealer will now begin the hand by dealing two cards face down to each player.

The player's two cards also referred to sometimes as "**pocket cards**." When you hear seasoned players talk about what they have in their pockets, they're talking about the two cards that they have in their hands. When a player says, "I went out with pocket jacks," it means he folded even though he had a pair of Jacks in his hand.

THE FIRST ROUND OF BETTING

When the cards have been dealt to every player, everyone looks at their cards and sizes up the strength of their hand. Then, it's time to increase the stakes by making bets.

Since the first two players to the left of the dealer have already put down blind bets, the player sitting just to the left of the big blind is now the first one to act, and then the betting continues clockwise around the table.

So let's say you're the one sitting to the left of the big blind, and it's your turn to bet; what are your options at this time? You must call, raise, or fold. 'Wait, can't I just check, and not bet?' Not in this case.

"Checking" means that you are choosing not to make a bet. However, right after the dealer has dealt the cards, a player cannot simply check; you must match the minimum bet in order to keep playing. Why is this? Since the blind bets have already been placed; meaning there are already existing bets on the table. Therefore, you have to 'call' the existing bet, match the big blind bet by putting down $10, if you wish to play the hand. Everyone who chooses to keep playing will be required to bet at least the $10 minimum bet.

You can also raise with a larger bet, or you can simply fold out of the hand. If you decide to raise, then other players have the option to match your bet, to fold, or raise it even higher. If another player raises the bet again, then it will be up to you to match the new larger bet, or fold.

When the betting has gone around the table and reaches the blinds, the small blind, having already placed half a minimum bet before the deal, will now be responsible for the other half of the bet if he wishes to remain in the hand, along with any other raises that have been made. The big blind, having already placed a full minimum bet, now has the option to check if no other player has raised the bet, or he must match any raises to stay in the game. If no one has raised, then the big blind has the option to raise the bet, but if he checks, then the round of betting has ended, and the dealer will move on to the "flop."

THE FLOP

The dealer now burns one card, and then deals three. To "**burn**" (or "bury") the first card means to discard the top card on the deck. The dealer must always burn the top card before dealing. Having burned the first card, the dealer will now deal three cards to the center of the table, face up. These cards are known as the "**flop**." The three cards on the table, and the two cards in your hand, together represent your potential hand. Of course, the three flop cards are also community cards, so they are also part of everyone else's hand. Be aware that those three cards support the other players as well. For example, if there are two aces in the flop, then you know that every other player has, at least, a pair of aces as well.

So now that the flop has been revealed, the next round of bets will ensue, beginning this time with the small blind, the player to the immediate left of the dealer.

THE TURN AND THE RIVER

The next two rounds will happen much the same way. After the bets have been completed, the fourth card is going to be flipped face up, (don't forget to **burn and turn**,") and placed in the center of the table. That fourth card is known as the "turn." Another round of betting takes place. Then the fifth card, which is known as the "river," gets flipped and placed on the table. Now that all five cards have been laid in the center of the table, the final round of betting takes place, and then it's time for the showdown.

THE SHOWDOWN

When all the bets have been placed and met, it's time for the players to reveal their hands. Of the players who are left standing, (the players who have not folded,) the winner is the player who holds the best hand, using a combination of the five cards in the center of the table and the two cards the player has in his hand, or his "pocket cards." Whoever can make the best 5-card hand, using those seven cards, wins the pot.

Congratulations! You have just completed your first hand of Texas Hold'em poker.

Strategies in Texas Hold'em

Once you understand how to play Texas Hold'em, it's time to cultivate a few strategies. This is where the fun begins.

When you're a beginning player, you'll be concentrating on your hand and trying to put together the best hand you can between the two in your hand and the five on the table and you'll make bets based on the strength of the hand. A more seasoned player, however, realizes that the real game is about reading the other players. Knowing what the other players are doing, and why, means everything in this game. With that in mind, you're going to cultivate some strategies.

Here are some things to consider when you're playing Texas Hold'em...

YOUR POSITION

Your position at the table may give you some power, and the "**late positions**" have the advantage. If you are one of the blinds, just left of the dealer, you're sitting in what is known as an "**early position**." As you go around the table, there are middle positions, and then late positions. When you're sitting in a late position, you have an edge. If you're one of the last players to bet, you've already seen what the other players have done. You'll already have seen who's folded, who's bet, and by how much. You can start to size up who may have weak hands and who may have strong hands. Poker is a game of information. The more information you can gather, the smarter you can play.

YOUR FIRST TWO CARDS

Your first two cards are critical. The two cards in your hand, (or in your pocket,) should be strong enough cards for you to continue. A poor player is going to keep playing as often as he can, staying in when he shouldn't, and keeps getting knocked out quickly. One of the keys to this game is survival, and a smart player chooses his battles carefully. So your first two cards are your first important decision. Winning a game of poker means making good decisions. If you have the beginnings of a strong hand in your first two cards, then play on.

Some players will say that any two cards can win. This may be true, but if you want to play smart poker, make sure your first two cards are strong ones. For example, let's say you were dealt a 2, 7, unsuited; this is statistically the **worst pocket combination** in poker. (The 2, 7, have the lowest numerical value, they cannot be turned into a straight, and no matching suits means no potential flushes.) Naturally you fold. But, then the flop turns over a 7, 7, 2; if you had stayed in you would have been holding a full house. A novice player might interpret this as a sign that he needs to be more aggressive, but a mature player knows that bad pocket cards are still bad pocket cards. Stay sharp, and bet only on strong hands.

There are facts to consider when you are deciding how strong your two pocket cards are. As we said, your position may help to reveal information that makes your pocket cards seem a little more promising. You may even find yourself in a situation where most of the other players have folded out; so if you are playing against nine other players, and you have just seen six or seven of them fold, suddenly your odds of winning have gone up, so the pair of 4s that you might have normally have folded, have just gotten a little sweeter.

Other factors to consider are the odds of getting that miracle hand. For example, if you have cards that can be turned into a straight or a flush, you should consider the gaps between the cards. For example, the Jack-10 combination is slightly better than the Queen-10 combination, or the King-10 combination. All three of these sets can help you make a straight, but if you have the Jack-10, you have a little more flexibility in terms of which cards you will need to make the straight.

PLAYING THE FLOP
Once you've made the decision to bet on your pocket cards, the flop is probably the most important moment in the hand. The flop will make or

break your pocket cards. You may end up with a great hand, or two strong pocket cards could have been rendered useless due to a bad flop. Make sure that the flop fits your hand. Only two more cards will be turned over, so at this point in the game, you should make sure that you have strong enough cards before you start matching or making bets.

Be sure to look at the flop carefully to look for possible combinations. Not only are you looking for combinations that might give you a strong hand, but you are looking to see what other players might have too. If you see three spades on the table, then you have to be aware that other players might be holding a flush. (Or, they might play strong just to make you think they've got it.)

PLAYING THE TURN

The turn is where you might hear some big betting going on. Look at the cards on the table closely, because this is where players might have just completed straights or flushes. If you feel that you're ahead at this point, make bets. If you're behind, fold. This is not where you want to make large bets if you're holding out for that miracle card.

PLAYING THE RIVER

All five cards have now been dealt, and you now know what kind of a hand you hold. It's not a potential hand anymore; it's a hand. As long as you've been playing smart cards up to this point, you're almost never going to fold here: You've been playing well up to this point, your money's in, and you're going to ride it out through the showdown.

Your Poker Face

In the film *Ocean's Eleven,* Brad Pitt's Rusty asks his novice poker players, "Guys, what's the first lesson in poker?" Answer: Leave emotion at the door. It's easy to make mistakes when your decisions are based on emotion. A novice player, having been dealt a series of boring, lifeless combinations, might grow impatient and start throwing chips away on bad cards just to get in the game. A few losing hands might cause a player to grow overly cautious and miss out on some good opportunities. And even a player on a lucky streak might get overly confident and start chasing too many long shots. A mature poker player acts on set rules and principles, not emotions.

PATIENCE

A good poker player is patient. Remember, winning isn't a 50/50 proposition, and to win a round of poker, you have to out-match every other player at the table. Depending on how many players are facing you, those could be some tough odds. Yes, folding can get boring, but patiently waiting for the perfect time to strike is the way to stay consistent, and the way to win. As we said, choose your battles carefully, and don't go for the long shots.

COURAGE

On the other hand; don't get bullied! While caution is always wise, especially for novice players, it's also important not to let the more experienced players count on your conservatism, so that they can scare you into folding at the sight of any strong bets. Again, keep watching how each player plays. Aggressive players will prey upon more timid players to "buy the pots."

Balance is key. When you do get that perfect hand, go after it. Don't become so patient that you grow fearful when the time comes to make a move. When you find yourself in a strong position, be confident. Making bets will apply pressure to the other players. When the time comes, let them know you're not here to watch, you're here to play.

So always remember the things to consider with every move: And am I in a good position or a bad position? How are my opponents playing? What are some of the hands my opponents are likely to hold? What do my opponents think that I have? These are the things to think about before you bet, raise, check, or fold.

For more on this, check out of the books that came highly recommended to me while I was preparing this chapter, Phil Gordon's 'Little Green Book: Lessons and Teachings in No Limit Texas Hold'em.'

Once you understand how to play to the strength of your hand, it's time to start playing your opponents. Watch your opponents and get to know their playing style. As we said earlier, the real challenge of Texas Hold'em poker is not about getting a good hand, that part is the luck of the draw; it is reading the other players. A fierce poker player can dominate a table if he just reads the other players correctly.

Bluffing and Tells

In *Casino Royale,* James Bond masterfully lures his opponents into doing exactly what he wishes. How does he do it? Observe these two scenes:

While at the exclusive Bahamas getaway, the Ocean Club, James Bond takes a seat at the poker table opposite the sinister Alex Dimitrios. In a particularly interesting hand, we can see that the flop has already been dealt, revealing a 9♦, 3♥, A♣. The fourth card is turned over to reveal a 7♥. Bond checks, but Dimitrios bets $5,000. Bond calmly calls his bet, placing $5,000 in chips in front of him, which the dealer then counts and slides into the main pot. When the fifth card is turned over to reveal a K♣, Bond checks once again. The villain immediately goes "all in," and even tries to raise the bet to $20,000. When the dealer objects, citing "table stakes," he tries to bet his car – a gorgeous 1964 Aston Martin –

and he tosses his keys into the pot. When the dealer objects once again, Bond gives an easy smile and convinces the dealer to "give him a chance to win his money back," and Bond slides all of his chips into the pot. At the showdown, Dimitrios flips his cards to reveal a hand of **K♠**, **K♦**, and along with the king on the table, he smiles confidently with his hand of three kings. James Bond calmly flips his cards to reveal **A♦**, **A♥**, and with an ace already on the table, Bond's hand of "trip aces" trumps the three kings.

Once the scene has unfolded, and the hand has been played out, we can now see that Bond had successfully lured Dimitrios into a false confidence. When the scene opened, and the **9♦**, **3♥**, **A♣** had already been flipped, Bond would have already been holding the best hand possible. No other combination can beat his hand, at least not yet. When the seven was turned over, Bond still held the best hand, and the chances of his hand being beaten had grown even slimmer, yet Bond calmly checked. When the final King was revealed, Bond knew that no other possible combination could beat his "trip aces." Even knowing that he held the best hand possible, Bond still checked. Dimitrios, knowing that he held a very strong (though not the strongest) hand, and not having detected any strength or confidence coming from his opponent, felt certain that he held the best hand, and he went all in.

Seasoned poker players will probably tell you that Bond's strategy of checking was extremely risky in this case. Perhaps he should have been making strong bets, as this might have been his only chance to take full advantage of his superior hand. But, his ability to conceal the strength of his hand pays off, and his opponent leapt at the chance to go all in.

James Bond would later employ this same technique during the high-stakes poker tournament at the Casino Royale in Montenegro:

During the game, Bond carefully observes LeChiffre's playing style, and begins to uncover a 'tell.' LeChiffre tends to twitch and touch his eye when he tries to bluff his way through a weak hand. Bond's strategy is to use this knowledge to his advantage, and ultimately outwit his opponent by betting strongly when LeChiffre reveals his weak hand through his tell. Bond's strategy backfires however; after observing the 'tell' once again, Bond goes all in. But he is shocked to find that the villain was holding a strong hand after all. Bond loses it all.

Later, after Bond has bought back into the game and seems to be holding his own. The last hand is dealt, and there are now four players left, including Bond and LeChiffre. When the fourth card has been dealt to reveal A♥, 8♠, 6♠, 4♠, Bond checks. Then the final card has been dealt to reveal an A♥, 8♠, 6♠, 4♠, A♠. Four of the cards are spades, so we can see that several good hands can be made with what is shown on the table. Bond checks, and two of the players have gone all in, with four and five million respectively. When it is his turn to bet, LeChiffre raises the stakes to $12 Million, causing Bond to look pensively at the bet that has just been placed. Bond looks up at LeChiffre and begins to stare into his eyes. Having been unsuccessful at reading LeChiffre's tells earlier, Bond seems to be contemplating LeChiffre's motives. Bond makes the bold move of going all in, raising the stakes to $14.5 Million. LeChiffre seems taken by surprise, but looks at his cards once more. Holding an ace-six combination, giving him a full house, LeChiffre confidently calls Bond's bet. The first player flips his cards, to reveal a flush. The second player flips to reveal a full house. LeChiffre flips his cards to reveals pockets cards of A♣, 6♥, to make a higher full house, A♥, A♣, A♠, 6♠, 6♥.

James Bond doesn't look well as his bet has been called. He sheepishly slides his cards toward the dealer, perhaps to quietly fold his cards. But, he flips his cards to reveal a 5♠, 7♠, creating a 4♠, 5♠, 6♠, 7♠, 8♠

combination; a straight flush – not only the highest hand possible on the table, but one of the highest hands in all of poker.

Just as he had done in the Ocean Club, Bond waited until he had the best possible hand at the table, and masterfully gave an aura of weakness, coaxing his opponents to attack, and then took full advantage.

This technique is known as "bluffing."

You'll notice in *Casino Royale,* that bluffing is a technique that James Bond observes in others, and also employs himself.

Be aware that other players will be observing your body language and facial expressions, so this is where you will put on your "**poker face**." When you get dealt a pair of pocket aces, don't scare the fish away with a triumphant smile. Stay cool.

One of the most effective techniques you can employ in Texas Hold'em is observing your opponent. This is one of the elements in poker that really makes it exciting. Think about what motivates the other players. Try to figure out what state of mind your opponent is in. Look for betting patterns. And last but not least, look for tells. Being able to successfully read your opponent is what turns a good player into a great player.

The Yin and Yang of Bluffing

There are essentially two types of bluffing. If a player is acting, either he is holding a strong hand and wants you to believe he has a weak hand, or he is holding a weak hand and wants you to think he's holding a strong hand. If you feel a player is acting, then you must decide what they want you to do, and disappoint them.

If a player acts like he has a weak hand, then he might have a strong hand, which means he want you to put money in the pot; you will need to counter them by checking or folding. A player who's acting strong may be weak; and he wants you to fold or check, and you will disappoint them with a bet or a raise.

A "**tell**" refers to another player's inadvertent indication that they are bluffing. Tells are usually not as obvious as a twitch, or touching one's face; rather, tells are usually seen in how the player behaves and reacts to the events as they unfold. Many "tells" are a variation on the "weak equals strong" and "strong equals weak" theme. A player with a really strong hand will immediately be conscious of the fact that he might look too excited. So what does he do? He looks calm, maybe even uninterested. Maybe he sinks back in his chair and looks around and pretends he's paying only casual attention. On the other hand, the player who has a weak hand might try to look eager and aggressive. Maybe he can scare enough of his opponents into folding.

Signs to Watch For

ATTENTIVENESS AND PASSIVITY

If a player is eager and attentive, he's trying to show that he's anxious for the next move, because he has such a great hand. He's probably trying to cover up a weak hand. On the other hand, if the player is passive, casual, relaxed or almost bored, he's probably trying not to let on that he's got a great hand.

OVER-CONFIDENCE AND DESPERATION

The extreme weak equals strong move. If a player is visibly excited, as if he's finally got the hand he's been waiting for all night, he's probably trying to scare you off. On the other hand, if he's disgusted, maybe he goes all in as if he's just looking to go home. He's probably got the goods.

QUICK BETS AND SLOW BETS

Again, strength equals weakness, and vice-versa. If your opponent is eager to make a bet, and bets quickly, he's probably trying to show you confidence. He's trying to scare you off. And if he's slow to bet, unsure, as if he can't quite decide what he wants to do, then he's probably trying to show a lack of confidence, hoping that you will attack and bet big.

DIFFERENT SIZED BETS

A simple 'tell' is the size of an opponent's bet. Say it's the first round of bets, and a player who typically sticks to the minimum bet, suddenly bets big; maybe he's got a great hand, but maybe not. Watch your opponents; maybe they play conservative cards and bet according to the strength of their hands, or maybe they are trying to throw you off. This can also be true if the player has been playing conservatively, and suddenly gets more aggressive. As the hand plays on, his opponent hasn't folded yet, so he makes a desperation move and bets big, hoping to terrify the other player into folding. This can often be a 'Hail Mary' move. As Rusty says in *Ocean's Eleven,* players may try to buy their way out of their bluffs.

BETTING OUT OF TURN

If a player starts throwing chips out before it's his turn to bet, it could be that he's made a simple mistake. Or, he's trying to show aggressiveness, and make people think he's got a great hand and can't wait to bet.

LOOKING AT THEIR CARDS

Sometimes called a 'suit check.' After the flop, a player takes another look at his pocket cards to refresh his memory. Most people will remember the numerical values of the cards in their hand, but the suits can be a secondary consideration. If the three flop cards are all hearts, and a player looks at his cards, it's a good bet that both of his pocket cards are both red, but he forgot which card was which suit.

LOOKING AT THEIR CHIPS

I've been caught doing this. When the cards have been flipped, at the flop, the turn, or the river, and a player looks down at his chips, it's a good bet he's got a good hand, and his first thought was, "How much do I have to bet on that?"

LOOKING AT MY CHIPS

Similarly, when a player has a good hand, he may start to size up the other player's chips to see how much he might be able to take away from him. Maybe he wants to see how much you'll be willing to gamble with, before you get cautious and fold.

Then again, if he's way too obvious – acting smug as he eyeballs the other player's stack – perhaps he's actually got a weak hand, and needs to scare you into folding. Continually observe the other players, and get to know their playing style. Monitor how much they bet, if they are conservative or aggressive with their bets, consistent or erratic. Make mental notes; watch when a player gets caught in a bluff, and how they tried to bluff.

For an extensive look at tells, be sure to check out 'Caro's Book of Poker Tells,' by Mike Caro, which was quoted in 'Phil Gordon's Little Green Book: Lessons and Teachings in No Limit Texas Hold'em.'

Rules of Etiquette

DON'T SPLASH THE POT

The term "**splashing the pot**" refers to a player haphazardly tossing chips into the pot, rather than sliding his chip stack forward, neatly and clearly displaying his bet. Splashing the pot makes it impossible for the dealer to verify the size of your bet. Just place your bet directly in front of you, so the dealer can count your chips and then place them in the pot.

DON'T STRING BETS

A "**string bet**" occurs when a player reaches into his stack more than once while making a bet. For example, let's say a player is intending to bet twenty chips, and he slides the first stack of ten chips forward, pauses, then reaches back to slide a second stack of ten forward. If this were legal, a devious player could slide the first stack forward, then pause to gauge his opponents' reactions, and then reach back for more chips. Place your bet in one motion, and speak up; get into the habit of clearly saying, "call," and "raise," when it's your turn to act.

DON'T TALK ABOUT THE HAND

"Hey, are two aces good?" There's no reason to announce what you have verbally or physically while your hand is at play. If you are a beginner and you're setting out to learn the game of poker amongst friends, that's one thing. But, in a real game with seasoned players, (and especially in a casino setting) calling out your hand will seem like you're trying to gain information, and gauging the reaction of the other players, by talking about your own hand. As Mom would say, "keep your hands to yourself."

OTHER RULES OF ETIQUETTE TO REMEMBER

Keep your cards on the table at all times; it's bad form to pick up your cards off the table. Watch the other players and observe how they lift the cards slightly and peek down at what they have, and protect your hand from wandering eyes when you look at your cards. Don't intentionally act out of turn; make bets, or fold when it's your turn to do so. Don't intentionally stall the game; everyone occasionally needs a little time to contemplate, but don't get carried away and get annoying. Don't order someone to turn up their cards face up at the showdown; you may ask someone to show their cards, but it's the dealer's job to tell them. Telling players to see their cards too frequently is considered bad form. Finally, show both your cards if it's required at the showdown.

Time to Play

WHERE DO WE GO FROM HERE?

Watching "The World Series of Poker," or any poker games online or live on TV is a great way to become more familiar with the game of poker. Bear in mind, shows or videos tend to highlight the more exciting hands. Your own poker experiences will require much more patience in waiting for the great hands.

Before you play a real game with real players, you could try an online game. There are dozens of apps by now for playing online poker, which is a great way to get your feet wet, and see if you find any elements to be confusing or challenging.

Once you've conquered some online poker games, you should be ready for a real game with real players. If you know some people who play Hold'em poker, try to get yourself invited to play a game. Otherwise, try to find a few people who know how to play and set up your own game. A low-stakes poker tournament can make for a really fun Friday night. Also, many bars and pubs will hold poker nights. Typically you aren't play- ing for actual money, since gambling in bars in most states is illegal, but you can play for fun. Be sure to be friendly and say, "this is my first time playing," or, "I'm still just learning." You might run into the occasional patron who doesn't get out much, and takes the game a little too serious- ly, but the vast majority of other players will welcome you to the game and be more than happy to share insights and helpful advice.

And when you do play for real money, be sure to keep your games "low- stakes" as you begin to gain experience. As Paul Kyriazi points out in his seminar *"How To Live The James Bond Lifestyle,"* there's a huge difference between "gambling" and "gaming." If you are playing with money that you can't afford to lose, then you are "**gambling**." However, if you play with money that you have budgeted out for your evening's entertainment, then you are "**gaming**." Don't put yourself in a position to have to stress about losing money. Play with a limited budget, and do not go over.

And remember, good players are always working on their game to become better players. Talk about the game with other players, practice, analyze your strategies, and work to improve the weaknesses in your game.

Further Reading

If you're interested in reading up on more poker strategies, one of the books that I used in preparing this article was 'Phil Gordon's Little Green Book: Lessons and Teachings in No Limit Texas Hold'em,' by Phil Gordon. I also referred to 'Poker for Dummies' by Richard D. Harroch and Lou Krieger, and of course, 'Caro's Book of Poker Tells,' by Mike Caro.

That concludes this chapter on Texas Hold'em Poker. Remember, great poker players are not made overnight; but with knowledge, practice, and a little luck, you'll soon be playing like a pro.

Order yourself a Vesper – and good luck!

Skiing

"There was the starting point of the Gloria Run, the metal notices beside it hatted with snow. Bond didn't pause. He went straight for it and over the edge.

"The first vertical drop had a spine-chilling bliss to it. Bond got down into his old Arlberg crouch, his hands forward of his boots, and just let himself go. His skis were an ugly six inches apart. The Kannonen he had watched had gone down with their boots locked together, as if on a single ski. But this was no time for style, even if he had been capable of it! Above all he must stay upright!

"Bond's speed was now frightening. But the deep cushion of cold, light powder snow gave him confidence to try a parallel swing. Minimum of shoulder turn needed at this speed–weight on to the left ski–and he came around and held it as the right-hand edges of his skis bit against the slope, throwing up a shower of moonlit snow crystals. Danger was momentarily forgotten in the joy of speed, technique, and mastery of the snow."

– Chapter 16, On Her Majesty's Secret Service, 1963

What is it about skiing that is so quintessential to the world of James Bond? Skiing is part adrenaline, part sensuality.

ADRENALINE

The pure excitement of hot skis slicing through the cold snow is unforgettable. You're not even thinking about how you're going to stop at the bottom. Maybe you will carve a few turns as you swing around the curves of the giant mountain slope. Perhaps you will shrink into a racing tuck with your skis flattened and your fists held out in front of you. You accelerate to a speed that is just beyond your control and hang on for dear life as you bounce over the ridges of the lower slope. It isn't until you reach the bottom that you realize how hard your body has been working. Your muscles burn, your back is aching from the tightness of your tuck, and you're gasping for breath. You look back at the mountain that you just conquered and admire the awesome power of nature.

SENSUALITY

Imagine cruising down one of the wide, well-groomed slopes, alone or with a companion, breathing in the mountain air, while enjoying the warmth of the sun and the cool air on your face. You'll stop at a beautiful mountainside cafe for a hot-spiced wine with the unmistakable smell of lemon, clove, and cinnamon stick. And, don't forget the unbeatable experiences beyond the skiing too. Consider the strange experience of sitting in a deck chair getting a sun tan at 24° degrees. Or enjoying an IPA and listening to a live band on an outdoor restaurant terrace, surrounded by snow-capped peaks under the bluest sky you have ever seen, and looking out across a mountain range that fills the entire horizon and watching the clouds drift beneath you. The après ski brings out the best in people; a wonderful group spirit descends every evening over groups of ruddy faces and cheery spirits. You find yourself with a hunger that you never thought possible, and that hearty dinner never felt so satisfying.

As this unknown writer points out, you don't go skiing just for the skiing; you go for that rush of adrenaline, the glorious scenery, the amazing mountain air, and of course, the après ski.

No matter who you are, you can learn to ski.

Like every topic we explore in **Being James Bond**, we will prepare you for your first day on the slopes, and to provide a few insights that will let you know what you can expect as a beginning skier. As with everything else, hands-on experience is the key, especially with a physical activity like skiing. An entire article about skiing won't add up to five minutes on the slope with a qualified instructor. But fear not; we can't get you down the slope, but we can help you to get there, and be ready.

We'll discuss what your basic expectations should be for your first day of skiing, try to answer a few of those burning questions, and tame those fears a little bit. We'll talk about how you should prepare for your trip. We'll discuss the exercises that are going to help you to get ready for a day of skiing. Then we will talk about clothing, and what you should wear for your first day on the slopes; having the right clothing can definitely make or break your first experience. We'll talk about gear; how to choose the right skis, the right poles, and what you need to look for in a pair of boots; having the right boots with the right fit is essential. We'll talk about how to navigate a ski area; we'll talk about ski lifts, how to look for the beginner slopes, and how to identify the intermediate and advanced slopes. Then, we will discuss actual skiing techniques, and offer up a few concepts to keep in the back of your mind on your first day of navigating the slopes. And last, but definitely not least, we are going to make a stop

over to Piz Gloria, located atop Mount Schilthorn, near the village of Mürren, in the Bernese Oberland region of Switzerland – a location that is
central to the world of skiing, and to the world of James Bond.

Expectations

What are the burning questions that people have when they consider
taking on skiing? The first question is usually, "Will I fall?" and closer to
the point, "Will I get hurt?" The answer to the first question is of course:
"Yes, you will fall." Just as in life, if you are not falling, you are not challenging yourself. Falling is simply a part of learning.

But more importantly, "Will I get hurt?" Generally speaking, when you
fall, the thing most likely to get bruised is your ego. If you have ever
watched Olympic skiing on TV, you've seen some spectacular crashes,
and the skier typically stands up, brushes himself off, and walks away.
You will certainly bounce off the soft snow many times as a beginner,
but you won't be cruising anywhere near the speed of a professional skier.
If you use your head and listen to a qualified ski instructor, you will avoid
any type of serious injury.

The next question is usually, "Will I look silly?" You'll see people falling
all over the slopes, all day long, so you won't stand out. Don't be afraid of
looking silly. Even the most advanced skier was once a beginner.

Next question: "When I fall down, will I have trouble getting up?" The
answer is "yes." But, there are ways to help you to get back up a little
easier, and we'll talk about those.

"Will I be cold?" I can honestly say that the answer to that is no. If you
have the right clothing and the right gear, then you should be able to stay
warm for several hours on the ski slope.

So then what are the hurdles you will need to overcome as a beginning skier? Well for starters, you'll find that as a beginner, you can only go at two speeds: too fast and too slow. This essentially means that, on your first day of skiing, you can expect to feel either bored or terrified. But as you progress, you'll find that sweet spot right in the middle, which is both exciting and fun. As with all the activities we discuss at **Being James Bond**, there's absolutely nothing to be afraid of. Bond shows no fear, and neither should we. So let's get going!

Getting in Shape

First things first. Let's get your body ready for the first day on the slopes. In addition to being fun, skiing is an excellent form of exercise. However, you don't want to wait until you are on the slopes to get into reasonable shape. Stamina is your friend. I've found that the best secret to a great day on the slopes is being prepared physically. You will take to skiing much faster, and your time on the slopes will be longer, if you are in pretty good physical shape. You don't need to be in phenomenal shape, as skiing shouldn't be that physically demanding, but on the other hand, if you have already slipped into your winter hibernation, then you'll definitely want to shake that off before you go out for a full day of physical exertion.

So how should you get in shape for skiing? Focus on good stretching, cardiovascular exercise, and strength training.

FLEXIBILITY

One of the easiest ways to avoid injury is to improve your flexibility. When you focus on stretching, consider which muscle groups will be called upon when skiing. This means focusing on your back, legs, hips, and shoulders. Keep your muscles flexible, but strong.

CARDIOVASCULAR AND ENDURANCE TRAINING

Good cardiovascular training is going to help you ski longer and stronger. Whichever type of cardiovascular exercise you do is totally up to you. Exercises such as like running, swimming, and bike-riding are all good forms of exercise for improving cardiovascular health. You can use videos like P90X Cardio or P90X Plyometrics, or even break out mom's old Jane Fonda workout tapes for some good old-fashioned aerobic exercise. Cardiovascular or aerobic training is most beneficial when it's done three to five times a week, and for about 20 to 45-minutes each.

STRENGTH TRAINING

I can't emphasize enough the importance of strength training before going skiing. Personally, I've had some great days on the slopes, and some lousy days on the slopes, and strength training seemed to make the difference. So which muscles should you focus on? Concentrate on your outer and inner thighs, your quads (the group of larger muscles on the front of your thighs), and your hamstrings (the muscles on the back of your thighs). Also, you want to focus on your calves, and even your shins. We tend to forget that we have muscles on and around our shinbones, but a skier who has his weight too far back and uses his feet to pull himself forward, will rely on those shin muscles.

As skiing is particularly hard on your leg muscles, what can you do to develop those muscles? The two exercises that are going to help you most are **squats** and **lunges**. If you have membership to a gym, or access to weight-training machines, you can also do **leg extensions** and **leg curls**. And, since you are going to have your arms extended most the day while holding up those ski poles, you might also throw in a couple of arm raises with those lunges to build up your shoulders a bit.

Skiing is a sport that favors power more than strength. What's the difference? **Power** is the ability to generate force quickly, combining strength and speed. If you stand up from a chair slowly, you don't exert much power. If you leap up from that chair quickly, you exert a lot of power. Based on that simple explanation you can deduce that weightlifting workouts involving many fast repetitions of moderate weight will better prepare you for skiing than workouts using slow repetitions with maximum weight.

Skiing has another interesting characteristic. It requires your muscles to work in eccentric motions, much more than other sports. **Eccentric** muscle effort occurs while a muscle is extended, becoming longer; as opposed to **concentric** muscle effort, where the muscle will contract. When you stand up from a chair, the muscles are contracting, or getting shorter, so the muscles are working concentrically. When you lower yourself into a chair, your thigh muscles extend, and are therefore working eccentrically.

Because skiing places heavy eccentric demands on your leg muscles – meaning your muscles are lengthening under tension – traditional gym machines like the stair machine or stationary bike aren't the most effective ways to prepare. A much better way to train for these specific demands is to take the elevator to the top of a tall building and walk down the stairs. As counterintuitive as it may sound, descending stairs does more to build the eccentric strength you'll rely on while skiing.

Another great exercise is to modify your squats for better results. When doing squats with moderate weight, push up using both legs as usual, but on the way down, lower yourself slowly while placing more emphasis on one leg at a time – alternating legs with each rep. This controlled descent mimics the kind of muscle engagement skiing requires. A few weeks of consistent training will help build the endurance and control you need to hit the slopes with confidence.

Clothing

When your body is ready, the next thing to consider is your clothing. Having the right ski clothes will be essential to staying warm and dry, and you get the most enjoyment out of your day. One of the advantages that modern skiers have today is the clothing. If you know anybody who ever skied in the 1950s or '60s, they can tell you that in the old days, skiers were cold. If you need any further proof of how far skiing apparel has come, just check out *On Her Majesty's Secret Service* and look at what James Bond was wearing on the slopes. Be glad you don't have to wear that when you ski.

If this is your first time skiing, you have two choices when it comes to proper ski clothing. One choice would be borrowing some ski clothes from a friend (if you have a friend in your size). On the other hand, if you're confident that skiing is something you want to invest some time in, then go ahead and buy yourself a respectable ski outfit.

A good time to hit the ski shops is mid-week, and before the ski-season is well under way, so that you are not rushed, fighting crowds of people, and a knowledgeable salesperson can take the time to assist you in finding exactly what you need. A good salesperson won't steer you wrong when it comes to picking out clothing.

As we said earlier, with today's modern ski apparel, there is no reason for you to ever be cold or wet on the ski slope. I've spent entire days on the ski slope and never got cold and never got wet, and that wasn't because I didn't fall, because I fell often.

When it comes to keeping warm, layering is the key. Personally, I tend to be somewhat 'old school' when it comes to ski gear. I wear a ski jacket with good insulation, which I can comfortably wear on and off the slopes.

The modern thinking tends more toward layering; meaning, instead of a thick insulated jacket, you would wear a few layers of warm clothing, under a thin, waterproof, outer shell. You can go whichever route you want and neither one is wrong, as long as your outfit is going to be warm, but not so thick that you can't move. After all, you want to remain flexible.

Your clothing isn't just about style – it's your first line of defense against the elements. Clothing has to perform three functions: pull moisture away from your body, prevent the cold air from coming in, and trap warm air close to your body. Layering will serve these purposes.

The basic ski outfit goes like this: Closest to your skin, you'll want thermal underwear – both top and bottom – made of moisture-wicking materials like merino wool or synthetic fabric. Over that, add your insulating layers, such as a fleece or wool sweater. On especially cold days, you can throw in an extra layer like a lightweight insulated jacket or vest for added warmth. These layers create a flexible system that keeps you warm, dry, and ready for whatever the mountain throws at you.

On the outside you have a waterproof shell jacket and shell pants. Finally, you will have your accessories; gloves, socks, headgear (either a hat or earmuffs, or both), a pair of goggles and probably sunglasses, and also neckwear, or a "gaiter." Let's break them down.

BASE LAYER

Your base layer will be a set of long, thermal underwear. The job of your base layer is not to keep you warm, but to keep you dry. To do this, your base layer must pull moisture away from your body. You need to keep your skin dry. It's for this reason that you must avoid cottons at all costs. Cotton has a tendency to stay cold and stay wet, so when you're buying long underwear for your base layer, think polyester, or polyester variant.

MID LAYERS

It's the job of your mid layer to keep you warm, and trap warm air next to your body. The way to stay warm is to keep the heat that your body is generating from escaping. Trapped warm air is the best insulator. A great mid layer is possibly a wool sweater or maybe a fleece jacket or a fleece vest. Think about loose synthetic fibers. One cautionary note; don't overdo it. If you get too hot you can start to perspire and the moisture on your body is going to get cold. Think loose breathable layers, so if you get too hot you can always take something off.

OUTER LAYER

The next layer would be your outer layer or ski jacket. A ski jacket will probably be the most expensive purchase you'll make when it comes to your ski clothes, and it's also the most important. As I mentioned earlier, your ski jacket is going to come with different levels of insulation. Whether you want a thickly insulated ski jacket, or a thinly insulated shell jacket is strictly up to you. Just make sure to layer accordingly.

What should you look for in a ski jacket? First, look at the collar. Before you purchase, try it on and zip it up all the way to see how it feels around your neck. Be sure it isn't so tight that it feels constricting. It should be tall and roomy enough that it covers your chin and cheeks when zipped up all the way. If you are planning to buy like a fleece vest with a collar, then try on the jacket and the vest at the same time to ensure a good fit. Also, make sure the top of the zipper is not touching your skin so it doesn't scrape your chin raw. The same thing goes for the main zipper in the front of the jacket. The zipper should be hidden under a piece of fabric so that the wind is not going to get through the zipper and to your skin.

A nice feature to look for in a jacket is a lot of **pockets**. You'll have personal items to keep track of, and having pockets will be helpful. One of my pockets is usually holding my iPhone so I can listen to James Bond music while I am skiing down the mountain. But, of course, I always keep the music low so I can always hear other skiers around me.

You also want to ensure that your sleeves are the correct length. When you are trying on your jacket, zip it up, crouch really low and reach forward as far as you can. Your sleeves have to be long enough so there are no gaps between them and your gloves.

Another nice feature to look for is something called "pit zips." **Pit zips** are exactly what they sound like; they are zippers next to your armpits, so that if you start to feel a little warm you can open up the zippers and give yourself a little extra ventilation.

Remember, the task of your outer layer is to keep you dry, so it needs to be waterproof, and it needs to keep you warm, so it needs to fit correctly to keep the cold out. The same theory that applies to your jacket also applies to your pants. So get a good pair of nylon, waterproof, ski pants. Your ski pants need to be loose enough to fit outside your ski boots, and your ski boots are going to be pretty big. You might see some people trying to get away with tight fitting pants, but I would definitely stay away from pants that tuck inside the boot. The fit of your boot is very important, so don't compromise the fit of the boot by stuffing the pants in there. Also, tucking your ski pants into your boots may allow snow to get inside. Stick with pants that fit outside your boots, and with elastic cuffs that will wrap and stay snug around your boots, preventing any snow from going up the pant leg. And if you get a pair of moderately insulated ski pants you can probably get away with just wearing your thermal underwear under your ski pants. As long as you can keep any snow from getting into your pants or boots, your legs will stay nice and warm.

Another alternative to the usual ski jacket and ski pants combination is to get a one-piece ski suit. Consider what James Bond wore in *The World Is Not Enough*. Perhaps Bond chose a one-piece ski suit because he knew he would be **heli-skiing**; when you take a helicopter to the top of the mountain, jump out, and ski down the mountain. Because of the intense wind that comes from the helicopter blades and the snow that's kicked up, a one-piece ski suit does a great job at keeping snow out.

The downside to the one-piece is that they are less versatile. You can't walk into a ski lodge and just take off your jacket if you have a one-piece. So unless you're expecting a high-wind situation, you may want to go with tradition and stick with a ski jacket and pants. Again, when you opt for several layers, you can always take off individual layers depending on how hot or cold you are.

GLOVES

With your basic ski outfit out of the way, you now need to accessorize. The most obvious accessory you will need is a pair of gloves. Most any pair of gloves you pick up in a ski shop will do you fine, but there are a few possibilities to consider. Do you want to go with gloves or mittens? Some suggest that mittens will keep you slightly warmer than gloves as they can trap heat more effectively. On the other hand, mittens are also pretty clumsy. You'll be using your hands for more than just gripping the ski poles, and you'll be taking mittens off more often. Personally, I have never been cold in a good pair of gloves.

Consider insulation. Stay away from downs, such as goose down. Down gloves or down mittens sound quite comfortable, but down tends to be very slippery, and you want to have a good grip on your poles. Also, if down gloves ever get wet, they're completely useless. Stick with synthetic fibers or synthetic furs.

Consider how they fit. You don't need very tight-fighting gloves, because they won't keep you as warm as slightly roomier gloves. A little room inside the gloves will trap warm air. Try the glove on and make a fist. If it's snug around the back of your hand, then the warmth that would otherwise be trapped there is gone, and your hands will be in a gripping position for most of the day. Also, buy your gloves around the same time you buy your jacket so you can try them on together. The cuffs on the jacket and the cuffs on the gloves should work well together to keep your wrists covered at all times. Finally, consider the material. Gloves tend to come in either leather or fabric. Personally, I would stay away from the leather, as it doesn't hold up as well in wet conditions.

SOCKS

What about socks? Again this is your base layer, so as we mentioned, stay far away from cotton, and move toward synthetics. Thermax and Thermolite are good synthetics for socks. Wool socks make a decent second choice. Make sure your socks come up higher than the calves on your boots, at least halfway up your calves. As far as thickness goes, that's really a matter of personal choice. It seems like that most experts can't decide if thicker or thinner socks are better, so go with whichever you find more comfortable. You're going to have some room in your boot anyway, so it won't matter very much. Worry instead about getting the correct material.

Naturally, get more than one pair of socks, especially if you're going to be skiing more than one day. Aside from the obvious reasons for wearing clean socks (stinky feet), your feet are going to perspire and your socks will absorb and retain some of that moisture, which means on the second day, they're less able to keep your feet warm. Always start your day with fresh ski socks.

HEADWEAR

Next, you'll consider headwear. Depending on where you're headed, and how warm or cold it will be, you may be able to get away with just a pair of earmuffs. You definitely want to keep at least your ears covered. For colder weather conditions, go with a wool or fleece hat. Fleece is actually said to work better in wet climates. If you are going to ski in extremely cold weather conditions, consider a tightly woven fabric like nylon. Just like mom used to say, *"Keeping your head warm will keep your entire body warm."*

NECKWEAR

One last item you will need for keeping warm will be neckwear, and your best bet here is a gaiter. A **gaiter** is nothing more than a small, tube-shaped piece of thick material, usually made out of polyester or acrylic fleece. You could mistake it for an over-sized headband, but it actually goes around your neck. This is a far superior alternative to a scarf, because scarves generally hang loose, and can snag and pull tightly around your neck. The gaiter will do a great job at keeping your neck warm, and will give you extra protection from any snow getting down inside your collar. If you're going with a jacket with a tight collar and maybe a hood, then you might not need the gaiter. Decide on neckwear when you are buying your jacket and your other accessories.

EYEWEAR

Before you leave the ski shop, don't forget some eyewear. You will prob-ably be choosing between goggles and a simple pair of sunglasses. Per-sonally, I would keep both on hand, as one or the other will probably be more suitable for different weather conditions on the slopes. If you're skiing on a bright sunny day, your sunglasses will do just fine. For con-ditions that are cold and windy, you'll definitely want a pair of goggles.

When you buy goggles, make sure they have double lenses to keep your goggles from fogging up. Be careful how you handle your goggles on the slopes. For example, you might be tempted to take off your goggles and put them on your forehead while you're on the ski lift. Try to avoid doing this. The heat and moisture from your forehead is going to rise up and fog up the inside of your goggles. Make sure the goggles fit snuggly so moisture won't get inside. And take special care of the inside of the lenses. The anti-fog coating on the inside of the lenses tends to smear and scratch easily. Only rub the goggles with a chamois or special cloth. You can pick these up when you're purchasing your goggles.

With your ski wear and accessories all taken care of, it's almost time to head off to the slopes, but before we go we should pick up just a few more items. Pack some skin lotion. You'll be spending the afternoon in very cold, dry air, and this can dry out your skin, so be sure to keep your skin moisturized. By the same token, grab a lip balm, like Chapstick. The cold, windy air can chap your lips pretty quickly, so keep them covered. Also, even on more moderate ski slopes, a higher altitude can contribute to dehydration, so pick up some water on your way to the slope, and stay hydrated.

Now that you've gotten yourself into some good shape for skiing, and you've chosen some ski clothing that would make James Bond proud, it's time to head to the slopes.

Hitting the Slopes

When you finally get to the ski resort, the first thing you'll do is hit the rental shop and sign up for a ski class. It's always best to scope out the resort before you go. Look on the resort's website and get as much information as you can, and be sure to look into ski classes. Find out what lessons are available, at which experience levels, when they are offered, at what times, and how to sign up. It's also a pretty good idea to call ahead before you go, even if you've already looked online, just to make sure none of the information the website has changed or become outdated. Be sure to ask how crowded the classes tend to be, and how fast they fill up. You might want to get there a little early, particularly if it's a busy season.

Renting Equipment

When you show up for your first ski lesson, you'll be expected to show up with equipment in hand; this refers to your skis, poles, and boots, so grab your rental equipment before you go to class.

While you may be anxious to make the commitment to becoming a skier, it's still a good idea to avoid making any major purchases before you actually try it at least once. Spend a few days on the slopes, getting the feel of the skis, getting the feel of the boots, and understanding what type of equipment works best for you. This will help you make a smart purchase when you do eventually buy equipment.

WHERE TO RENT

So how and when do you rent your equipment? You have three options: The first would be to find a local rental shop close to home, rent your equipment, and then bring your rented gear to the ski resort, but this option presents problems. If you get to the resort and find out there's something wrong with the equipment, or you just need an adjustment, you can't get back to the shop until you get home. Also, you have to transport it to the ski resort. So unless you're planning on buying a ski rack for your car, this is probably not the best way to go.

The next option would be to rent the equipment at a shop near the resort. This is a slightly better route if you're planning to use the equipment for several days. When you rent just a little away from the resort, you tend to get better prices, better service and better attention from the salespeople. The shop is still relatively close to the resort in case you need to have some adjustments done. But again, the downside is that you still face the problem of traveling with the equipment, and the need to leave the resort and go all the way back to the shop if you have any issues. The prospect of dragging everything back to a nearby rental shop might be frustrating enough to send you to the lodge for the remainder of the trip.

Your best option might be to rent your equipment at the slopes. If you choose this option, you can arrive at the resort, hit the rental shop, and sign up for your class all at the same time. If there's any downside, it's that you can count on crowds in the rental shops. They'll be moving a lot of people through that rental shop pretty quickly, but a reputable resort staff should be able take care of your needs, and they won't send you out with the wrong equipment. If this is your first day on the slopes, and you have yet to see if you take to skiing, then this option will probably be your best. Also, if you're with a group of people, then chances are that at least a few of them will be doing the same thing, so you can just follow along.

Choosing your Equipment

Once you are in the rental shop, it's time to choose your equipment. The first bit of gear you're going to need is a pair of ski boots. A professional skier will tell you that your boots will be your most important piece of equipment. One author illustrated this point by saying, if he were on a flight to a ski resort and had to lose either his boots or his skis, the choice would be simple – goodbye, skis!

SKI BOOTS

If you feel that you're ready to purchase a pair of boots, then this is where you'll want to invest some time and care into choosing the right pair for you. Do this at a reputable ski shop and take time to talk to the salespeople. But for now, what should you look for when you're renting boots?

Many beginners renting boots for the first time will make the mistake of getting them too big. A ski boot is not a 'shoe,' and should not fit like one. When you ski, your actions are communicated from you to your skis through your boots. Your boots should feel like they've been molded to your foot and lower leg. In other words, when you try the boot on for the first time, it's going to feel really tight, but tight is good. Not so tight that they cut off your circulation, but they should definitely be very snug. If your boots are too roomy, you will end up having less control over your skis. This forces your legs to work harder to make the skis do what you want them to do, and your feet will actually hurt more at the end of the day, both due to the extra strength needed, and because your feet have been jolted around inside the boot. When trying on ski boots, err on the side of tight.

When you try your boots on, make sure that the heel fits snuggly, and that your shin is pressed firmly against the front. Your toes can move a little bit, so long as they're not floating too far back, nor pressed against the front of the boot. It may surprise you to find that it will take some strength to buckle your boots, but this is correct, and it means you've chosen wisely.

One last thought on boots: Once you've been out on the slopes for a while, you might feel that your feet are settling in a little bit. This may mean that it's time to stop and check to see if you need to tighten the buckles a little bit. Don't wait for your boots to start to feel roomy; make sure you keep the buckles tight.

That should keep you covered as far as renting boots goes, but remember, when you feel confident enough to invest in ski boots of your own, do this when you have enough time to spend making your purchase. Be ready to try on several pairs, from several different manufacturers, and for several different ability ranges. And once you have chosen your boots, you should reserve some time to have them properly adjusted. But for now, let's move on to your skis.

SKIS

Compared to picking out boots, picking out skis is a relatively simple process. In the last ten years, almost all skis have become "shaped" skis. Long, thin, perfectly parallel skis have become the minority. When you inform the person at the rental shop that you are a beginning skier, you'll notice that he immediately offers you a pair of skis that are shorter and more hourglass-shaped. And the more inexperienced you are, the shorter and more "shapely" the skis will be.

The "**side cuts**," which refers to the shape along the sides of the skis, are designed to make skiing much easier. Smaller skis also make it easier to navigate. Getting around with long skis attached to your feet will feel awkward enough when you first get on, so give yourself a break and go with the shorter skis.

BINDINGS

Another skiing term that you've probably heard, or will soon hear when you hit the rental shop, is "bindings." The **binding** is the part that keeps your ski attached to your boot. They're also adjusted to give way and let go of the skis under a given amount of pressure. Let's say you fall and find yourself rolling down the slope; the bindings will release the skis, so they won't get tangled up, and your legs won't get twisted and cause injury. Correctly fitted bindings will let go of your skis at just the right moment, and keep you free from injury.

When it's time to rent your skis and boots, the salespeople at the rental shop will adjust the bindings for you and make sure they're just right for your boot. The only other thing you need to know about bindings is how to step in and out of them.

STEPPING INTO YOUR SKIS

You will be carrying your skis right up until you begin your ski class, or board a ski lift. When the time comes, drop your skis to the ground, tap your boot with your ski pole to knock loose any snow from the bottom of your boot, and be sure the heelpiece of the binding is cocked in the open position so that you can step into the boot. You'll know this is open when the back lever is pointing up toward the front of the boot. You want to slide your boot into the front part of the binding, and then clamp down on the heel. When you hear that click, you know your ski is firmly in place. Then, do the same thing with your other boot; knock the snow free, step in with the toe of your boot, and clamp down on the back until you hear the click.

To release the bindings when it's time to take your skis off, the lever behind your heel should be pointing upward, toward the back of the ski. Place your ski pole down into the notch on the lever, and push down hard. The binding should click up and release your boot. Do the same thing with your other boot, or you could use your free boot to step down on the lever, releasing your second boot.

SKI POLES

We seem to be headed towards the ski slope without one thing: ski poles. I've heard different schools of thought regarding beginners and poles.

The first time I broke down and signed up a lesson, I went to rent my equipment, and I was surprised to see that they didn't give me any poles. When I asked about this, they told me I didn't need them. The instructor said that I didn't need any poles because poles were for advanced skiers. He said that the primary use of the poles is for when skiers drop down to an angle, and the poles touching the ground will let the skiers know how much room they have between their bodies and the ground. He continued by saying that if you're a novice, the poles just get in the way and confuse the whole operation.

They gave me two short skis, and I was on my way. Much to my surprise, the instructor was correct. I didn't really find myself missing the poles at all. Whenever I fell, I pushed myself up with my hands normally, without the awkwardness of the ski poles attached to my wrists. The only time I could have used poles might be to help me push forward when traversing flat areas. Poles will help you push off and slide a little bit. The lesson being; always follow the advice of your instructor.

If you do decide to go with a poles, the only thing you have to consider is the height. If you're not sure which height is right for you, here's a good rule of thumb: look for a pole that seems to come up just a little past your waist. Turn the pole upside down, rest it on the floor, and grip it just under the "**basket**" (the little round part at the bottom of the pole). If you grip it, your forearm should be parallel to the floor. If you're using a pole, make sure you grip it correctly. Always put your hands through the straps so that when you fall, you aren't chasing the poles over the slope when you fall.

Now, you're dressed and ready. You've got all your gear. It's finally time to go skiing.

The Importance of Taking a Ski Lesson

Let's say you're on the fence about taking a lesson; you're on your first ski trip with friends who all know how to ski. At least one friend will tell you to skip the lesson, and that he'd be happy to show you the ropes. Before you follow him to the ski lift, let me share a story with you:

Years ago, I was watching a well-meaning father attempting to teach his son how to ski. The boy was about ten years old and still very awkward on skis, as all beginners are. He was headed down the bunny hill and didn't get far before he fell. Like all beginners, he couldn't quite figure out how to get up. The father explained to his son the best way to stand up, and his explanation wasn't all that clear. The father basically refused to help his son get up, telling him that getting up was an essential fundamental of skiing, and that he would need to teach himself to stand up by himself. A few minutes went by and this poor kid still hadn't gotten himself up. He sat there in the snow getting cold and growing more and more frustrated. The moral of the story: I'll bet you an Irish Coffee that this was the last time that poor kid ever tried skiing.

What's the first thing you need to learn about skiing? You need to learn that you love to ski. Beginning with a qualified instructor will start you off on the right foot. If that father had done all he could to make the day more enjoyable, and his son had discovered that he actually enjoyed skiing, then I'm willing to bet he would have figured out how to stand up.

If this is your first experience on the ski slope, by the end of the day, you'll either love it or hate it. If your first day is filled with obvious mistakes, falling down a lot, not being able to get up, and sitting for a long time in the snow, you'll walk away from your first day with a bad taste. Let me make a personal plea: tell your well-meaning friends that you'll catch up with them in a little bit, and take a lesson!

Incidentally, most ski areas will offer packages that allow you to purchase your lift tickets, rentals, and ski lessons, all at the same time – and at a pretty reasonable price. Hopefully, that might be a further incentive to actually take the lesson.

The Fundamentals Are the Key

Once you've walked away from you first lesson, you should have a good grasp on the fundamentals, a new sense of confidence being on skis, and a good idea of what you should be doing. Knowing the basics will give you a clear sense of when you're doing things right, when you're doing it wrong, and how to fix it. Concentrate on how you feel when you're doing it right. Your instructor will be able to tell you when you're doing something wrong, so when that happens, focus on how you feel, so that you can recognize and make adjustments. When you feel you have those basics down, you're on your way to becoming a skier.

As you can probably gather, once you've been handed off safely to an instructor, we've covered just about all we can cover in this chapter. Once you're on that slope with your instructor, you can officially call yourself a skier, because as we said at the beginning, you'll learn a hundred times more with an instructor than anything I can tell you about skiing technique, but here are just a few more insights that will help you on your way.

Just Like Riding a Bike?

As I put this chapter together, it struck me that discussing skiing is much like explaining how to ride a bike. Remember the first time you tried to ride a bike? Everyone else made it look easy, and you thought you could just jump on and do it too. Then, the first time you got on the bike and started to pedal, it felt completely foreign. You had this contraption attached to your body and you didn't know how to communicate with your body, in order to get your body to communicate with the bicycle. It felt strange the first time you went forward on a bicycle. You knew that you weren't telling the bicycle where to go; the bicycle was telling you where you were going. The same thing happens with skis. The first time I put on skis and went down a small incline, I felt like the skis were going forward, and I was just going along for the ride. It was like I had slipped on a banana peel and just kept on going. Your body tells you that something feels wrong, and you fall as quickly as you can. The parallels between riding a bike and skiing don't end there.

Just going forward on a bicycle felt like the most difficult thing you've ever tried. Next, you tried to turn and actually navigate the bicycle, and that was a whole new nightmare. You learned very quickly, and probably the hard way, that simply turning the handlebars left or right was not the proper way to change course. You learned about balance. You figured out that you have to lean into the turns, and navigating to the left or the right had a lot more to do with leaning your body than just turning the handlebars. Suddenly, you find that you're actually turning the handlebars only slightly, but you were turning your body quite a bit. Skiing is very similar, and you're probably going to experience the same range of emotions as you learn to ski. Initially, the skis are going to feel heavy and clumsy. But, just as you taught yourself a sort of communication system with a bicycle, you're now going to teach your body to communicate with your skis. Suddenly, you're not following where the skis are going; the skis are there to help you navigate the slope. And ultimately, the skis will simply feel like an extension of yourself – just like riding a bicycle.

Skiing Basics

Comic-genius Stephen Wright used to joke, "You know that feeling when you're leaning back in your chair, and you lean too far back, and you almost fall over backwards, but then you catch yourself at the last second? I feel like that all the time…" Well, once you are actually standing in the snow, with the skis attached to your feet, you'll be feeling like that all the time. When you first realize that you can't hold your balance the way you normally could, this is the moment when terror strikes, and everything you were taught about skiing goes out the window. But take heart, and remember these tips about navigating on skis.

GETTING AROUND ON SKIS

How are you supposed to get around with these things on your feet? Walking forward is just one foot in front of the other, you'll just take bigger steps. If you opted for ski poles, they will help you to keep steady.

But, what happens when you're walking uphill on a small slope? You can try taking "**Herring Bone**" steps. This is when you point your skis out at an angle, separating the front of your skis, and forming like a "V-shape," while pressing the edges down into the snow a little bit to get some grip, and trying not to step on your own skis. For sharper inclines, you might have to do a **side step**. Turn to the side, perpendicular to the slope; move your first ski up, get a good grip, and then bring your other ski up next to it.

COMING TO A STOP

Usually, the first question on every beginner's mind is "How do I stop?" For the absolute beginners, the best way to stop is usually to simply fall down. For example, if you start down the slope for the first time, and you start picking up speed, don't panic and lock up. Just bend your knees, and drop gently to the ground.

The basic way for all beginners to stop is usually a "**snowplow**," also called a" **wedge**," and sometimes the younger kids call that a "pizza." What's happening here is, you're going to bring the tips of your skis together to form an arrowhead. This is where you want to keep your legs strong, because you don't want your skis to cross and overlap each other. You're pushing against the snow to slow down, so you're also going to apply pressure to the outside edge of your skis, enhancing that snowplow effect. You can apply this method more gently if you just want to slow down a little bit. Now, while you're learning to do this basic snowplow, it's also interesting to know that this is one of the simplest ways to turn.

TURNING

Let's say you're going down a gentle slope, and you decide you're going to snowplow to slow yourself down. While you're snowplowing, put a little extra lean on your left leg, applying pressure down onto the inner edge of the ski. You'll find yourself gliding a little more towards the right. Naturally, if you apply a little more to your right ski, you'll find yourself gliding towards the left. Suddenly, you realize that you've just learned how to make a turn. It's literally as simple as that. Of course, this is only the beginning.

By watching the more experienced skiers going left and right down a steep slope, you'll soon realize that the snowplow is only going to get you so far for so long. Keep in mind, as you watch those advanced skiers come down the slope; they are simply using a more exaggerated method of the principle we just talked about.

They're coming down harder and faster. So whereas we just applied a little bit of pressure to one ski to slow down and turn, they're going to have to apply a lot more pressure. To make that left turn, they're going to have to throw all their weight down onto the right ski; in fact, they will have to lift up that left ski, and throw both skis down so they are traveling in the same direction. This is why skiers must keep their legs bent and stay flexible, because they need to be ready to give a little bounce when they want to change course. This is also when you'll be happy you did some strength training in your legs. This action of shifting your balance and throwing your weight on different skis, is the way you slow your body down, and change course. Essentially, that's what skiing is. It's the art of slowing yourself and changing direction, to easily navigate the slope.

This is, of course, completely counterintuitive to a beginner's first instinct to throw down the skis, pointing towards the bottom of the slope, and just go forward. You're going to be in a constant state of motion where you're changing directions and slowing yourself down periodically. It's very rare that you see a skier just pointing straight down the mountain. Even when you see an advanced skier doing that, he's never going faster than he can handle. He knows that he will need to slow himself down. He might go forward for a little while, then apply pressure to his skis to change direction and slow himself back down.

The name of the game is staying in control.

This is why we start out on hills that are not very steep. As you're learning to control your skis and stop yourself, only go as fast as your stopping ability will allow, and as you get better at stopping, and better at changing direction, you can start to tackle steeper hills.

As I mentioned earlier, there are only two speeds for a beginner; too fast and too slow. But, as you start to get better, and as you learn to control yourself on the skis, you start to move toward that sweet spot in the center; that middle ground where skiing becomes exciting and fun.

That's the science of skiing as I have come to understand it. Now, how about a few more practical techniques before you head off to the lift to catch up with your friends and show them what you've learned?

GETTING UP FROM A FALL

The first time you fall and try to stand up in skis, you'll feel like a turtle on its back. So, what's the best way to get back on your feet? Here's a helpful tip: whenever you need to stop or take a break – whether due to a fall or to adjust your equipment – always position your skis perpendicular to the slope. This keeps them from sliding, as they won't be pointing uphill or downhill. Step one in getting up is to align yourself this way.

The next step is to position your skis downhill. Try to rotate your body so that your skis are pointing downhill while your head faces the top of the slope. This is the first step in getting yourself upright. Since gravity is already pulling your feet downward, your body is naturally closer to an upright position. In other words, if you're lying on a steep incline, you won't have to push yourself up as far to stand. So, whenever possible, position yourself so that your skis are facing downhill.

If your skis are more or less still parallel to each other, you're in good shape. Try to position your skis perpendicular to the slope. Now, you want to pull your inside leg up a little bit higher. When I say "inside leg," I mean the leg that's closest to the ground. For example, you're laying down on your right side, and your head is pointed toward the top of the slope.

Looking down, your skis are pointed toward the right side of the slope, and are now perpendicular to the slope. You're going to pull your right leg up a little bit, and now if you push up with your arms, you should be able to get yourself on top of the two skis to stand up. You can use your ski poles to help you by pushing yourself up on the poles to get yourself upward.

When you get your skis tangled up, try this: Roll onto your stomach, get your thighs and knees flat on the ground, bend your knees, so your skis will go up in the air and straighten themselves out. If you can turn your ankles in the same direction, keeping your skis parallel, then roll to your side and push yourself up normally. If you're having trouble getting to your side, then twist your feet so that your heels are coming together and your toes are pointed out, you can now put your legs down so that your skis are back on the ground, forming a V-shape. Then, you'll come back up on your knees and try to push yourself up. You should be able to push yourself off; get your rear end up in the air, and then stand up. It's not very graceful to look at, but neither is sitting in the snow for too long.

RECOVERING YOUR SKIS

What happens if you fall and lose one of your skis? What's the trick to getting the ski back on? The rule of thumb is that it's always easier to step uphill. If you try to step downhill into your ski, it's going to be really easy to lose your balance. Place the ski next to you so that it's perpendicular to the slope, then turn around or move your ski so that the ski is uphill, and then step up into the ski.

Now, with that out of the way, I think you're ready to hit the lifts, and join the rest of your crew who are already tearing up the slopes.

Ski Lifts

Your first time on a ski lift might be a little intimidating, but you'll be surprised how easy it really is, and how enjoyable the ride to the top really is. As the chair comes closer, stay alert, and keep moving forward in line. When it's your time to board, you will be directed where to stand, and you'll know exactly when it's time to sit down, as the chair will simply come up behind you and scoop you up. The silence is refreshing as you enjoy the peaceful ride to the top.

Getting off is just as easy. You'll always know when it's time to step off. As you get to the top, and it's almost time to step off, you'll scoot up to the edge of the chair, and when your skis meet the snow, you'll know it's time to stand up and slip off.

Navigating the Trails

When you're actually on your own and navigating the slopes, depending on the size of the ski area, you might want to keep a trail map with you. Every ski trail has a trail map so you'll know which ski trail is the easiest, which are intermediate, and which trails are the most difficult. You'll be able to identify the trails according to their markings. The trails are always clearly marked according to their difficulty levels, and the markings are usually universal. The easier trails are marked with a **green circle**. The intermediate trails are marked with a **blue square**. Of course, the more difficult or expert trails are marked by a **black diamond**, or for the really difficult trails, two black diamonds, or a **double black diamond**. Naturally, you want to start off on the greens. Stick to those until you're ready to tackle the blues, and then, when you're ready to ace the blacks, that's when you're going to feel like James Bond trying to outrun the villains.

Knowing When to Hit the Lodge

After you've been carving up the snow for a few hours, if you find yourself falling down more often, and you're getting a little bit frustrated, take heart; your skiing ability isn't slipping away from you. Your body is just telling you that you're getting tired, which basically means it's time to hit the lodge and warm up with a cold beer, a hot chocolate, or a nice Irish coffee.

Once you discover that après ski after a long day of carving up the slopes, you can officially call yourself a skier.

Ski Destinations

As we said earlier, after your first day, you're either going to love skiing, or you're going to hate it. My guess is that you're going to love it. Maybe you'll get so good that you're going to venture off to some more challenging ski locations. If you're on the East Coast, the best skiing is in New England, in states like Vermont, New Hampshire, and Maine. Of course, for the best skiing in the United States, the real skiing is out in Colorado.

Once you've mastered the U.S. slopes, you can really follow in the footsteps of 007 and head to Europe; specifically the Alps, which is basically the Mecca of skiing. Countries like Austria, France, Italy, and of course, Switzerland are the major Alpine countries, and Bond has skied most of them. What this all means is that, if you find yourself being seduced by skiing, if you learn to love it, you'll go often, and you'll get better. Once that happens, the possibilities are endless. The world is your oyster. One day, you might even find yourself carving up the Swiss Alps, just like James Bond.

Safety and Etiquette

As a beginner, you'll find that the other skiers are generally very forgiving of honest mistakes – everyone remembers what it was like to be new. But there's a world of difference between making a mistake and being reckless or careless. With that in mind, here are a few important things to remember as you set out onto the slopes:

KEEP CONTROL

Always keep control and be able to stop when you need to, especially when close to objects or other people. If you find yourself going too fast, and you just can't get control, bend your knees and drop to the ground. That hurts a lot less than crashing into another skier.

KEEP YOUR EYES FORWARD

People ahead of you have the right of way. It's your responsibility to avoid them, just as the people behind you are responsible to avoid you. Keep your eyes forward and stay sharp.

DON'T STAND AROUND THE SLOPE

Try not to stop or stand around in the middle of the trail so that other skiers have to try to avoid you. If you need to pause and catch your breath or get your bearings, just move to the outer edges of the slope, and always keep visible.

LOOK BEFORE MERGING

Whenever you're stepping onto a trail midway, or your trail merges with another trail, be sure look uphill and yield to other skiers.

HOLD ONTO YOUR EQUIPMENT

Always use devices to prevent runaway equipment. Keep your hands through the straps of your poles so you don't lose them, and if you find yourself losing your skis a little too frequently, your bindings might need an adjustment. Head back in the rental office and get them corrected.

READ THE SIGNS

Pay attention to the posted signs and warnings. Watch for signs indicating the trail's difficulty levels, and avoid the trails that are closed off.

BE AWARE AT THE SKI LIFT

Stay sharp when you're getting on and getting off the ski lift. Getting distracted when it's your turn to board the lift can lead to some embarrassing and possibly dangerous moments. Use your head, and follow what the other skiers are doing.

What About Snowboarding?

In my mind, if Ian Fleming's James Bond was a skier, then I am a skier; however, it would be remiss if I didn't mention snowboarding. After all, James Bond snowboards (technically) in *A View to a Kill*. In fact, you could even make the argument that James Bond did a lot to push snowboarding into the mainstream. At the time *A View to a Kill* was released in the mid-80s, the idea of somebody surfing on snow was so strange that the filmmakers even decided to highlight the absurdity by adding that awful surfing music that makes most Bond fans cringe. However, if James Bond can lose his skis and easily jump onto a snowboard, then it's something that **Being James Bond** should touch on.

Much of what we've covered so far about skiing, applies to snowboarding as well; including conditioning, clothing, and navigating the slopes. Snowboarding went from obscurity to being downright common in most ski areas. In fact, you might even find the snowboarders outnumbering the skiers. You should have no trouble finding snowboarding classes.

So, what are the differences between skiing and snowboarding? I've heard different schools of thought when it comes to the similarities between skiing and snowboarding, but one thing is for sure; just because you have good skiing experience, doesn't mean you can switch easily over to a snowboard. (And, I can vouch for that. The first time I tried to snowboard was an absolute fiasco.) On the other hand, if you do have some experience carving up the snow, you at least know a few general principles, but don't expect your body to communicate with the snowboard in the same way it communicates with skis.

If you are an absolute beginner about to set out on the slopes for the first time, it might be good to decide up front if you want to be a skier or a snowboarder. Here are a few of the differences that you should consider before making the choice:

Stopping and standing on a snowboard is a little bit awkward. Snowboarders are always exerting energy to stay on the edge of the board if they want to keep from sliding. Either that or they have to sit down. Plus, you don't have the poles to keep you upright and stationary. Snowboarding tends to be easier on the knees, and injuries are a lot less common on snowboards. On the other hand, snowboarding can be rough on your wrists as you tend to land forward on your hands; protective wrist guards can help. Flat surfaces can be particularly frustrating because you don't have your poles to move you forward. The only way to get around on a snowboard is to take one foot out and just walk.

Another difference between snowboarding and skiing is that snowboarding works better in deeper, softer snow, whereas skis are much better handling bumps and ice. Also, they say that getting up on a snowboard is easier than getting up and getting yourself together on skis.

Now, if you're learning to ski as a way to get your adrenaline going, it might surprise you to know that skiers get a lot more velocity than snowboarders, so factor that in when you're making your decision.

I hope I didn't show too much bias in this explanation, but as I love to remind my snowboarding friends, if Fleming's Bond skied, I ski! Of course, there's plenty of room on the slope for all of us, so whatever you decide to do is fine. Both activities will give you a great feeling at the end of the day, as you're relaxing in the lodge.

Where do we go from here? Of course, there is no better way to learn than hitting the slopes and taking a skiing class with a qualified instructor. Even if you already have some experience, a few lessons should really bring out your personal best, and take your skiing ability to the next level.

Before this chapter on Skiing is complete, we need to make one stop. As promised, we're going to visit the absolute mecca of James Bond locations – Piz Gloria, located atop Mount Schilthorn, near the village of Mürren, in the Bernese Oberland region of Switzerland.

Piz Gloria

The following is based on two separate visits to this magnificent location, spaced roughly twenty years apart, and as you will see, these two experiences were almost perfect polar opposites of one another, in every way, but both will contribute to a complete picture of what you might expect, and how you can get there for yourself.

When it comes to skiing, Switzerland is unmatched, and when it comes to Bond locations, there is one that I contend is absolutely second to none. The grandfather of all Bond ski chases started at Piz Gloria, and descended down the side of Mount Schilthorn, in Mürren, Switzerland.

I can't think of any single James Bond location quite as perfect as Piz Gloria, and for several reasons. Based on what many would argue is Ian Fleming's very best novel, Piz Gloria was the fictional mountain top lair of James Bond's greatest foe, Ernst Stavro Blofeld. When location hunting began for the film version of *On Her Majesty's Secret Service,* the soon to be realized Piz Gloria was the perfect fit. It's a magnificent location in one of the most magical parts of the world, and even if it didn't have a Bond connection, is a marvel in its own right. Additionally, not only is this one of the few classic locations to withstand the test of time, and still look as timeless as it did during the 1969 production, but the current proprietors of Piz Gloria have taken great care and investment to make this iconic place a celebration of the one of the greatest James Bond films of all time.

The iconic location was first conceived in the early 1960s as a state-of-the-art revolving restaurant at 2,970 meters (9,744 feet) above sea level, to attract visitors to the Schilthorn region. Piz Gloria was engineered to rotate, offering visitors a panoramic 360-degree view of its breathtaking surroundings, including iconic peaks like the Eiger, Mönch, and Jungfrau. Construction began in 1963.

The producers discovered the yet unfinished project during their location scouting, and decided it was the perfect stand-in for Blofeld's mountain top lair. Eon invested in the completion of the building, adding several story-specific elements, including the helipad. Construction was completed in time for the filming, and this magnificent mountaintop sanctuary and restaurant was opened to the public soon after, now enjoying the notoriety of having been in the latest James Bond movie. The name "Piz Gloria," was later adopted by the real-life restaurant.

Getting to Piz Gloria can be half the adventure, and has many James Bond inspired stops along the way. You begin the journey in the beautiful nearby town of Interlaken, which is accessible by car or rail, and you'll embark on a scenic 20-minute train ride that offers breathtaking views of the Swiss Alps, leading you to Lauterbrunnen. A picturesque village in the Bernese Oberland region of Switzerland, Lauterbrunnen is nestled in a lush valley surrounded by towering cliffs with waterfalls cascading from sheer rock faces, and snow-capped peaks.

As you step off the train in Lauterbrunnen, you are already retracing the steps of James Bond, as this is indeed the very same station where Bond exits the train in the opening frames of the Switzerland scenes of *On Her Majesty's Secret Service.*

The village of Lauterbrunnen is also home to a few other iconic scenes. When Bond and Tracy are being pursued by Irma Bunt and Blofeld's henchmen, the red Cougar passes a small church at the southern entrance of the village.

"Nearest post office to contact London." Near the center of the village you'll find an elevated parking lot between the Kloppelstube and the Hotel Jungfrau; this is where Bond reaches the phone booth to contact London. The call is cut short, and Bond jumps into Tracy's car right in front of the Hotel Jungfrau. The phone booth is not actually there, as this prop was placed there for the film, but the view of the raised lot is unmistakable.

From Lauterbrunnen, you'll take a cable car to your next stop, the town of Mürren, which is home to James Bond lore, both on and off the screen.

During the filming of *On Her Majesty's Secret Service,* most of the cast and crew stayed at the Hotel Eiger. A charming alpine retreat since 1886, this family-run hotel offers breathtaking views of the Alps, and provides cozy rooms, an exceptional dining experience featuring locally inspired cuisine, and offers a perfect nightcap in the Tächi Bar. The Hotel Eiger is also conveniently located, only a short walk to the Schilthorn cable car.

Mürren also provides some amazing hiking. As you're trekking along the side of the mountain, look sharp and you can see the ghost of the bob-sled chase from the finale of *On Her Majesty's Secret Service.* The outline of the former track is still visible in several spots.

After exploring Murren, it's time to board the next cable car and continue the ascent up Mount Schilthorn. The first leg of this journey is a five-minute cable car ride from Mürren to your first stop. Recall the helicopter trip which brought 'Sir Hillary Bray' from Lauterbrunnen up into the alps and to Piz Gloria. As the helicopter soars upward, Bond looks down to observe a large chalet with an expansive outdoor terrace, bustling with skiers and tourists soaking up the sun. Prominently displayed along the side of the building, inscribed in bold letters is the word, "BIRG."

High above Mürren, Birg serves as a gateway to the iconic Piz Gloria on Mount Schilthorn. This mountain station is perched at an altitude of 2,677 meters (8,783 feet), and offers spectacular panoramic views of the Alps. Featuring a large sun terrace and a cozy bistro, guests can relax and take in the breathtaking alpine scenery. Birg is also home to the Thrill Walk, a heart-pounding cliffside pathway with glass floors. Birg serves as a perfect prelude to the final ascent to Piz Gloria.

Finally, there's one last five-minute cable car ride; the final stretch of a journey culminating in the arrival at the iconic summit station.

As I mentioned, I've had two visits to this magnificent location. About twenty years ago, on (another) business trip to Switzerland, a much younger man took a train from Geneva to Interlaken, with stops in Lausanne and Bern. At that time, there was a funicular that connected Lauterbrunnen to Grütschalp as part of the route to Mürren, traversing diagonally up the steep mountain incline. The funicular has since been dismantled and replaced. Continuing on the short train ride into Mürren, I reached the first cable station, where the operator actually tried to dissuade me from continuing. It was a spring afternoon, and the warm weather had created a disappointing dense fog that obscured the normally awe-inspiring views. Naturally, a Bond fanatic was not to be deterred.

Two cable cars later, I was stepping off and into Piz Gloria. It was practically deserted, with only a skeleton crew inside. The silence at this altitude was deafening. On the bright side, I had the place to myself and could explore as much as I wanted. Once inside, it felt like little had changed since James Bond was here. Walking up the stairway, along a familiar gold balustrade to the revolving restaurant, would make even the mildest fan of *On Her Majesty's Secret Service* feel as if they had stepped back in time.

I've always said this about Piz Gloria; as much as we enjoy visiting iconic Bond locations, Piz Gloria truly embraces being one. At that time, the proprietors had created a charming 'Tourist-O-Rama' beneath the main rotunda. Pressing the '007' button in the center of the large circular room would cause the window shades to lower with a soft mechanical hum, and a panoramic slide show would begin. The presentation highlighted the preparation and filming of *On Her Majesty's Secret Service,* followed by a video montage showcasing the film's Swiss highlights. After exploring every inch of the legendary stronghold, I stopped off in the gift shop to see the airbrushed murals of Bond and Tracy, grabbed a few souvenirs with the 007 logo as reminders of the day, and made my way back.

In 2019, I would take my second trip to Schilthorn and to Piz Gloria, as part of *'OHMSS50: The On Her Majesty's Secret Service 50th Anniversary Celebration,'* created and organized by Martijn Mulder and an extensive crew of dedicated and creative people. This visit would be (excuse the language) orgasmic.

My perspective might have been slightly jaded. After all, I had just come away from the first leg of this trip which was a week in Portugal – this could be an entire chapter unto itself, but here are just a few highlights: We stayed in the amazing Hotel Palácio in Lisbon, where Bond stayed and enjoyed a rendezvous with Tracy – and yes, when I checked into my room, I strolled onto the balcony and said, "This will do. This will do me nicely." We went to Praia do Guincho, or Guincho Beach, near Cascais, Portugal, where Bond rescues Tracy (I braved a nasty undertow and plunged into the ocean with my clothes on to reenact this moment). We visited the bullfighting ring where Bond meets Draco and Tracy, along with the courtyard where the two became Mr. and Mrs. James Bond, and we drove along the scenic coastline where Tracy met her tragic end. And speaking of romance, what could be more appropriate than having two of our companions actually get married in the courtyard of the Palácio. By the way, George Lazenby also stayed in the same hotel, and we all ended up in the hotel bar at the end of each day, so we got to know him well, and we all walked away with some funny drinking stories.

I'm already walking six inches taller, and thought nothing could possibly top this extraordinary week.

The large group boarded a plane bound for Switzerland, where we hopped on a set of charming old buses and headed off. There would be several stops before finally reaching our destination, and to the grand finale at Piz Gloria.

The first stop was the Hotel Schweizerhof in Bern, notable for the scene where James Bond breaks into Gumbold's office and cracks the safe. The interior shots were filmed in the studio, but the balcony where Bond emerges, observing the clock tower in the center of town, and awaiting a package lifted by crane from the construction site below, were all filmed on the balcony of a fourth-floor room of the hotel. The historic Schweizerhof Hotel & Spa has been in operation since 1859, offering luxurious rooms and suites, the only hotel spa in the city, the French restaurant Jack's Brasserie, a bar and cigar lounge in the lobby, and the rooftop Sky Terrace overlooking the city of Bern. We all were able to visit the room and the balcony, overlooking the building that was under construction during filming, and the familiar clock tower.

Continuing on our journey, the bustling cityscape soon turned into lush green rolling hills that seem to stretch endlessly. We entered the town of Heiligenschwendi, and slowed down at the top of a hill above Lake Thun, at what seemed to be a farm with a large chalet with a ramp on one side leading up to a barn. The owners came out to welcome us and everyone gathered around the barn entrance to take photographs. Just then, a familiar red Mercury Cougar appeared, turned down the long driveway and drove up to the barn door.

The passenger-side door opened and James Bond, dressed in the familiar blue and plaid, emerged and ran up ahead to the barn door, opening it, allowing the Cougar to proceed inside. The driver emerged gracefully, revealing a stunning yet familiar ensemble of tan, yellow and gold that shimmered in the light. It was a perfect recreation of the scene when Bond and Tracy hid themselves and their car inside the barn to avoid the heavy snowstorm. The parts of Bond and Tracy were played by the owners of the car, Wolfgang and Piroska Schnetzer.

We were invited inside the barn to explore and take photos, and the owners of the property treated us to a buffet of meats and cheeses that were made on that very farm. It was a wonderful moment that cemented this location perfectly in our minds.

The expedition continued on, with the red Cougar now joining us and following behind. There wasn't a single moment that you could refer to as uneventful. We stopped for lunch in the town of Grindelwald, in the very same town square where the ice rink was constructed for Bond's reunion with Tracy. An additional Bond car met us in Grindelwald; a white Lotus Esprit owned by Gernot Wolf, who along with the Cougar, then followed us to our next destination – what a charge it was seeing the Cougar and the white Lotus following the buses, and then overtaking us!

A few more hours of driving, and two cable cars later, and we finally arrived in Mürren. At an elevation of 1,638 meters (5,374 feet), Mürren is something to behold – a picturesque, Alpine village offering breathtaking panoramic views of the magnificent Swiss Alps. Like something out of a childhood storybook, Mürren's narrow cobblestone streets are lined with traditional wooden chalets adorned with colorful flower boxes, breathing charm and tranquility.

We checked into our respective hotels, and continued on with the days' events. We toured the nearby Lauterbrunnen, seeing all the local Bond locations and retracing Bond and Tracy's escape route. Later, we visited a nearby airplane hangar, where inside was a selection of James Bond cars; an Aston Martin DB5, a copper/red Lotus Esprit complete with ski rack, and the Mercury Cougar and white Lotus Esprit that joined us previously, with all of the owners present to talk about their cars. Just outside the hangar was an unassuming open field; it turned out this was the same field where the stock car race was filmed, where Tracy eluded the goons. Every moment of the day was filled with memorable discoveries. The evening concluded with a welcome dinner where we reunited with old friends and made some new ones, and of course a nightcap; a few pints at the bar in the Hotel Eiger.

By the way, after all this, I haven't even gotten to Piz Gloria yet.

The day finally arrived for what would be the actual *'OHMSS50: The On Her Majesty's Secret Service 50th Anniversary Celebration,'* Everyone arrived at the cable car station dressed with an emphasis on sophistication and adherence to tradition, decked out in evening gowns, dinner jackets and tuxedos, and we began our journey. Our first stop was Birg, and unlike my previous visit, the outdoor terrace stretching out over the Alps was bustling once more, packed with visitors reveling and soaking up the sun. Our first reception was here, and it was our first opportunity to really meet and mingle with all of the evening's celebrants. I was thrilled to finally meet some familiar faces which had previously only been virtual at best. I made a ton of new friends on this trip.

Then, it was time to begin our final ascent.

The Swiss locals had told us that the weather over the past few weeks had been abysmal; nothing but dense fog and sleet. But on this day, the sky stretched wide with a brilliant canvas of soft cerulean blue, dotted with billowing cumulus clouds.

You could feel the anticipation in the air as the cable car drew close to the familiar shape of Piz Gloria appearing in front of us. As the car arrived, and we all stepped off, the excitement was palpable. Anticipation became exhilaration and joy as we ascended the escalators and staircases which would bring us back in time and into the very familiar setting.

It's hard to describe the sensation of this moment without sounding over-dramatic or hyperbolic; I'm standing in what is probably the most quintessential James Bond location ever, which was the key setting in my all-time favorite James Bond movie. I'm nearly 3,000 meters above sea level, and surrounded by panoramic views of the Bernese and Valais Alps. I'm immersed in a crowd of over 200 of the most hard-core fans of James Bond and *On Her Majesty's Secret Service,* as well as dozens of cast and crew from the film.

Without trying to sound blasphemous; I'm in my church.

As I mentioned, the current proprietors of Piz Gloria have taken great care and investment to make this place a celebration of one of the greatest James Bond films of all time. The previous attractions have all been up-graded and the atmosphere is one of 'pride' in being a Bond location; if you doubt me, just visit the bathrooms. The theme here is 'fun.'

The evening began with dinner in the rotating restaurant; sitting in the very same spot where 'Sir Hillary Bray' enjoyed a malt whiskey and branch water, and a steak Piz Gloria, with the lovely 'Angels of Death.' Many of the cast were scattered among the tables, and sitting at our table was Jenny Hanley, who played the Irish Girl, and could not have been more lovely. The restaurant makes a complete rotation around its own axis every 45 minutes, giving you an incredible view of the surrounding alps. Between the view outside, and the one inside, it was tough to play it cool despite my best efforts. I was continually scanning the room taking in all the familiar faces.

After dinner, the sun was beginning to set, and I promise you you've never seen a view quite so spectacular. We were soon led into a dark viewing room where we were to be treated to a video presentation; a tribute montage of the film. When I heard the name of the artist who created the video, I immediately perked up. Tom Waldek, of Passionfruit Cine Promos, was well known to me for his previous video montages celebrating James Bond; my particular favorite being *'James Bond & The Vesper Chronicles'* made not long after the release of *Quantum of Solace,* perfectly blending the mood of Daniel Craig's first two Bond films.

Waldek's three-and-a-half-minute tribute to the greatness of *On Her Majesty's Secret Service* was supernatural! This montage presented the film in a fresh, exciting way. The pulsating and heart-pounding rendition of the familiar musical score immediately has you tapping your foot, and the interesting chronology of events were finessed and reworked in such a way that it gave the story new focus and meaning; it feels as if you're seeing the film for the first time all over again. It was electrifying and a perfect tribute. Be sure you check out this video on his YouTube page.

The sun continued to set, turning the sky into a warm golden yellow, as the rest of the evening progressed, characterized by a great deal of celebration and socializing; I made sure to grab a few more photos with my friend Terrance Mountain who I had the great privilege of meeting and getting to know in Portugal. *"Put your hands behind your head. Move!"* Terry played Raphael in the film, who holds Bond at gunpoint on the beach, and then grapples with Bond in the surf. What a great human being Terry is! Very generous with his time and attention; when you talk with him he makes you feel like you're the only person in the room! It was a privilege to spend time with and get to know him.

The meeting and mingling continued; I got the chance to gush to John Glen about my love for (in my humble opinion) his best Bond film. I told him I thought *Octopussy* had the most Hitchcock-style intrigue; he responded by telling me he likes it for its comedy. Walking outside to get some air, I saw that a curling game had been set up in the same area as was seen in the film. I joined a group of people who were huddled up chatting, and Steven Saltzman, son of Harry Saltzman, had his phone out and was sharing behind the scenes photos from the filming of *Live and Let Die*. Inside, several gambling tables had been set up around the room, so I couldn't pass up the chance to play a little blackjack with a few other fans. I lost a few hands and had a few laughs as we listened to the band warming up just down the nearby staircase. By now, the sky was a breathtaking palette of fiery oranges, soft pinks and purples.

Then, Q the Music began to play.

As I've said many times to Warren Ringham, the musical director of Q the Music, I lack the language of music to properly articulate just how magnificent this group and this performance really was. But, as one might say about the visual medium; I don't know art, but I know what I like! I'll just say it, Q the Music was off the hook!

The 13-piece band started off strong with a medley of several different tracks from the *On Her Majesty's Secret Service* score, all seamlessly blended into one harmonious movement. They meticulously re-created each track to sound virtually identical to the original, but seeing it all played out in person – watching every tap on the key, the contribution of each instrument – to see and comprehend the work coming together to form the finished symphony was extraordinary.

They continued with an eclectic repertoire of Bond music; performing an impressive setlist of popular theme songs, as well as the lesser-known gems that only real fans know, and even a few more rather obscure oddities; I have to confess, only Q the Music could warm my cold heart to such gems as *'Another Way To Die'* or *'Dirty Love.'*

The finale was truly mind bending. After performing a smoky, brassy rendition of an iconic, cinematic score from the 1960s, the band broke out with the electronic fusion remix of the *On Her Majesty's Secret Service* theme by the Propellerheads. I couldn't imagine pieces of music any further apart on the spectrum. I didn't know this was a thing that a 13-piece band could do.

By the way, I mentioned that we were nearly 3,000 meters above sea level; several guests had already left the party early, feeling lightheaded from the altitude. Q the Music's lead singer Kerry Barnard Schultz was a consummate professional and belted out the classic Bond ballads without missing a beat. (Yes, she was able to hold the final note from '*Goldfinger*' so long it would have made Shirley Bassey jealous.)

Is it any wonder that I began this recollection by calling it 'orgasmic?' This was the absolute climax of a lifetime of fandom. The planets aligned perfectly, and everything about this experience was flawless. It was transcendent. This was an adventure that I will never forget! Thank you to Martijn Mulder and all the people who made this event possible!

Further Reading

While nothing can replace hitting the slopes and taking a lesson, there are several other resources that can help you grasp essential skills and techniques, as well as sources for tracking down Swiss Bond locations on your own:

'The Essential Guide to Skiing: 201 Things Every Skier Must Know'

Ron LaMaster has created a comprehensive book packed with authoritative advice on every aspect of the sport. For novices, you'll learn how to walk in ski boots, when and where to rent equipment, and where to attach a lift ticket, while more experienced skiers can learn how to find the shortest lift lines to the best slopes, discover the best goggle lens colors for flat light, and uncover the best powder stashes even when the mountain looks skied out.

'Harald Harb's Essentials of Skiing'

In his seminal and highly influential work, Harald Harb describes and demonstrates the essential movements of expert skiing, and presents lessons to improve your ability to perform these key movements. The essentials are universally applicable and beneficial. Whatever your current level, working on the essentials will accelerate your progress, giving you command of any terrain.

'On the Tracks of 007'

Hands down, this is the bible for anyone traveling overseas in search of Bond locations. I have two; one autographed copy that sits on the shelf in my office, and another that's beat up and dog-eared and covered with the dust of several countries. Martijn Mulder does extensive work on Piz Gloria and its surrounding areas, as well as the rest of Swiss Alps. If you don't have a copy already, put this one on your list.

www.onthetracksof007.com

'The Making of OHMSS50'

There seems to be nothing Martijn Mulder cannot do. After creating the definitive work on James Bond locations, Martijn moved on to creating incredible events. This 136-page commemorative photo booklet about the 2019 event, detailing how the event came about and each day's events. It includes personal words from cast & crew members including George Lazenby, Joanna Lumley, Terence Mountain, Catherine Schell, Vic Armstrong, and John Glen, among others. Written by Martijn Mulder, and beautifully photographed by Sascha Braun.

www.onthetracksof007.com/shop

For more information on Piz Gloria and Mount Schilthorn, look them up on the web at www.schilthorn.ch.

As we wrap up this guide to learning how to ski, you should now have a solid understanding of what it takes to prepare for the slopes; from choosing the right gear and getting in shape to mastering essential techniques. More than just a sport, skiing is an experience that combines skill, adventure, and breathtaking scenery. And if you're lucky enough to find yourself carving down the legendary slopes of Switzerland, you'll discover firsthand how skiing can be as much about the journey as the destination. Whether you're a first-timer or looking to refine your skills, the mountains are calling. So gear up, embrace the challenge, and enjoy every exhilarating moment on the snow.

And with that, that concludes this complex (and often self-indulgent) chapter on skiing. Good luck, and I'll "see ya back at the lodge!"

Drinks & Mixology

"A dry martini," he said, "One in a deep champagne goblet."

"Oui, monsieur."

"Just a moment, three measures of Gordon's, one of vodka, half a measure of Kina Lillet. Shake very well until it's ice cold then add a large, thin slice of lemon peel. Got it?"

– Chapter Seven, Casino Royale, 1953

It's hard to believe that it was a whole fifty-three years later that Daniel Craig ordered that very drink in the exact same way in the film version of *Casino Royale,* thrilling the Ian Fleming purists everywhere – myself included. Hearing such complete respect for the original material gave me one of the biggest charges I've ever gotten at the movies.

There's just something about ordering a cocktail exactly the way you like it. When James Bond orders a cocktail, his attention to detail tells us two things: He possesses an extensive knowledge about cocktails, and he's a man who knows what he wants. Anybody can walk into a bar or a club and order the same drink that everyone else is drinking; either a light beer, or a boring vodka drink made with whatever brand happens to have the best marketing campaign at the time.

"I take ridiculous pleasure in what I eat and drink," said James Bond in the same novel.

Rather than follow the undemanding masses, we're going to explore the world of mixology, and expand our horizons. By the time we are finished, hopefully you won't order or prepare a cocktail exactly the same way again.

What would the potential James Bond need to know about Mixology, and what's the best way to make this knowledge and skill your own? This chapter will make a few assumptions. We'll assume that you enjoy the occasional cocktail, and would like to know more about the various types, and how they're made, so that you can choose cocktails to suit the setting, and suit your mood. We'll assume you would like to be able to mix various cocktails on your own should the need arise. We'll assume that even if you don't want to be a bartender by trade, you might like to have a few insights as to how professionals mix their drinks. We'll assume that you want to be prepared to mix cocktails in your home, and to offer impressive cocktails to guests, even surprise guests. We'll assume that you may want to have several guests over for gatherings, and you'd like to be able to serve a selection of cocktails.

Note: This chapter goes into serious detail; in fact, the word 'overkill' might come to mind at some point. But hopefully, this chapter will speak to your interests and needs, and you may choose to skim past certain parts, but it's all here as and when you need it.

So let's get started!

Types of Liquor

Let's start by taking a look at the liquors that will be the primary ingredients in our cocktails. The five primary liquors used in making drinks are vodka, gin, rum, tequila and whiskey. We'll begin with the most obvious and most popular liquor behind the bar, and James Bond's choice, vodka.

VODKA

The word "vodka" comes from the Slavic word "voda" meaning "little water." Vodka is distilled from a fermented mash of grain; it is distilled at a high proof (190 or above) and then processed even further to remove all the flavor. While quality can vary from brand to brand, vodka is meant to be a neutral spirit, and does not have any characteristic flavor, aroma or color. The neutral quality of vodka makes it very versatile, and it can be easily added to juices and sodas to create cocktails, such as Screwdrivers, Cape Cods, Bloody Marys, Vodka Tonics, etc.

GIN

Gin is also distilled from grain, but this liquor receives its unique flavor and aroma from juniper berries and other botanicals and spices, with each gin producer creating its own special recipe. The flavor and quality of gin will vary, but the most typical style is London Dry. Gin's unique flavor goes well with tonic and certain citrus drinks like the Tom Collins.

RUM

Rum is distilled from molasses and is generally produced wherever sugar grows, which would explain the popularity of the Mojito in sugar-rich countries like Cuba. Rum is distilled at a lower proof, which allows it to retain its distinct flavor, and is usually aged in oak barrels. Rum can be broken down into various classifications, including rhum and cachaça (which are made from raw sugar cane instead of molasses), and flavors such as light, dark, gold, spiced, and flavored rums such as coconut rum.

Rum goes well with cola, creating the Cuba Libre (if you add a slice of lime), and is also often associated with tropical drinks such as the Mai Tai, the Daiquiri, and the afore-mentioned Mojito.

TEQUILA

Tequila, the primary spirit of Mexico, comes from the fermented juice of the Agave plant, giving it a very distinct flavor, and is aged in oak barrels. Tequila comes in different styles including blanco (meaning "white") and plata ("silver") which have been aged under two-months, oro ("gold") which has caramel added for coloring, reposada ("rested") which is aged between two-months and one-year, and añejo ("aged") which is aged over one-year. Because of its very distinct flavor, tequila isn't used in as many cocktails as other liquors and will generally be served neat. Exceptions include the Margarita and the Tequila Sunrise.

WHISKEY

Like vodka, whiskey is distilled from a fermented mash of grain, but the two liquors differ in the methods of distillation. Unlike vodka, which is distilled at a high proof, whiskey is distilled at a very low proof to retain its natural flavor, and most styles are then aged in wood. Whiskey is seldom used as an ingredient in cocktails, and usually consumed neat; a few cocktail exceptions would include the Mint Julep and the Sazerac, but in both cases, the whiskey is the primary ingredient with only a few minor ingredients added to season the liquor. Whiskey can also be very confusing to many drinkers, as it's often better known by its distinctive varieties, including Bourbon, Scotch, Rye, Tennessee whiskey, Canadian whiskey, and Irish whiskey. Many drinkers believe that Whiskey, Bourbon, and Scotch, are individual spirits.

Those are the five basic types of liquor. You could also add brandy to this list. The term brandy comes from the Dutch phrase *'brandewijn,'* meaning 'burnt wine.' Brandy is the spirit that is distilled from fermented grapes at a medium proof (between about 70 to 120).

What did I mean by distilled, fermented, and proof? Let's take a closer look at brandy to understand the process.

Fermentation, Distillation, and Proof

Liquor is created through two processes, fermentation and distillation. **Fermentation** refers to the conversion of sugar to alcohol; this is how wine, beer, and even vinegar are produced. For example, when a grape is crushed, the sugar inside reacts with the natural yeasts on the skins, and becomes alcohol; thus begins the process of turning grapes to wine.

Distillation, is simply a method of separation. If the fermented grape juice we just created is distilled, meaning that the water or juice is removed from the wine, what remains is only the pure alcohol, which is where we get brandy.

So what does it mean to distill at a certain proof? Before science figured out how to test booze to see how much ethanol was in it, the liquid would be mixed with gunpowder, and then someone would try to light it. If it burned, it was considered "proof" that it had high enough alcohol content, which they referred to as "100-proof."

While methods have grown more sophisticated, proof is still known as the way we measure the alcohol content. We understand that distilling refers to the removal of the non-alcohol from the mixture, so if we've distilled at a high proof, then more of the non-alcohol has been removed. The higher the proof, the more alcohol is present in the liquor. Proof is directly related to alcohol percentage. For example, liquor that is 100-proof is 50% alcohol by volume, and therefore 200-proof (100% alcohol by volume) would be the highest possible proof. So any liquor with a very high proof has a very high alcohol percentage.

Now that we've got the science out of the way, let's talk about cocktails.

What are the different types of drinks you can make? To keep things simple, we can sort the majority of cocktails into one of these categories: one liquor (and mixer) drinks; two-liquor drinks; cream drinks; sour drinks; and of course martinis. If you've seen a typical cocktail menu, you know that some drinks will throw in everything but the kitchen sink, falling under several categories – or none at all – but let's start with the basics.

Categories of Cocktails

ONE-LIQUOR DRINKS

These are usually the simplest cocktails, and even the name of the drinks will usually tell you what's in it; such as a 'Rum and Coke' or a 'Gin and Tonic.' They traditionally served over ice, and in tall glasses. While most drinkers know these very simple cocktails by their ingredients, they often have names that you might not have heard of like a Cape Cod (which is simply vodka and cranberry), or a Greyhound (which is vodka and grapefruit juice). The next time you wander into the tavern, try ordering a Cape Cod or a Greyhound just to see if your favorite bartender really knows what it is.

TWO-LIQUOR DRINKS

The most popular example of a two-liquor drink is probably the Black Russian, which is simply vodka and Kahlua, and no other mixers, no soda, no juice, etc. Since this drink is made only with liquor, these drinks can be extremely potent, so they are generally served over ice and in smaller glasses. A variation on the Black Russian is the White Russian, which is vodka and Kahlua, but with some milk or cream added, diluting its potency. This brings us over to the next category...

CREAM DRINKS

Cream drinks are seldom heard of these days and are called cream drinks because they use either cream or milk as a key ingredient. These old-fashioned drinks are typically served in small glasses, and include the White Russian, the Brandy Alexander, and the Grasshopper. Very few people ever order cream drinks these days, but if you ever run into an old school bartender and you are in the mood for something different try asking for a Grasshopper; it has a sort of mint chocolate chip flavor that might just hit the spot, especially in colder weather.

SOUR DRINKS

Sour drinks are cocktails that use lemon or lime juice (or both) and sugar. Most bars today will use a pre-made sour mix, but you can just as easily (maybe even easier) use fresh citrus juice and sugar or homemade simple syrup to get a far better outcome. By using fresh ingredients, you can achieve a perfect balance between your base alcohol, your sour ingredient, and your sweetener. (More on sour mix and simple syrup to come.) Sour drinks are much more popular than you might realize. In addition to classic sour drinks like the Whiskey Sour and Amaretto Sour, sour mix is also used for popular warm-weather drinks like the Margarita, the Collins, the Daiquiri, and the Long Island Iced Tea.

MARTINIS

In the last decade, the martini culture has made a serious comeback, and has grown far more creative. A martini used to mean three measures of gin, plus one measure of vermouth, and served ice cold. But, these days a bar might offer up an apple martini, or a watermelon martini, or a chocolate wedding cake martini. Some bars will call anything a martini these days, so long as they serve it in a martini glass. But, long before these new creations came to be, there were traditional martini drinks, such as gin martinis, vodka martinis. This category could also include the Manhattan and the ever-popular Cosmopolitan. Martinis can be served in a glass with ice, but they are more widely known for being prepared and chilled in a separate shaker, and then strained into tall, stemmed cocktail glasses.

Expand your Horizons

The best (and most fun) way to get to know the various types of cocktails is to try them. Don't ever be afraid to ask a bartender for something different. Unless you are in an overcrowded bar, in front of an overworked bartender, he or she is probably dying to make something a little out of the norm. If you think a cream drink is something that might interest you, then ask him to suggest one. Maybe you are in the mood for something salty, or maybe something fruity. Ask your bartender if he has any specialties; you will get to try something new, and trust me, the bartender will be happy you asked.

Getting Behind the Bar

To truly understand the cocktail is to see how they are constructed. And to make this skill your own, it wouldn't hurt to pick up a few good bartending techniques. Where to begin? Let's start by making a simple mixed drink, but let's learn to do it the way the bartenders do. For this example, we'll look at one of the simplest mixed drinks, the Rum and Coke.

To make a proper cocktail, the name of the game is getting your percentages correct.

Drink recipes are usually explained in one of two ways: they list the ingredients in liquid measurements, (typically ounces or milliliters,) or they use 'parts' (or 'measures'). For example, in *Casino Royale*, James Bond describes his cocktail as *"three measures of Gordons, one of vodka, and half a measure of Kina Lillet."* Since the recipe is given in measures, it doesn't matter what unit of measurement is used. You could make one cocktail, or a batch of cocktails, using ounces or pints or gallons, and as long as the percentages remain accurate, the drink will taste right.

However, many Rum and Coke recipes will simply instruct you to pour in actual measurements, as in; pour one or two ounces of rum, and then fill the glass with Coke. As you might be guessing, for the percentages to be correct, this brings in another factor: the glass. For this trick to work, you have to know your glassware. You might have noticed that the glasses at your local watering hole are a lot smaller than the glasses you have at home. That's because the bar is most likely serving its mixed drinks in the traditional Highball glass, which holds, on average, about 8- to 12-ounces.

If you start with a 12-ounce Highball glass, fill it to the top with ice, pour 1- or 2-ounces of light rum, and then fill the rest of the glass with Coke, your drink should taste just right. Not too strong, and not too weak. (Note: This doesn't mean 1-ounce of rum, and 11-ounces of Coke, because the ice takes up a lot of the volume of the glass. More on that in a few.)

As I mentioned, the glassware you'll find at most bedding and bath stores will be much larger than what most drink recipes call for. (The smaller glass in most sets is already about 12-ounces.) You can always experiment with different sized glasses to get the proper percentages down. But, another way to try and maintain your percentages is simply to "eyeball" it.

When you fill a Highball glass with ice and add 1- to 2-ounces of rum, you'll find that the rum takes about between 1/3 and 1/2 the glass. (Don't worry, that seems like a lot of booze, but as we mentioned, the ice is taking up a lot of space.) So when you are dealing with different sized glasses, if you keep filling the glass to the top with ice as you would with smaller glasses, and you eyeball a 1/3 to 1/2 with booze, then your percentages should stay roughly the same, and your drinks will taste the way they should.

Ice is Your Friend

Don't be shy about filling the glass to the top with ice. When I was a bartender, I regularly had cheap customers complain about the amount of ice in the glass, to which I always replied, "The ice is your friend." There are several reasons why this is the correct way to prepare a drink.

First, a full glass of ice serves as a self-insulator, and will prevent it from melting. If you were to pour yourself a glass of Coke, and throw two or three ice cubes in, the ice would probably be almost completely melted before you finished your drink, whereas is you completely fill the glass with ice, it will do a better job keeping the drink cold, and a cold drink won't melt the ice as quickly, and therefore won't water it down.

Second, a full glass of ice is already factored into the standard cocktail recipe. For example, a typical Rum and Coke recipe calls for one ounce of rum and topped with cola. If you are making this cocktail in a 12 oz. highball glass, and you neglected to add the ice, then your drink would be one part liquor and eleven parts soda, creating be a very weak cocktail. So as I would tell my cheap customer, this drink is based on one shot of liquor. If he really prefers no ice, he'll end up with a lot more Coke, instead of more booze. (And if he thinks he's going to complain his way to a triple shot of rum for the same price, he's drinking in the wrong bar.)

Measuring Out a Shot

So if we know we need exactly an ounce, or an ounce-and-a-half, what's the best way to pour it? One way is to take a shot glass (which is typically 1.5 ounces) and fill the glass and pour it in. Or you could use a **jigger**, which is a useful bartending tool, and will typically measure out 1.5- ounces and .75-ounces. You can use one of these to pour 1.5-ounces of liquor and then drop it in your glass. This is a great way to get a perfect measurement every time.

If speed is a factor in your cocktail making, we could do what many bartenders do. If you look at the rows of liquor bottles behind most bars, you will notice that they never have caps; they always have speed pourers. **Speed pourers**, which come in metal or plastic, are the little spouts that fit on the top of most 750ml bottles, and allow you to control the pour. These are great when pouring out one or more cocktails at a time and will help you pour an accurate measure, but be sure to save the caps and screw them firmly back onto the liquor bottles for long term storage.

By the way, stay away from **measured pourers**. In bartending, a measured pourer (also known as a measured liquor pourer or precision pour spout) is a small device attached to the top of a liquor bottle that controls the amount of liquid poured. It's typically designed to dispense a specific amount – like 1 ounce, 1.25 ounces, or 1.5 ounces – every time the bartender tips the bottle. A lot of novice bartenders and cheap bar owners will use these, especially for their higher-end liquors. Personally, I hate using measured pourers. They never work correctly, and even when they do, you'll often make drinks that use more than an ounce and a half of booze (like martinis) and there's nothing more frustrating or unprofessional looking than flipping the bottle up and down three or four times to get the correct measure for a certain drink. So stay away from measured pourers. Speed pourers are cheaper and they work better.

Without using a jigger to measure out an ounce, in order to pour a perfect shot using a typical 750ml bottle and a speed pourer, bartenders will generally pour a "four-count."

A "**four-count**" refers to the length of time a bartender will tip the bottle, in order to pour exactly a shot. When the bartender tips the bottle upside down, and a thin, heavy stream of liquor pours out, he counts to four. As he begins to tip the bottle he thinks, "one, two, three, four." When he is about at 'three' he is starting to tilt the bottle back up so that on the word "four," not one more drop comes out of that bottle. When a bartender does this correctly, he has poured exactly an ounce of liquor.

Now you might be thinking, my four-count might be faster or slower than your four-count. Exactly! This is why you need to practice.

PRACTICE!

If you want to pour booze like a professional bartender you should get yourself a 750ml empty bottle of booze, and fill it with water. Place a speed pourer on the top of the bottle, and grab yourself a shot glass. Then, you can practice filling the shot glass with water using your four-count. Remember: don't tip the bottle a little bit to gently dribble water out of the bottle. You want to hold it upside down so a steady stream of liquid comes out. Start on zero and stop dead on four. Once you've poured your shot a few times and gotten a feel for the four-count, try pouring the same four-count into a cup or a shaker, and then pour the water from the shaker into the shot glass to see how accurate you were. (Avoid practicing pouring into a clear glass, because you'll start getting used to pouring to a certain level on the glass. Practice pouring into cup or a tin that you can't see through, and focus on your timing.) You'll probably end up a little short, or a little over, but with a little practice, you will get a perfect shot every time.

The Size of Your Bottles

Speed pourers work best (and often only) with medium-sized bottles, about 750ml. So what do you do when a friend is nice enough to bring over a bottle of vodka, but instead of getting the medium-sized bottle, he goes the extra mile and gets an over-sized 1.75 liter bottle of Absolut. Besides the fact that these oversized bottles look very unsophisticated on your bar, they're generally too heavy and bulky to maneuver smoothly, and the pourers probably won't fit on the necks of these bottles.

What to do? If you still have the original 750ml. Absolut bottle, then in this situation, I would marry the bottles. **Marrying the bottles** refers to pouring the contents of one bottle into another. Grab a funnel and pour your oversized bottle of Absolut into your medium-sized bottle and keep the extra stored away. This will allow you to keep using your speed pourers and generally just keep your bar looking nicer. (By the way, it's actually illegal for professional establishments to marry bottles. This is to prevent a disreputable bar owner to pour the cheap stuff into a bottle of Stoli, and then charge for the good stuff. Even two bottles of the exact same liquor and the exact same brand. The law views this as "tampering." So only marry bottles behind your home bar.)

Creating a Home Bar

In my humble opinion, a great way to live like James Bond, and to practice your bartending skills, is to create and maintain a modest home bar.

I'm not suggesting hiring a contractor to come in and build a bar in your living room, (unless you have the resources and eccentricity of course,) or even to purchase one of those smaller mobile bars, unless you so choose. What I am suggesting is to keep a moderately-well stocked collection of your favorite spirits, along with a few mixers and garnishes, with a re-spectable set of glassware, and a few handy bar tools.

Let's start with the liquor that every home bar should have.

Needless to say, it can get expensive to stock a complete supply of liquor. When you belly up to a bar, you are probably staring at thousands of dollars' worth of bottles. A fully stocked bar will take time to grow, so here's a good rule of thumb: start slowly. Begin with the spirits that you enjoy, and then follow that up with what your friends or family enjoy, and go forward from there.

Personally, I think it's a great Bond moment when a friend drops by, and you can place their favorite cocktail in front of them, without even asking. As you begin to stock your bar, stock it with yourself, and your friends and family in mind. I always make sure to keep a good tequila, gin, and some prosecco on hand for particular friends and family members.

To take this a step further, consider inviting friends over for cocktails. When I was learning to bartend, I used to throw small cocktail parties as 'bartending practice.' I made a menu of the cocktails I was learning, so I knew exactly what liquors, mixers, and garnishes I would need to have on hand. We even got creative with a bar menu, slipping names of friends into the drink names (Luna's Electric Lemonade) or throwing in some inside jokes (The Fuzzy Pool Boy). The highlight was a caricature of yours truly that a friend had drawn. Everyone loved it.

People also like the bar menu because it gave them more choices. By setting up a menu, you're letting them know that they don't have to stick to the usual beer, wine, or vodka, and it might introduce them to cocktails that they haven't tried before. So if you or a friend is planning a party, think about putting together a bar menu.

LET'S STOCK YOUR BAR

Beyond a few favorites, what should typically make up your home bar stock? A good groundwork will at least cover the five basic liquors: vodka, gin, rum, tequila, and whisky.

Let's begin with that traditional staple, **vodka**. The brand you choose depends simply on your personal preference. Personally, I keep it 'old school' and keep a bottle of Stolichnaya (or Stoli) on hand. Many of the favorites these days are Absolut, Ketel One, and Grey Goose, among others, and with the explosion of flavored martinis, you could always grab a few flavored vodkas. For example, if you think you are going to make a lot of Cosmopolitans, a bottle of Absolut Citron would come in handy.

The next liquor to stock is **gin**, which as I mentioned earlier, comes in different varieties. Personally, I keep at least two bottles of gin; one for martinis, and the other for gin and tonics. My personal favorite for martinis is Bombay Sapphire, and for a gin and tonic I prefer Tanqueray, but I'm recently discovering Hendrick's with cucumber instead of lime. If you want to keep it basic, a good bottle of Bombay or Beefeater will work just fine. And of course, be sure to keep a bottle of Gordon's on hand if you plan to make a proper Vesper.

The next liquor is **rum**, and different rums work better for different drinks. You want to start with light rum, which will be clear. For a traditional rum and coke, Bacardi light is a great choice. As your stock grows you might want to consider some rum varieties. Many people will frequently ask for Malibu, which is a coconut flavored rum (for drinks like the Malibu Bay Breeze) or Captain Morgan, a spiced rum, (for the Captain and Coke) so those brands are good to keep on hand. If you really want to be complete, Myer's dark rum is a staple in many exotic and tropical drinks.

When it comes to **tequila** you can usually get by with Jose Cuervo or Sauza, but if you want something really smooth, try a bottle of Patron. Also, tequila seems to be rising in popularity lately, so maybe one or two higher-end "sipping" tequilas, like maybe a Clase Azul Reposado Tequila which has a decorative bottle and always looks nice on a home bar.

"I prefer bourbon." Finally, you will want to stock some **whiskey**, but as we mentioned, this one can be very confusing since many whiskeys have come to be known by their varieties. For example, **American whiskey** is better known by its top three most-recognized styles: Bourbon, Rye, and Tennessee whiskey.

For **Bourbon**, you could choose Maker's Mark, Wild Turkey, Jim Beam, or the popular Woodford Reserve. For **Rye** whiskey, you could pick up Old Forester, Rittenhouse, or Knob Creek. At one point, there were only two brands of **Tennessee whiskey** left on the market, Jack Daniel's and George Dickel, as a Tennessee whiskey must be made in Tennessee and is distinguished by a maple charcoal filtering process called the Lincoln County Process. Other Tennessee whisky's have been cropping up, but it's still a protected style, and has been since 1941.

Scotch is another key variety of whisky, though many Scotch connoisseurs don't even realize they're drinking whisky, and is broken down into **Blended Scotch**, and **Single-malt Scotch**. Popular Blended Scotches include Chivas Regal, Dewar's, and Johnnie Walker. Some popular Single Malts include Glenfiddich, Glenlivet, Macallan, Talisker (which incidentally, can be seen in M's office in *The World is Not Enough* and *Die Another Day*,) and one that came highly recommended, Laphroaig. **Irish Whiskey** will include Jameson's, Bushmills, and Tullamore Dew. And finally, some popular choices for **Canadian whisky** include Crown Royal, Canadian Club and Seagram's VO. (Author's note: Noticing the different spellings of 'whiskey' and whisky'? Both are correct spellings of the word for the alcoholic beverage. The difference is in the country of origin. 'Whiskey' is used in the United States and Ireland, so you will see it when referring to American whiskeys like bourbon, rye, and Tennessee whiskey, and also for Irish whiskey. 'Whisky' is used for spirits from Scotland, Canada, and Japan, (The word comes from the Gaelic and Scots word *'uisce beatha,'* which means "water of life.") so you will see it used when referring to Scotch or Canadian Whisky.

Keeping these basic liquors on hand will give you a great start.

To help you round out your collection, we could take a cue from a typical bartender's speed rack. The **speed rack** is right behind the bar where the bartender can easily reach, and typically hold the most commonly used liquors. Along side the vodka, gin, rum, and tequila, Triple Sec is usually the next bottle you'll find. **Triple Sec** is an orange-flavored liqueur, and is used in many mixed drinks including the Margarita, Cosmopolitan, and the Long Island Iced Tea. You'll be surprised how often you'll use Triple Sec in making cocktails. If you are looking for an exceptional orange liqueur, you could use Cointreau instead of basic Triple Sec. Cointreau will give you a top-shelf Cosmopolitan, Margarita, or Side Car, every time. (By the way, "**top shelf**" generally refers to the higher-quality and more expensive booze, and as the term implies, and it gets its name because it's known for being kept on the top shelf of most bars and even liquor stores.)

A typical speed rack would also have **Sweet Vermouth** and **Dry Vermouth**, which are both fortified wines, flavored with aromatic herbs and spices. The Dry Vermouth would be used for mixing martinis, while Sweet Vermouth is used in drinks like the Negroni, the Americano and the Manhattan.

A quick note about Vermouth: Since it's a necessity for making martinis, no well-stocked bar should be without it. But, as we mentioned, Vermouth is a fortified wine, and as such it has a limited lifespan. Most bars are keeping bottles of Vermouth way past their prime, uncapped and not refrigerated (which also might be why an increasing number of martini drinkers are shunning Vermouth altogether). A few simple rules will help you keep Vermouth on hand. Always buy the smaller bottles of Vermouth (375ml). They are very inexpensive, so you can always purchase a fresh bottle when you are expecting guests. Also, be sure to cap the bottle tightly after opening, and keep the bottle refrigerated after opening, the same way you would with a bottle of white wine. Sealing it with a VacuVin should keep Vermouth fresh for about four to six months.

There are two others that are completely optional, but complete the traditional bartender's speed rack; they are Lime Juice and Grenadine, which are both non-alcoholic mixers. **Lime Juice** is used in many drinks, including Margaritas, but for a home bar, I would just keep fresh limes on hand and squeeze fresh juice. The last mixer on the speed rack is always Grenadine. Real **grenadine** is made from pomegranate, though most grenadine today is just corn syrup with a cherry flavoring, and it's used in certain drinks like the Tequila Sunrise and other tropical-style cocktails.

Beyond those basic liquors and the mixers on the speed rack, you'll also want to start to build your collection of cordials, or "liqueurs."

What's a liqueur?

The difference between a **liquor** (LIK-er) and a **liqueur** (Li-KUR) is the characteristic added flavoring, as well as the added sugar. For example, Peach Schnapps is an alcohol, but it's considered a liqueur because it has been sweetened, and peach flavoring has been added. What are some typical liqueurs you will want to have in your collection?

There is a multitude of flavors of liqueurs, so you could easily drive yourself crazy trying to get all of them. But, if your focus is on mixed drinks, then these liqueurs will help you put together an impressive list of cocktails:

The first would be the afore-mentioned **Peach Schnapps**. This is (obviously) a peach-flavored liqueur, and you will find it in popular drinks like Fuzzy Navels and Sex on the Beach. **Kahlua** is a coffee-flavored liqueur used in Black Russians and Mudslides; and **Amaretto**, an almond-flavored liqueur you find in drinks like a Toasted Almond. **Sloe Gin**, which is actually not a gin at all, is a liqueur that comes from sloe berries and almonds, and possesses a cherry-like flavor (think: alcoholic Grenadine) that you will find in drinks like Alabama Slammers and Red Devils. Also, for people who are virgins to the world of mixed drinks, a Sloe Gin Fizz is very gentle. **Blue Curacao** is very simply Triple Sec with blue coloring added. Since you would already have Triple Sec on hand, the Blue Curacao is completely optional, but I find that anytime I use it to make a drink, everyone else perks up and becomes curious about what that person is drinking. So if you want to make an attention-getter, keep some Blue Curacao on hand.

That should be a good starting place. Beyond those five, the list of flavored liqueurs is endless. There are almost as many schnapps as there are flavors, like Apple Schnapps, Butterscotch Schnapps, Peppermint Schnapps, Crème de Banana, Crème de Cacao, Crème de Menthe, and so on. If your palate can recognize it, then someone has probably made a liqueur that tastes like it. These are also very handy if you are interested in flavored martinis. For example, an easy Apple Martini is simply two parts vodka and one part apple schnapps. Yep, it's really that simple. All these are available to you as you start to build your collection and get into more exotic drinks.

In addition to these flavored liqueurs, there are countless cordials that you could add to your collection, such as Frangelico, Nocello, Disarrono, Bailey's Irish Cream, Sambuca, Campari, Drambuie, etc. While many of them can be used as cocktail ingredients, most are served neat and after a good meal. Again, the list is endless and these would be solely based on your personal preferences.

Mixers

By this point you've got a pretty impressive collection of liquors and liqueurs. But before your home bar is complete, you'll need a few mixers such as sodas, juices, sour mix and even milk or cream. Let's explore the basics, and find the best ways to keep these on hand for everyday use.

SODAS

Any of the carbonated drinks will be referred to as 'soda.' The most commonly used sodas for cocktails include **club soda**, **tonic**, **ginger ale**, **cola** (Coke), **diet cola** (Diet Coke), and **lemon-lime soda** (Sprite or Seven Up). These are relatively easy to keep on hand even if you don't have much space, and since you are mixing your drinks over ice, they don't even need to be refrigerated. You can always keep two-liter bottles handy, but I find that one-liter bottles of sodas and mixers are much easier to work with, and easily store on or under any bar.

JUICES

The most common juices for mixing cocktails are **orange juice**, **cranberry juice**, **pineapple juice** and **grapefruit juice**. Juices don't have an indefinite shelf like soda, so depending on how often you might keep juices in the house for regular daily use, it's not always easy to keep them on hand and fresh. What to do? If you are dealing with larger numbers for a party or a get together, you could opt for using **juice pourers**, which are medium-sized plastic containers for holding juices. If I were bartending at home or for a small party, I would always use pourers. It's a great way to keep the bar neat, organized, and even professional looking. The tops are typically color-coordinated so you always know which juice is in which container, and they are also re-sealable so you can store whatever you don't use in the refrigerator.

If you are expecting company then you'll know in advance that you need to keep the juice stocked up, but what do you do if you want to keep some juice on hand for a spur of the moment craving, or a surprise guest?

One solution I found is to keep small cans of juice handy. For example, you will typically find pineapple juice in large 46 oz. cans. But, unless you're a regular pineapple juice drinker, the majority of the can will only go to waste. So I started picking up six-packs of 6 oz. cans of pineapple juice; so when a friend drops by who happens to like a Malibu Bay Breeze, one of these little cans usually gets me two drinks, and the other five go back into the refrigerator or pantry. Works perfectly!

SOUR MIX

In addition to sodas and juices, you are also going to need sour mix, which is essentially a mixture of lemon juice and sugar. As we mentioned earlier, sour mix is used in more cocktails than you might imagine. Sour mix can be purchased relatively easily in most liquor stores, but avoid the specialized mixes such as Margarita mix, etc. If you stick with basic sour mix, then it should work with all your mixed drinks that call for sour mix.

Of course, a far superior choice than store-bought sour mix is to stick with fresh ingredients, such as fresh-squeezed lemon or lime juice and sugar or simple syrup. Before sour mix came along, the old-school recipes for sour drinks called for lemon juice and sugar. Why buy a pre-made mix when you can get far better (not to mention less expensive) results from the real thing? You can squeeze fresh lemons and limes to make your citrus juice, and make simple syrup from sugar and water. Another bonus to using fresh citrus juice and simple syrup is the control you have over your sour and sweet. If your Collins is too sour, simply add more simple syrup, and vice versa. Wait, what is simple syrup?

SIMPLE SYRUP

Simple syrup is another ingredient than shows up in many old school cocktails, and as we mentioned, can be swapped out for sour mix in favor of natural ingredients. Because of the reemergence of classic cocktail recipes, simple syrup has been showing up on many store shelves. The name speaks for itself; simple syrup is just too simple to make to ever justify paying ten dollars for a bottle in the store.

Take one cup of water, boil it on the stove or microwave it in a Pyrex measuring cup, add one cup of sugar, and stir it until it dissolves. Put the mixture in the fridge until you are ready to use it. Congratulations, you've just saved yourself ten dollars.

MILK OR CREAM

While it's probably going to be incredibly rare, it's a good idea to have cream or milk on hand, on the off chance that somebody might ask you for a Toasted Almond or a White Russian, among a few others. If not, you've got milk for your coffee in the morning.

Again... Pace Yourself

If you were to purchase all the liquors and liqueurs and mixers on this list, you would have a pretty impressive bar menu that would even rival a professional establishment. Needless to say, getting everything in one shot is probably overkill. Build your stock gradually, with your own personal tastes and the tastes and preferences of your friends in mind, and in a way that's going to express your own personal tastes.

Garnishes

Adding the proper garnish to your cocktail is a simple and easy step that brings flair and professionalism to your drinks and makes them look complete. The most typical drink-garnishes include lemons, limes, oranges, cherries, and olives, but can be as exotic as apples, bananas, pineapple, star fruits, onions, coffee beans, celery, sugar cane, fresh herbs, etc. The list is endless.

Lemons and limes will probably go into the majority of the drinks you make. I personally always keep lemons and limes on hand for myself or for others since it's relatively inexpensive to keep a few around. Whenever I go grocery shopping, I pick up a few lemons and limes and keep them in a bowl on my kitchen table, just in case I'm in the mood for a cocktail that calls for a lemon or lime as an ingredient or garnish. Jars of cherries and olives are also very easy to keep on hand, and will last a long time in your refrigerator. Mint leaves is another must-have if you are planning on making Mojitos or Mint Juleps, two classic James Bond cocktails. They tend to wilt quickly so buy mint leaves on the day you plan to use them; if you need to refrigerate them, place them in a loose plastic bag and keep them in the crisper drawer, but better yet, just leave them on the counter and put their stems in some water to prolong their shelf life.

How much of each? Again, I try and keep maybe three lemons and three limes in a bowl, but if you are expecting friends, about 10 - 12 each of lemons and limes should be more than enough, as well as a few oranges. There are only a few drinks, such as an Old Fashioned, that call for an orange slice, or sour drinks that call for an orange and cherry skewered, but sometimes I'll use an orange to change things up a little, especially for the fruitier drinks. One jar of cherries and one jar of olives should probably do you fine, unless your party is going to emphasize martinis, in which case you should probably pick up two or three jars (or one large jar) of olives. And I tend to go overboard on mint leaves, because I never seem to make one or two Mojitos; once I make the first one, everyone always wants the same, especially on warm days. So pick up no less than three bunches of mint leaves.

Cutting Up Your Lemons and Limes

Is there a 'proper' way to cut up your fruit? Again, it depends on your needs, and how much you want the flavor to accentuate the cocktail. For example, a bartender will typically cut up a lemon or a lime into small wedges, getting the most mileage out of each; by cutting off the top and the bottom, standing it vertically, quartering the lemon vertically and then quartering each section, so one lemon makes roughly 16 wedges.

This works fine, but for personal use, I cut my fruit a little larger. In fact, I usually just keep a cutting board and a knife nearby and slice the fruit as I am making the drink, so the fruit remains as fresh as possible. Depending on the cocktail, the fruit usually contributes a lot of flavor. For example, when I am preparing a gin and tonic I always cut and squeeze a large piece of lime. I find that the fresh, citrus quality really accentuates the gin. Of course, wedges work best when you plan to drop the fruit into the glass. Other situations will call for different cuts, such as cutting long spears to top a bottle of beer, like adding a lime to a Corona.

If you want your garnishes to be decorative as well, cut them into wheels, or half-wheels. Just cut the lemons or limes into round slices, and cut a slit halfway into the slice, so you can sit it on the rim of the glass. This way your guest can leave the slice on the glass, drop it into the cocktail, or remove it and put it aside.

"…and then add a thin slice of lemon peel."

And of course, no self-respecting James Bond fan would dream of serving a martini without the proper garnish – a thin, elegant slice of lemon peel. It's not just about taste; it's about presentation, tradition, and a little showmanship. If someone asks for a slice of lemon peel, they're not asking for a clumsy wedge of lemon – they're asking for a delicate ribbon of the skin itself, carefully sliced away with a knife, a sharp vegetable peeler, or, for the purists, a channel knife.

Using a vegetable peeler will give you wide, luxurious strips of lemon peel, perfect for squeezing gently over the drink to release the oils, then dragging around the rim of the glass to coat it with a whisper of citrus before dropping it in. A simple move that makes a lasting impression.

For a thinner, more refined garnish – the kind seen in *Casino Royale* and *Quantum of Solace* – a **channel knife** is your tool of choice. Designed specifically for cutting slender zests, it lets you glide effortlessly around the lemon, carving out elegant, narrow spirals of skin. One or two quick passes around the lemon is all it takes. Drop the finished peel into the glass with a touch of style.

In *Quantum of Solace,* when Bond is getting sentimental on the airplane and polishing off his sixth Vesper, if you look sharp you can spot the bartender cutting slices of lemon peel using a channel knife.

With garnishes out of the way, it must feel like I've exhausted everything there is to know about cocktails, but believe it or not there is still a lot more. The combinations of ingredients, techniques, and garnishes are as endless as the list of drinks. One of the great things about the world of cocktails is that there is always something more to learn.

Bar Equipment

Every good setup will need a few good bar tools, so here's a few staples you shouldn't be without, and a few more that are just fun to have around.

MARTINI SHAKER

One of the first pieces of equipment that the James Bond enthusiast will gravitate towards is probably the martini shaker. While there is certainly more than one way to chill a cocktail, the **martini shaker** (also known as a "Cobbler Shaker") is ideal for preparing drinks that are served straight up. By the way, the term "**straight up**" (or just "**up**") refers to a drink that is chilled with ice, but then strained into a glass with no ice; as opposed to "**on the rocks**" which of course refers to a cocktail served with ice, and **"neat"** which refers to a liquor poured directly from the bottle, not chilled, served without ice. *"That's extra, man!"*

When you are preparing a martini, we obviously want to chill the cocktail before serving it, so we have to prepare it in a separate container and agitate it with the ice, and after it's ice cold we then strain it into the empty cocktail glass

As elegant as the martini shaker might look, most bartenders have mixed emotions about using shakers. As you probably know, shakers come in three pieces; the body, the lid with a built-in strainer, and a top that keeps the shaker sealed tight while shaking. For the bartender on the move, this is usually too many pieces to keep track of. Also, when you are using the shaker to mix a Martini, or any drink for that matter, you will shake the drink until it is ice cold. When this happens, the cold causes the metal to contract, and the top becomes difficult to take off.

What should you look for in a cocktail shaker? While I used to avoid the traditional three-piece shakers, I recently stumbled on some more modern three-piece shakers that changed my mind. A few things to look for: Check that it's insulated, making the shaker comfortable to handle even when it gets very cold, and also keeping the tin from sweating so your hands don't get wet. Also, a good top is magnetized so it stays firmly in place, and it's shaped so that it hugs the shaker on an angle, making it much easier to remove when it gets cold. The inside of the top could also be marked for specific measurements; at 1-ounce, 3/4-ounce and 1/2-ounce measurements, so you can use the top for measuring out your liquor.

But my local bartender doesn't use a martini shaker, so how would he mix a martini? The other way is to prepare the martini in a pint glass, and seal it with a Boston shaker to shake the drink. Personally, even if I'm eventually going to transfer my cocktail to a martini shaker, I prefer to do my preparation in the pint glass, primarily because I want to see what I am doing, and if I'm working behind the bar, I also want my customer to see what I am doing. Once you've placed the ingredients and the ice into the mixing glass, you'll then pop a Boston shaker snuggly on top of the pint glass, give it a solid tap to form a seal, grab both ends, and shake it good.

A **Boston shaker** is simply a metal cup (that looks like a traditional martini shaker with the top missing), which would be used in conjunction with a pint glass (or similar-sized mixing glass). The cocktail is prepared in the mixing glass with ice, and then the Boston shaker is placed on top of the pint glass. Giving the shaker a solid tap will form an airtight seal, so you can shake the two pieces together without fear of spillage. After the cocktail has been thoroughly shaken, tapping the shaker lightly will usually set the shaker free.

The best way to break the seal on your Boston shaker: Hold the shaker in your hand with the metal shaker on the bottom and the glass sticking up. Have your top two fingers on the top glass and your bottom two fingers on the metal shaker as well as your thumb wrapped around. You'll see looking into the side of the shaker where the glass meets the inside of the metal. This is where you want to tap. While putting pressure from your top two fingers, tap with the palm of your other hand on the side of the metal shaker right where the glass meets it in the inside. The glass will tilt from the pressure of your fingers and you've just broken the air seal. Now simply lift the glass up.

Once you have shaken the cocktail, you would then use a **Hawthorn strainer**, which fits snuggly over the top of most metal shakers, and strain the drink into the glass. Hawthorne strainers work best when straining cocktails from the tin, as opposed to the pint glass, because liquid tends to cling to the glass and then dribble and spill. If you opt to stir your cocktail in the pint glass, a julep strainer will be your best friend. A **julep strainer** looks like an oversized spoon with holes, fitting on top of the pint glass, allowing you to strain your drink with no spillage.

SHOT GLASS

Once you've got your martini shaker is squared away, you can move onto a few other useful tools. As we already mentioned, one of the first gadgets you'll need is a shot glass. Why only one shot glass? You can always buy more if you so choose, but you need at least one to help you practice a "four-count." Remember, you are going to take an empty liquor bottle and fill it with water. Put a speed pourer on top of the bottle and pour out your four-count. Practice this till you feel like you've got it just right.

SPEED POURERS

Again, the simpler the better and stay away from those measured pourers. Speed pourers are relatively inexpensive so buy at least one for each liquor bottle, and keep a few extras on hand. And don't leave the speed pourers on for extended storage.

JIGGER

If you are still practicing your four-count, you can always pour an accurate measurement by using a jigger. A **jigger** typically measures out 1.5 ounces and .75 ounces, though some will measure out 1 and 2 ounces. These are especially useful for recipes that are given in parts or measures.

BAR SPOON

If you plan to offer your martinis shaken or stirred, you'd better be prepared with something to stir the cocktail, and for that you would need a bar spoon. A **bar spoon** is a multi-functional tool that comes in handy for multiple tasks. It's extra-long to reach the bottom of many tall glasses, and most bar spoon handles are curled for stirring without chipping the ice. The spoon itself is generally for spooning out ingredients (like sugar), but the back of the spoon is also useful in creating layered drinks and shots.

BOTTLE OPENERS

Another obvious, but indispensable bar tool is the **bottle opener** for opening wine bottles as well as beer bottles, (corks as well as caps,) so you can get one of each type, or get one that's universal. For opening wine bottles, you'll have a variety of openers to choose from. I'm not crazy about the popular **butterfly** or **winged corkscrew**, as they are bulky and typically don't lift the cork all the way out of the neck. I prefer the **waiter's corkscrew**, or the "**waiter's friend**," which looks more like a pocket knife. You can get this traditional corkscrew for next to nothing, and they have a blade for cutting the seal or foil around the neck of the wine bottle, as well as a built-in opener for beer bottles.

CUTTING BOARD AND KNIFE

You should also have a **cutting board** and a **knife** to cut up your fruits and garnishes. As we mentioned earlier, you can always cut up fruit in advance, but if your evening is going at a casual pace, you can just keep fresh fruit handy, and a cutting board and knife nearby so you can cut your fruit as you're making and garnishing your drinks. It makes a good impression too.

MUDDLER

Ever since the explosion of the Mojito (thanks, *Die Another Day*) the muddler has become an essential piece of bar equipment. A **muddler** typically comes in wood or stainless steel, and looks like nothing more than a tiny baseball bat, and it's used to crush or "muddle" ingredients like mint leaves, limes, sugar, and cherries, for cocktails like the Mojito, the Mint Julep, the Caipirinha and the Old-fashioned. It's a very inexpensive tool and is much more effective than trying to muddle with a fork or a spoon.

JUICER

If you are planning to avoid the store-bought sour mix, then you'll need fresh citrus juice, and you can't get any fresher than using a juicer. You would use a **juicer**, obviously, to extract the juice from lemons and limes. They come in all sizes, including electric juicers, but I find that a handheld juicers to be perfect for making single cocktails that use citrus juice, such as a Collins.

JUICE POURERS

When you are dealing with speed and volume, you could always purchase **juice pourers**. Commonly called 'Store 'n Pour', these might be something that you pick up later as you start to build your bar setup. Be sure to get the ones that are the one-quart containers and have the different color-coded lids, so you always know what's inside. (Orange and cranberry are obvious, but grapefruit, pineapple, and sour mix look almost identical, and can get confusing.)

ICE BUCKET AND SCOOP

And of course you will need something to handle your ice. An **ice bucket** will work fine to keep your ice cold and insulated, but will probably need to be refilled regularly, which means you will need some extra ice on hand, so make room in the freezer. **Ice tongs** are popular with ice buckets for placing ice into glasses, but unless you feel like dropping one ice cube at a time, go with a medium-sized **ice scoop**.

BAR TOWEL

The last item that every bartender should keep on hand is a good bar towel to keep your area neat and also keep your glasses polished. You don't want tiny little shards of paper towel getting into your glasses, so keep a good fabric bar towel handy.

That's a good basic list of some things you are going to want to keep around your home bar. As you continue to explore, you might add a few more to your collection, but these tools should definitely set you in the right direction. You will be surprised how inexpensive some of these are. You can probably purchase everything on this list for about the same price as one high-end bottle of liquor.

Glassware

Right about now you have everything you need to put together some serious cocktails, except for the glass to serve it in. So to make your bar complete, you need a good set of glassware.

A good set of glassware is not necessarily an expensive set. In fact, when it comes to glasses, I would err on the side of being frugal. This doesn't mean you have to be obscenely cheap, but this is the one time when I would go for quantity over quality. Why? If you plan to entertain, glasses will break. So you don't want to spend a lot of money on glassware, only to spend your evening completely terrified that a glass might break. You also want to have enough glasses so that you don't run out. You don't want half your party with expensive glassware, and the other half drinking out of red plastic cups. Not very James Bond. Buy enough glassware.

Incidentally, I'm far more inclined to preach the virtue of higher quality glassware if we're talking about wine glasses. While none of them are really sure why, virtually all wine experts will tell you that quality glassware will make a serious difference in the wine tasting experience. But, the flavors in cocktails are not nearly as subtle and complex as the flavors in wine, so you don't need to go overboard on expensive cocktail glasses.

WHICH GLASSES?

As we mentioned earlier, depending on how the recipe is constructed, the correct glass becomes a key ingredient in getting the cocktail percentages correct. So you'd better get the proper glasses, right? After all, professional bartenders know their glasses as Collins glasses, highball glasses, and rocks glasses. But if you set foot in most bedding and bath stores, you'll see sets of tall "soda" glasses and stout "juice" glasses.

While the choices for attractive glasses are endless, you'll probably find that the sizes just don't line up with the sizes of traditional cocktail glasses. These days, everything is 'bigger and better.'

One solution would be to go directly to the source, and buy your glassware from the same places that bars and restaurants buy theirs. Restaurant supply companies offer a wide selection of restaurant grade glassware, and at lower prices than department stores. A possible downside (depending on your needs) is that they typically sell in bulk. An order of cocktail glasses will probably be sold in cases of 24 or 36. This might be overkill for many casual consumers, but you get a much better price per glass, and if one breaks, who cares because you have a bunch more.

If you decide to go with glassware that you found in your favorite department store, is there no hope for an accurate cocktail? Don't despair. The truth is that even the pros can't seem to decide the exact size of most glasses. Do a search for a Collins glass on the net; you'll find that this glass can be as small as 8 ounces and as large as 16 ounces.

You will need to get acquainted with your glassware. If your drink recipe calls for one-ounce of rum, topped with Coke, and the drink specifies an 8-ounce highball glass, and you happen to be using a 16-ounce glass, then obviously you can double your rum to two-ounces and top with Coke, and ideally the cocktail will still taste perfect. It's a good practice to experiment with your cocktails to be sure they are properly balanced. A good cocktail should have balance. When you are drinking a Rum and Coke, you shouldn't taste the rum, and you shouldn't taste the Coke. A well-balanced cocktail will take on its own unique flavor.

For example, I recently purchased a set of over-sized Collins glasses that actually held a full pint. When I use them for Mojitos, I double most of my ingredients. I drop a healthy 10 or 12 mint leaves into the glass, half a lime that has been cut into quarters, and a full ounce of simple syrup. Once I've muddled them, I fill the glass with ice and add two ounces of rum, and top with club soda. After I give that a quick stir to chill it and combine the flavors, I usually drizzle the top with just a splash of rum, and a small splash of simple syrup. I generally find that to be the perfect combination for my 16 oz. glass.

The moral of the story is, once you've read and understood your drink recipe, you should get acquainted with your glasses, and experiment with the balance of your cocktails.

So which glasses should you have in your collection, and how will we deal with the discrepancies between the size of the glasses that your drink recipes suggest and the sets of glasses that you can easily find in the local shopping malls? Let's try and bridge the gap.

Books of cocktail recipes will tell you that you need both Highball glasses and Collins glasses. (We already mentioned that opinions vary on glass sizes, but lets discuss a few general rules.) **Highball glasses** generally hold about 8- to 12-ounces and are used for preparing one-liquor mixed drinks on the rocks such as Rum and Cokes and Gin and Tonics. **Collins glasses** are taller and thinner than the Highball, and hold about 10- to 12-ounces, and are generally used for cocktails with more ingredients such as the Collins (obviously), Juleps, Mojitos, etc.

Most department stores have merged these glasses and called them "soda glasses" or "coolers," and usually hold much more liquid; up to 16- ounces. So pick up a few of these tall glasses for your Highball and Collins drinks, and experiment with your cocktails to achieve the correct balance. These are also the glasses you are going to use if anybody is just drinking water or cokes, so have enough of the tall glasses.

Next you should have smaller, stouter drinking glasses. Again, bartenders will call these rocks glasses, but the department stores will call these juice glasses, or "double old fashioned" glasses. (Their smallest glasses are called "doubles." Go figure.) Traditional **rocks glasses** (also called "lowball" or "Old Fashioned glasses") will hold 6- to 10-ounces, while your department store glasses will typically be 10- to 14-ounces.

Fear not, these glasses are generally for serving liquor on the rocks, (think: scotch on the rocks,) and for the two-liquor drinks such as the Black Russian, so you shouldn't fall victim to the percentage problems of the Collins glasses, as most of these cocktail recipes will be given in parts. As we mentioned, the parts can be as small as ounces and as large as gallons, and the drink will still work if the percentages remain consistent.

The next set of glasses you'll want is fairly obvious; the **martini glasses** or your **cocktail glasses**. I don't even need to describe these; martini glasses are the signature James Bond glasses and these are for all your martini cocktails, including gin and vodka martinis, and their variations such as the Manhattan or the Cosmopolitan. Traditional stemmed cocktail glasses held about 4.5-ounces (which would have perfectly held a Vesper if her measures were ounces), but have grown to hold anywhere from 7.5- ounces to 10-ounces.

You definitely want to keep these on hand because, depending on your crowd, once one person sees the martini glasses everyone is going to want a martini.

Try to stick with the small or medium-sized martini glasses for the simple reason that you want to keep your martini ice cold. Most martinis are usually served straight up, so they will warm up over time. The larger the glass, the longer it will take to finish, and can warm up before you finish, and warm vodka is rough stuff. Also, martinis are extremely potent by nature, as they are made up of 100% hard liquor, so unless your mission is to get your guests destroyed after one or two, stick to smaller glasses.

This covers all your mixed drink glasses, but you are also going to want to keep a good set of **wine glasses** on hand, and be sure to distinguish between white and red wine glasses, and also pick up a few **Champagne flutes** for special occasions. Remember, if you are a true wine aficionado, go with high-quality glasses. (More on wine and wine glasses to come in 'Being James Bond: Volume Two.')

You might also want to pick up some **beer glasses** too. Keeping nice glasses on hand will look a little more attractive than drinking from bottles or cans. Avoid mugs and lean toward more sophisticated looking beer glasses like **pilsner glasses**, which are the tall, thin beer glasses that get a little wider up at the top. And if you 're serving stout beers, like Guinness, you might want to keep some **pint glasses** on hand.

Those glasses should definitely have you covered. But of course, you can venture into other sorts of glasses for specific drinks like Irish coffee glasses, and also brandy snifters for brandies and Cognacs, and if you really find yourself getting creative you could try Margarita glasses. Go wherever your imagination takes you.

We've got our liquors, some liqueurs, our mixers, juices, garnishes, some bar tools and our glasses ready. So what do we do now?

Now We Make Drinks

Even if you are a complete beginner at mixing cocktails, everything we've covered so far will probably give you some knowledge of how to prepare drinks. There are literally thousands of cocktail recipes in existence, so to try to list even a small portion of those would be crazy. But, rather than discuss specific recipes, we'll review a few of the basics and the cocktail groups, and through that you'll be amazed how many cocktails suddenly become crystal clear.

By now, we've thoroughly exhausted the Rum and Coke recipe; fill a tall glass with ice, add 1 oz. of light rum (or 2 oz. for a 16 oz. glass), top with Coke. This same rule will apply for all your **one-liquor drinks**, which are cocktails that consist of one liquor and a topping; such as Gin and Tonic, Vodka and Club, etc. Don't forget, **juice drinks** also qualify as one-liquor drinks and follow the same rules, so fill a tall glass with ice, add 1 to 2- oz.

vodka, and top with orange juice to get a Screwdriver (aka: Vodka and Orange), or with cranberry juice to get a Cape Cod (aka: Vodka and Cran).

For **two-liquor drinks**, we mentioned that these recipes generally come in parts as opposed to ounces, primarily because it doesn't incorporate a "topping" like juice or soda – it's strictly booze. Our example, the Black Russian, consists of two parts vodka, and one part Kahlua (or other coffee flavored liqueur). You'll find that most two-liquor drinks will follow this same pattern of two-parts liquor and one-part liqueur, such as the Brave Bull (or Brahma Bull), which is two-parts tequila and one-part Kahlua. Since these drinks are made up solely of booze, these powerful drinks are typically served over ice, and in smaller glasses.

Cream drinks are usually variations on the two-liquor drink style, and therefore are constructed in much the same way; 2-parts liquor, 1-part liqueur, and about 1-part milk or cream. A typical example is the White Russian; 2-parts vodka, 1-part Kahlua, and about 1-part cream. Or a Brandy Alexander, which is 2-parts brandy, 1-part crème de cacao, topped with cream. Don't be tricked into regarding the cream as a "topping," as you might regard Coke as a topping in the Rum and Coke. Unless you would drink cream the same way you might drink Coke, then treat the cream sparingly, and stick to the smaller glass. And, always shake cream drinks into a nice froth, and never garnish.

Some recipes actually suggest using a tall glass for sour drinks, but to me that's insane. A **sour drink** follows the same principle, unless you would drink a glass of sour mix, use it sparingly, and use a smaller glass. Sour drinks are very simple as they are made up of liquor with some sour mix, like a Whisky Sour, an Amaretto Sour, a Midori Sour, etc. Stick to 2-parts liquor and 1-part sour mix (pre-made or home-made), and shake into a froth. To maintain balance in our cocktails, we'll offset our sour with a little bit of sweet, so we garnish our sour drinks by dropping a maraschino cherry into the cocktail, or try a traditional '**flag**' garnish, which is an orange slice and a cherry skewered together.

A variation on the sour drink that does call for a tall glass is (naturally) the Collins. As we touched on, the **Collins** is a cocktail that has one liquor, and is then topped with sour mix and club soda, like the Tom Collins, Vodka Collins, and the Rum Collins that James Bond drank with Largo in *Thunderball*. Typically, the Collins is about 1-part liquor, with 1-part sour mix added, and topped with 1-part club soda. Again, experiment with your percentages and find the correct measurements that suit your glass size. You can follow the same rule as the sour drink and garnish with a cherry, but I prefer to garnish with a slice of lemon.

One category of cocktails that were once a lost classic, but have since been revived, is the julep, which is making a comeback thanks to cocktails like the Mojito. The classic julep is, of course, the Mint Julep, like the one James Bond is offered in Kentucky in *Goldfinger*. **Juleps** are traditionally cocktails that incorporate non-liquid ingredients, like mint leaves and requires muddling.

So try to remember these general rules about tall glasses versus short glasses. If the mixer is something you would drink straight, as with a Rum and Coke (Coke), Screwdriver (orange juice), or Vodka and Club (club soda), use a tall glass; if you would probably drink it sparingly, like a White Russian (cream) or a Whisky Sour (straight sour mix), then use a smaller glasses. If it uses more than two ingredients like a Tom Collins (gin, sour mix, and club soda) then it probably shifts back to the tall glass. You can now get an idea about how juleps work with the aforementioned rules for glasses. For the Mint Julep (mint leaves, simple syrup, and about 3-ounces of Kentucky bourbon), since it's almost completely booze, I stick to a smaller glass. (Though I have seen variations that top the julep with club soda, in which case you could use a tall glass.) For a mojito, (mint leaves, lime wedges, and simple syrup, rum, and club soda), since there are several ingredients, and my filler is club soda, I use a tall glass. See how easy this is? And of course, we use a cocktail glass (or martini glass) for drinks that are chilled, and served straight up. Any drink that is served "up" is served in a stemmed cocktail glass, so that the drinker can hold the glass by the stem, thus keeping the warmth from their hand away from the drink.

Expanding Your Knowledge

I think that about wraps it up. With your glasses, your ice, your liquors, your toppings, your garnishes, and your bar tools under your belt, you are ready to mix an impressive batch of cocktails. Now you can start expanding your knowledge of drink recipes. There are so many great venues for learning new cocktails, including books and social media.

Start your collection of recipes with a few good books. Pretty much any bookstore is going to have a lot of great books with cocktail recipes. Some are very good, some are very practical and some are just going to look nice on your coffee table. One book you are going to find most bartenders have on them is The Bartenders Black Book by Stephen Kitteridge Cunningham. It's a thin black book with spiral binding and will fit nicely into a bartender's back pocket. It's really inexpensive and it might be the only cocktail recipe book you will ever need, although there are plenty of great cocktail recipe books out there that are very imaginative, so just keep your eyes open and see what you like.

The Interwebs is another obvious resource for finding drink recipes, as well as how-to videos that will show you bartenders actually putting these drinks together. There are a ton of great channels on YouTube and Instagram with new drink recipes and videos on how to make them. Recently when my wife had a milestone birthday, I stumbled across two drink recipes that I knew would resonate with this particular crowd, and that I thought were perfect for this autumn celebration; a Smoky Harvest Apple Cider Margarita and an Autumn Aperol Spritz, and for both I froze large ice cubes with diced apple, cinnamon sticks, and star anise. They were both a huge hit.

Another interesting thing about finding drink recipes online is the variety. You'll quickly find that no two recipes are exactly the same. If I look for a recipe online, I make sure to check a few different versions so that I can find a general consensus, and then go with the one (or the combination) that I like best.

Finally, for those who really want to take this skill to the next level, or might even be considering bartending as a profession, you could always take a **bartending class**.

People tend to have mixed feelings about bartending schools, and with good reason, especially if you're assuming it will be the doorway to employment. They range greatly in price and quality, and almost all of them will tell you that they have job-placement, but I have yet to meet a person who was placed at a bar through a school's job-placement.

But, having said that, if you are starting from scratch and you don't have any contacts that could teach you the ropes, then a bartending school is probably a great place to start. Just be prepared to use the shotgun approach for job hunting. There are probably many more bars in your area than you have even considered; aside from neighborhood bars and clubs, there are restaurants, hotels, catering and reception halls, bowling alleys, arenas, airports, train stations, golf courses, ski lodges, etc. You get the idea. If you live near a shopping mall that has a few restaurants, chances are that's a lot of bars, and a lot of shifts. So there's almost always a bar looking to fill a shift.

The class I took was Monday through Friday from 6:00 to 10:00 p.m. for two weeks. It was a pretty intensive course, but also it was a lot of fun. You had to study liquors and liqueurs, and naturally that's where I learned how to do the four-count, and of course you had to memorize a lot of drink recipes. To graduate the class, you had to take a speed test, making ten drinks in three minutes, and you didn't know in advance which ten drinks they would be. The classes are usually offered at night, so this is an option available to you, whether this is something you would like to take on professionally, or just for fun.

Now grab your cocktail shaker...

How should we close out this chapter? You can probably make this one in your sleep by now, but let's put it all together by making the quintessential James Bond cocktail, the vodka martini, shaken, not stirred.

Grab your martini glass, set it on your bar (or table) and fill it with ice. Do this is to chill the glass; you are not going to serve the drink on the rocks, we are going to serve it straight up. While your glass is chilling, grab your pint glass and fill it almost to the top with ice. We are making a vodka martini so you are going to grab your preferred vodka and pour it into the pint glass.

How will you know how much vodka to pour? You can use an old bartender's trick.

As we mentioned earlier, you should get to know your glassware, so before you set out to make a martini, do this experiment with your martini glass:

Fill your pint glass with ice, then fill a martini glass about three-quarters with water (plan for a little vermouth and a little melted ice to fill more of the glass), and then pour the water from the martini glass to the pint glass. Now check out the level the water came up to in the ice-filled pint glass; that's where you should be pouring your vodka or gin.

The next step will be adding some dry vermouth. This is where you will hear the term "dry." Originally, the term "dry martini" had nothing to do with how much (or how little) vermouth you wanted in your cocktail, but instead, that you wanted a martini made with Dry Gin and French Vermouth. Before the traditional London Dry Gin came along, most gins were either Dutch Gin or Old Tom Gin (which was sweeter), and they were made with Italian vermouth and were considered just "martini." It wasn't until the silver screen, and when vodka started outselling gin, that vermouth started being used less and less and the term "extra dry" was used.

Today, the **dryness** of a martini refers to how much vermouth is preferred, and the drier the martini, the less vermouth. If someone requests a dry martini, I'll add just a dash of vermouth. If someone requests an extra-dry martini, I'll literally put a drop of vermouth. If I were making a gin martini, I would be a little less shy with the vermouth, and probably double what I would use for a vodka martini.

Now that you have your pint glass filled with ice, vodka and vermouth, you will either shake or stir your martini. As I mentioned earlier, I tend to stir my gin martinis, but I shake my vodka martinis. For a **shaken** martini, you will either transfer is to your martini shaker, or you'll grab your Boston shaker and pop it on top of your pint glass. Give your shaker a gentle tap to form a seal with the pint glass, then shake until it's ice cold. If you are using a non-insulated shaker, you should shake it until you've got frost on the outside of the tin, and your hands are almost going to be numb. They say shake it until your hands hurt, and then shake a little more. When your cocktail is good and shaken, you are going to pop the shaker free from the top of your glass. Give it a light tap to loosen it. Next, you'll put the Hawthorn strainer on top of the Boston shaker, dump the ice from your cocktail glass, and strain your martini into the glass. Your martini will appear cloudy because you've aerated the drink. All that shaking has put tiny air bubbles into your drink, and give it that frosty look. If you prefer your martinis clear, rather than the cloudy look of a shaken martini, you can always go with stirring.

For a stirred martini, just grab your bar spoon, and gently stir your cocktail until it's nice and cold, Stick to the rules of shaking, and keep stirring until your tin gets frosty. And try to use large ice cubes when shaking or stirring a martini, to avoid diluting the drink with melted shards of ice.

The only thing left to do is garnish your martini. How do you garnish a martini? Just think of the classic story, Oliver Twist. For classic martinis, the most popular garnishes are olives or lemon twist.

So which garnish goes better with your vodka martini? Typically, when a customer orders a martini, they will just ask for what garnish they want. In other words, there's no right or wrong answer.

An olive devotee might ask you for a "**dirty martini**," which means they want extra olive juice in their cocktail. Since they want to taste the olive flavor in their martini, you could even rub an olive around the rim of the glass. You could pour your olive juice into the cocktail glass before you strain your martini in there, but then you are going to warm up the drink. I prefer to add the olive juice into the vodka/vermouth mixture before you shake it up; that way you merge the flavors together. Old bartender's superstition: never put an even number of olives in a cocktail.

What other garnish goes well with a vodka martini? Take a tip from James Bond, and add a thin slice of lemon peel. A lemon peel in a vodka martini looks spectacular, and the hint of citrus flavor goes perfectly with the drink. Once you have strained your martini into your cocktail glass, gently drag your channel knife once around your lemon, and drop the lemon peel into your martini, and you have just made a medium-dry vodka martini, shaken not stirred.

Take a long sip, lean back, and enjoy.

As we reach the end of this chapter, hopefully you possess a broader knowledge of cocktails, you feel confident preparing a cocktail, and you understand the correct ways to follow cocktail recipes.

And not to be a drag, but don't forget that cocktails, especially martinis, are extremely potent, and can easily knock you off your edge if you aren't careful. There's nothing James Bond about being the guy with his head in the toilet because he threw back three martinis in two hours. Always eat a full meal before a night of drinking, and whatever you do, pace yourself. And if we learned anything from watching James Bond flip that gorgeous Aston Martin: remember, don't drink and drive.

And, don't forget to have fun and enjoy the experience of learning. Enjoy and experiment! Soon, like Bond did in *Casino Royale,* you'll come up with your own signature cocktail and give it a name. When you do, please send me your recipe, I'd love to try it.

Cheers!

MAN OF ACTION
Flying an Airplane

Ian Fleming's James Bond did not know how to fly an airplane, but the cinematic version of 007 is definitely a pilot.

Though, it took many years before Bond's piloting skills became obvious. In the early years, it was difficult to know whether or not Bond could actually fly, because anytime we saw him at the controls of an airplane, he was usually crashing it.

BOND, THE PILOT?

The first time we see James Bond grab the controls of an airplane is in *Goldfinger*. When the cabin loses pressure, Bond races into the cockpit of the Lockheed VC- 140B, already in a steep nosedive. Bond wrestles with the controls, but it's of no use, and the two parachute to safety just before the plane crashes into the ocean. In *You Only Live Twice,* Bond faces a similar situation. He manages to grab the yoke of the Meyers 200A, only to crash land the plane before it explodes. Does Bond crash the plane because he can't fly, or because Helga Brandt had damaged the plane before she escaped? (Maybe that lipstick is more than just a smoke bomb?) In any case, James Bond seemed to have an ill-fated relationship with flying.

Perhaps Bond's piloting skills developed over time. It wasn't until much later that we see James Bond definitely knows how to pilot an aircraft. In *The Man with the Golden Gun,* Bond flies a Republic RC-3 Seabee through Thailand's Phang Nga Bay cliffs to Scaramanga's hideout. In the pre-title sequence of *Octopussy,* Bond uses an Acrostar Jet to complete his mission and make his escape. After that, it was becoming downright common to see James Bond piloting an airplane. Never a stranger to airborne escapes, he uses a Cessna 185 seaplane to take off with Sanchez's cash in *License to Kill,* and in *GoldenEye,* Bond pilots two different planes: the Pilatus PC-6, which he skydives into and uses to escape from the weapons facility, and the Cessna 172 Skyhawk, which he flies into Cuba – only to be shot down, true to form.

It was in *The Living Daylights* that James Bond proves that his piloting skills go beyond light single- and twin-prop airplanes. Bond brings it up a notch during an escape from Afghanistan, by piloting the massive Lockheed C-130 Hercules. Also, Bond takes it to the limit when he commandeers a Soviet L39 Albatross fighter jet to make his escape in *Tomorrow Never Dies.*

James Bond's luck with piloting aircraft seems to have backtracked once again in recent years. In *Quantum of Solace,* James Bond flies – and narrowly escapes – a disabled Douglas DC-3. In *Spectre,* James Bond mysteriously commandeers a twin-engine Britten-Norman BN-2 Islander to chase down the Spectre goons who've just kidnapped Dr. Madeleine Swann. Naturally, the aircraft sustains heavy damage, losing its wings and part of its fuselage, but still manages to slide down the snowy mountain and take out the baddies and rescue Madeleine.

In *No Time to Die,* James Bond prefers to travel by boat, while Nomi pilots a Cessna A185F Skywagon into Cuba; an aircraft that he will later commandeer to deliver Obruchev to the CIA. And while James Bond does not personally pilot either aircraft, Bond and Nomi infiltrate Safin's island lair aboard a Boeing C-17A Globemaster III, which is equipped with a specialized stealth glider. Bond takes a back seat aboard the glider as it detaches from the Boeing mid-air to facilitate their covert arrival.

If it has wings, James Bond can fly it.

There are few activities that are quite as exciting as flying an airplane. Not sure that's true? Try sitting in a room full of pilots and listen to them reminisce about flying. Any pilot will tell you that whenever they get behind the controls of an airplane, it's just as exciting as the first time they flew. And I can tell you from experience, the first time I actually had my hands on the controls of an airplane was an absolute thrill. It's something everyone should try at least once. And just maybe, flying is something that could become part of your life.

To most of us, the idea of getting a pilot's license sounds about as crazy as the idea of becoming an astronaut. But you'll be surprised when you find out just how attainable a private pilot's license really is.

When you start training with a flight instructor, one of the first things they will do is take you on an **introductory flight**, where you'll sit in the pilot's seat and get hands-on experience flying the airplane.

So in this chapter of **Being James Bond**, we will walk you through your introductory flight, and give you a sneak peek at the things you'll experience. We'll discuss the parts of the plane, and explore the theory of lift. We'll tackle take-off and landing, and the fundamentals of maneuvering, including climbs, straight and level flight, turns and descents. We'll talk about what's involved in getting a pilot's license.

We'll talk about age and medical requirements, ground schools, flight hours, and flight tests. And finally, we'll talk about finding the right flight instructor or flight school. So with that said, please put away your tray table and return your seat to its upright position, and let's go flying.

"Welcome to The Bleeker Flying School, Mrs. Bell"

"Where's Mr. Bleeker?" You might recall the flying lesson that never got off the ground in *Live and Let Die.* If Mr. Bleeker hadn't been 'indisposed,' then Mrs. Bell's lesson might have gone something like this:

You'll notice that Mr. Bleeker uses a Cessna 140; a single-engine (single propeller), two-seat, light general aviation aircraft which is very common for flight training. Climb aboard, switch on your radio, and check the ATIS (Automated Terminal Information Service). The information it gives you about the current temperature, winds and visibility, all indicate that you have chosen a perfect day for your flight lesson. With your battery master switched on, you'll check your fuel pump, check the electric vacuum pump, be sure that the mixture is set to full forward, and that the carburetor heat is switched off.

Yell "Clear" and turn the key. The engine bursts into operation, and the propeller roars to life. Now it's time to check the oil pressure, and it's just right. You radio the tower, and they give you permission to taxi to the runway, so you apply a little throttle to get to taxiing speed, and you are on your way to the runway.

After taxiing to the starting point of the runway, you apply your parking brake to do your last minute, pre-takeoff checks. You bring up your RPMs, and check your gauges. They all check out okay, so you bring your RPM back down to idle. You grab the controls and check that your ailerons, your stabilizer, and your rudder, are all functioning and moving freely.

You check that the fuel is set, and the tank is full. The electric fuel pump is on, engine gauges have been checked, the flaps are set for takeoff, carburetor heat is set to off, mixture is full forward, your seat belts are fastened, your trim tab is set, the controls have all been checked, the door is latched, and your transponder is switched to on. You're ready to go!

The tower has now cleared you for takeoff, so you apply the throttle, sending the airplane hurtling down the runway. You glance quickly at the RPM and the oil pressure to make sure everything checks out okay as you adjust the left and right rudder pedals, making sure the plane stays centered down the runway. You are about to pull back on the controls to establish the plane into a climb attitude.

It's at this moment that you think back to your instruction on the theory of lift. In fact, before we take off into the wide blue yonder, this might be a good time to back up and talk about these basic principles.

How does an airplane fly?

To understand how a plane flies, you have to know how "**lift**" works, but before we get there, let's look at the airplane itself. Understanding the basic structure, design, and specific parts of the airplane is the first step towards understanding how it flies. Let's look at a very simple, single-prop (single-propeller) airplane like the Cessna 140 we just mentioned.

Everyone knows what an airplane looks like; you have the **fuselage**, which is the body of the airplane, and of course you have the **wings**. On the front of the fuselage you'll find the **propeller**, and then you have the **tail** with its two smaller wings and vertical fin, but let's get a little more specific. The smaller "wings" on the back of the airplane, at the base of the tail, is called the stabilizer. These small wings are much more important than you might guess; the **stabilizer** is responsible for creating the angle of the airplane, or more precisely, controls the attitude of the plane. The **attitude** of the plane refers to the vertical angle, and relates to the airplane's rate of climb or descent. We'll take a more in-depth look at these features in this chapter.

How does the stabilizer control the angle?

Let's begin with the simple idea that the forward momentum of the airplane is generated by the aerodynamic "pulling force" of the propeller. If we accept that the natural function of the plane is to pull itself forward, then we can understand that maneuvering the plane becomes an exercise in pointing the plane in the direction you want to go.

Anytime you've seen someone flying a plane, even in the movies, you know that when you pull the controls toward you, the plane goes up. What's happening here is, when the controls are pulled back, the rear end of the stabilizer, or the trailing edge, moves upward. In other words, the rear of the stabilizer is now angled higher than the front. So the air current streaming across the top of the stabilizer is striking the upward curve, and by forcing the air upward, downward pressure is applied to the stabilizer, and thus the current is pushing the tail of the airplane down. When the tail goes down, the nose of the plane begins to point upward, so the propeller is now pulling the plane in the upward direction.

Alternatively, if you push the controls forward, the rear end of the stabilizer moves down, and with the back of the stabilizer down, the air is now pushing against the bottom of the stabilizer, and forcing the tail upward. When the tail goes up, the nose points down, and the airplane descends. There is another interesting feature designed to make it easy to take off and to climb into a cruise altitude; this is a small section called the trim tab. The **trim tab** is controlled in the cockpit by a little wheel between the two seats, and it works with the stabilizers, and in a similar capacity, but will move up and down independent of the stabilizer. You can adjust the trim tab into a raised position, making it less necessary to pull back on the wheel to achieve the proper attitude. If the trim tab is set correctly, then the plane will now have a tendency to rise, allowing you to have a gentle touch on the controls.

Flying is not physically demanding. Thanks to its aerodynamic design, the plane is engineered to make flying remarkably easy – i.e., the aircraft is designed to fly itself, but more on that later.

So far, we've focused primarily on the rear of the airplane, and we now understand how the stabilizer is employed to affect climb and descents. The next concept is turning.

HOW DO YOU TURN AN AIRPLANE?

This is a good time to mention that there are two basic types of steering mechanisms ('the steering wheel') for an airplane, typically referred to as the control yoke or joystick, depending on the type of aircraft. The **control yoke** (or just "**yoke**") is more common in larger airplanes, and resembles a "U" shaped steering wheel. It is used to control the airplane's pitch (up and down movement) and roll (left and right movement). The **joystick** is found in many fighter jets, light aircraft, and some modern airliners. It's a single stick used for the same pitch and roll functions. But, back to how the aircraft actually turns:

You turn with the ailerons. If you look at the wings you will find that, just as the stabilizer has its trim tabs, both wings have two additional sections, or tabs, that move independently; these are called the **ailerons**.

The wings are obviously fixed in place, and the only parts that move on each wing are these two tabs.

Take a look at the left wing (the pilot's left). On the rear edge of that wing, there are two independent flaps that go up and down. There's one on the right, or inside (closest to the fuselage); this is called the **flap**. Both flaps on the left and right wing move together. Similar to the trim tab which is there to help you climb, flaps are used when descending or slowing the airplane. Lowering the flaps will create drag, thereby causing the plane to slow down. You also do this when you wish to descend; for example, when you are preparing to land the plane.

But, back to turning. Let's look at the other flaps; the other tabs located on the outside of the wings, are the aforementioned **ailerons**. Let's say you have your hands on the steering control, and you turn the wheel to the left. This action causes the left aileron on the left wing to tilt upward while the right aileron on the right wing tilts downward. Just as airflow interacts with the stabilizers to change the plane's direction, the ailerons adjust the plane's roll angle – tilting the plane left or right. Because the left aileron has gone up, the airflow now pushes the left wing down, and with the right aileron down, airflow is pushing the right wing up. Therefore, the wings have caused the plane to tilt, as if on an imaginary axis, and we have changed the angle of the plane.

Why does changing the angle of the plane cause the turn? Why can't the plane just turn or tilt on its side and keep going straight?

The answer to that question is "lift." To over-simplify a little; due to its design, the plane is perpetually moving (or 'lifting') in an upward direction; therefore, by tilting the plane to the left, you have just changed its angle, so that 'up' is now actually somewhere off to the left. You've banked the plane to its left side, and it's essentially just going 'upward' in that new direction. To understand this phenomenon, you need to know about lift.

Lift

When learning aerodynamics, you will be discussing weight and lift. Any college-level textbook will have plenty of mathematical methods for calculating lift. Two of the most common explanations are the Longer Path Explanation (also known as the Bernoulli, or Equal Transit Time Explanation) and the Newtonian Explanation (also known as Momentum Transfer or Air Deflection Explanation). The simplest way to understand lift is this:

Lift is the aerodynamic force that holds the plane in the air. For an airplane in motion, the angle of the wings create most of the lift required to keep the plane airborne. The principal concept in aerodynamics is the idea that air is fluid. Consider that, like all gases, air flows and behaves in a similar manner to water and other liquids. Even though air and water may seem like very different substances, both conform to the same physics and sets of mathematical relationships.

The other important concept is the fact that lift can only exist in the presence of moving fluid. It doesn't matter if the object is stationary and the fluid is moving, or if the fluid is still and the object is moving. What matters is the relative difference in speeds between the object and the fluid.

Consider that the propellers (and the wings) are forcing air behind, and beneath the plane to make it rise. For an aerodynamic aircraft, lift works in an upward motion, so envision the force of the lift going straight up and through the top of the airplane. When you turn the wheel, it causes the plane to bank. If the plane angles to the left, then that vertical lift is now pointing left, and 'up' is now somewhere over to the left.

So now we understand the parts of the wings and we understand how the ailerons affect and create turns; this would be a good time to wonder about the purpose of the rudder.

WHAT DOES THE RUDDER DO?

The **rudder** is the vertical wing on the back of the plane. The rudder on the plane works in a similar way to how a rudder works on a boat. (Remember, airflow and water flow follow the same principles.) Consider that the rudder is in the water behind the boat, so when you angle the rudder to the right or to the left, it changes the direction of the forward moving boat. The rudder on the plane works the same way.

But, we already established that the ailerons control steering, by controlling the angle of the plane; so why do I need the added rudder? Well, let's say you are turning to the right, so you turn the steering control right, and the left aileron goes down and the right aileron goes up, causing downward pressure on the right wing and upward pressure on the left wing, therefore banking the plane to the right. So far so good.

However, the air moving underneath the plane, which is holding the plane up, is now catching a little drag by that downward-pointed aileron on the left. So while we are trying to turn right, the left wing is now dragging a little bit, causing the nose to drift a little to the left, which is of course the opposite of where we actually want to go.

Here is where the rudder comes in. If you are trying to make a right turn, you apply a little right rudder to compensate for that left drag. You control the rudder with pedals at your feet, and applying the right rudder will actually turn the back of the rudder to the right, causing the airflow to push the tail end to the left, in essence pointing the nose to the right which is where you want to go. The rudder is compensating for that left drag.

So controlling the direction of an airplane becomes relatively simple.

We understand that pulling the yoke toward you will pitch the airplane into a climb position, and pushing forward on the controls will dip the nose into a descent position. Turning the controls right and left will tilt you into a turning position, and the rudder will assist in turning by reducing drag on the opposite wing.

Earlier we talked a bit about lift. We understand that air is fluid and the function of the plane is to push air behind and underneath the plane, allowing it to essentially float on top of the air. We understand the moving parts of the plane that control navigation. We know that the stabilizer controls climb and descent, while the ailerons control pitch, and thereby controlling the direction of the plane.

Back to Takeoff

After a briefing by the instructor and a walk-around inspection of the airplane, he or she will explain the actions the pilot takes to prepare for the flight. You will then strap yourself into the left front seat. This is the pilot seat, and believe it or not, you will actually do most of the flying. This is where they will go over the fundamentals of flying: climbs, straight-and-level flight, turns and descents.

One of the great things about learning how to fly is that it's something you are almost guaranteed to enjoy learning. As I mentioned earlier, when you start your flight instruction with a **certified flight instructor** (or **CFI**) they will take you on what is known as an introductory flight, which is a time-honored tradition.

Once you are in the pilot's seat and strapped in correctly, it's time to begin the takeoff, which brings us right back to where we began.

Before you begin, the throttle is pushed all the way forward, the mixture control is all the way up, and the carburetor switch is turned to off. The throttle is the mechanism for controlling the RPM of the engine, or simply, controlling how fast your engine is revving. This is how you control the speed of the airplane. '**Mixture**,' controls how much air is getting into your engine, and you will adjust accordingly depending on your altitude, as the air gets thinner as you go higher. Next, you will take a look at your instruments; when you get into an airplane, you'll quickly notice there are a lot more instruments on the dashboard than you're used to.

Instrumentation

There are six instruments that you are going to want to pay special attention to. The first would be your **airspeed indicator**; just like it sounds, it works like a speedometer, and indicates the airplane's speed through the air measured in knots or miles per hour.

Next is your **altimeter**, which displays the airplane's altitude above sea level, letting you know how high off the ground you are.

Then we have the **vertical speed indicator**, which tells you the rate at which the airplane is climbing or descending, in hundreds of feet per minute; simply, you how fast you are moving up or down.

Following that is the **attitude indicator**, which in essence shows you the angle of the airplane. More specifically, it displays the position of the airplane's nose and wings relative to the horizon.

Next, we have the **heading indicator**, which is essentially a compass. Also called a directional gyro, it indicates the direction of the airplane's nose, and is set by the pilot to align with the magnetic compass.

Last is the **turn coordinator**, which guides the pilot in use of the rudder to properly balance turns.

Those are the basic six instruments you are going to have to know when flying a plane, and everything else in the cockpit is support equipment ranging from radios to controls for aircraft systems, which would include instruments like the **tachometer**, which indicates your engine's RPM, or how hard you are pushing your engine, the **fuel gauges**, the **fuel pressure**, the **oil temperature**, and, of course, the **electrical switches** and **lights**. Your navigation equipment includes your **transponder**, which is essentially how the control tower radar can see your airplane, and of course your **radio control panel**.

Taxiing

With what you now understand about how the controls steer the plane, relying on the manipulation of the force of air flow, you can also conclude that the steering wheel has absolutely no effect on the ground. When taxiing on the ground at low speeds, the direction of the plane is controlled solely by using the rudder pedals.

The engine's propeller thrust will still pull the airplane forward. The **rudder pedals** at your feet control the rudder on the tail and, in most small airplanes, also control the steerable **nose wheel** or **tail wheel** (depending on the airplane design). The rudder pedals typically have brake controls built in, allowing you to control direction using **differential braking**; pressing the top portion of each pedal activates the brake for the wheel on that side. By applying brakes to one wheel, the airplane can make tighter turns, particularly useful during slow-speed taxiing or on narrow taxiways. If the plane is being pulled forward by the propeller, and you apply the left brake, leaving the right wheel to move freely, then the plane will slowly turn to the left.

Pilots will tell you that taxiing using only the foot pedals feels strange in the beginning, but you get used to it pretty fast. Now you have taxied up to the beginning of the runway, it's time to do that pre-flight check one more time.

Pre-flight Check

You've set the parking brake and now you are going to bring up your RPM. With your RPM high, you'll check all of your engine gauges to make sure they are functioning properly. Grab the wheel and check the controls; check the ailerons to make sure they are functioning and moving freely, and do the same thing with your stabilizer and your rudder. Make sure your trim is in the right position, and you make sure the doors are latched.

At this point you'll take out your pre-flight checklist and work your way down the list. Make sure your fuel is set on the proper tank, and that the tank is full. The electric fuel pump is set to on, your engine gauges have been checked, the flaps are set in the correct position for takeoff, the carburetor heat is switched to off, your mixture knob is set to full forward, seat belts are fastened, trim tab is set, you've checked the controls, the doors are latched shut, your transponder is on and you are ready for takeoff. You radio the tower and request takeoff, and the tower has cleared you.

Takeoff

We're now right back where we left off; the moment we've been waiting for. Slide throttle forward to start the plane moving. Take a quick glance at your RPM and your oil pressure to make sure everything is responding appropriately. Keep your feet on the rudder pedals, adjusting as needed to keep yourself centered as you speed down the runway. As you hurtle forward and hit the appropriate speed, you'll feel the controls become effective. Now, pull back on the controls, adjusting the stabilizers, and establishing the plane at the correct climb attitude.

You can now feel the powerful airflow as it lifts the plane off the runway, and suddenly, you are airborne!

You hold at the climb attitude and the airplane flies at the proper airspeed on its own. You'll continue to climb until you have reached your cruise altitude. This is where the trim comes in. Remember, the trim tabs are those movable sections on the back of the stabilizer which adjust up and down. Using the knob on the floor between the seats, you can adjust the trim tabs upward, and they will hold that position, so you are not tugging on the controls the whole time. As we said, flying a plane should not require strength, and adjusting the trim tab to help achieve a climb attitude is another way that the plane helps to remove some of the effort. Many beginning pilots tend to have a tight grip on the controls, when in fact you actually want to keep a very light touch. Remember, the reason flying is not strenuous is because the plane is designed to fly itself. The aerodynamics of the plane does most of the work.

As you climb to your cruise altitude, you will notice the other function of the rudder. Because the propeller goes clockwise, you would assume there would be a natural tendency for the plane to want to pull a little bit to the left. When you are in straight-and-level flight, the plane is designed to compensate for that factor, so the tendency is just to go straight. However, when you are in a climb attitude, the plane does have an increased tendency to pull slightly to the left. To compensate for this, you use the rudder to angle the plane a little bit to the right as you climb.

CHANGING DIRECTION

The first step in turning an airplane is the same as before turning a car; check your surroundings and look for oncoming traffic. It's worth noting that, while you must always remain vigilant for other planes, especially close to airports, it's actually very rare to see another airplane in flight. Flying is one of the safest modes of transportation – significantly safer than driving. Many pilots will compare flying to driving, pointing out that the drive to the airport carries more risk than the flight itself. *"Statistically speaking of course, it's still the safest way to travel."* Mishaps in aviation are generally very rare.

Once you've looked for traffic, turn the controls gently to the right. You will observe the right aileron shifting up, and the left aileron shifting down, causing the plane to bank on its axis to the right, and the plane will begin to turn right. When you're facing the desired direction, you naturally straighten the wheel out. However, after straightening the wheel, you see that the plane is still turning right. Why? After all, if you were driving a car and you were making a turn, you would simply straighten out the wheel when you've completed the turn to go straight.

With the plane banked right, you hold the turn until you are facing the correct direction; at which point you need to roll yourself back out of the turn. So you turn the wheel to the left, so that the plane will bank back to the left. When the plane levels off, you adjust the wheel to the right to straighten out, until you are going straight-and-level once again.

Now that you are out of your turn, and you've just about reached your cruise altitude, you will level off into some straight-and-level flying. You are going to adjust your trim back down, as you don't wish to climb anymore, causing you to level off and fly straight.

How do you know if you are going perfectly straight and level? One way to know for sure is to check your instruments. Your altimeter is stable, indicating that you are not climbing or descending, and your vertical speed indicator reads zero. Your attitude indicator reads that you are level with the horizon, your heading indicator is stable, and your turn coordinator is also remaining level.

While it is important to get the hang of reading and understanding the instruments, it's also important to learn to read your horizon; to be able to just look out the window and understand what your plane is doing. When you are straight and level, your nose is probably going to look just a little under the horizon, and you can also look left and right to see what your wings are doing in relation to your horizon as well.

Getting to Know the Aircraft

While you are going straight and level this is also a good time to play with the controls a little bit, and get to know how they respond. When you pull back on the controls, you know the plane is going to pitch upward, and you will see the nose go up and over the horizon. Pushing down on the controls does the opposite; the nose will dip down below the horizon.

This is also a good time to observe the plane's tendency is to fly itself. If you were to gently pull back on the controls, pitching the attitude back into a slight climbing position, and then just let go of the controls, you will notice that, because of the aerodynamic design of the plane, the plane will level itself back out. Again, the plane is designed to go straight and level, and possesses a natural inherent stability.

Learning to Fly

Why would the potential James Bond want to earn a pilot's license? The answer is quite simple: for the fun, for the freedom, and the adventure. In **Being James Bond**, we learn to do the things that James Bond does, so just as we would learn to ski in the Alps, or scuba dive in The Bahamas, we will also learn how to fly an airplane.

Just imagine that you and a friend were flying out to the Bahamas for a long weekend of scuba diving, and you were the one doing the flying! Flying is not only fun and exciting, but it can also be practical. Getting a pilot's license is definitely a serious investment financially, but saving on the cost of plane tickets can help to offset that cost, and you would have more freedom to get where you want to go, when you want to go. I have a friend in airplane sales who told me that sales had skyrocketed during the pandemic, as frequent flight delays and cancellations left many business travelers seeking alternative ways to fly.

What are the steps and requirements for getting your pilot's license?

As we mentioned earlier, one of the very first things a flight instructor will do with you is take you on an introductory flight, where you will sit in the pilot's seat and do most of the flying. It's after that first flight, that you are probably going to be very anxious to schedule your next lesson.

Any concerns you may have about the complexity or the long paper trails standing between you and becoming a pilot are highly exaggerated. According to many pilots, you probably had a tougher time getting a driver's license. One friend of mine actually had his pilot's license before he could drive a car. Aviation is a learn-by-doing proposition.

People train to be pilots under a variety of different circumstances, so there is a great deal of flexibility that exists for fashioning the kind of training plan that you need. If you are looking into flight schools, try to find out as much as you can about several schools in your area before making a decision. Consider the company's longevity, location, costs, and what kind of programs it offers. If you have time limitations, make it very clear to your instructor from the beginning, so you can put together a realistic training schedule.

Requirements for a Pilot's License

AGE REQUIREMENTS

You can begin your flight training at any age, but you need to be at least 16-years-old to fly solo, and at least 17-years-old to receive your PPL, or private pilot's license.

MEDICAL REQUIREMENTS

There are three classes of medical certificates, and the requirements depend on which class you need. First- and second-class medical certificates are required for commercial pilots. You need a **third-class medical certificate** to become a private pilot. To get this certificate you just need to be in reasonably good health, adequate vision and hearing, and have generally good physical coordination. Only in cases where you might have severe diabetes or severe epilepsy or anything that would cause sudden, severe incapacitation would prohibit you from getting a certificate. This medical must be renewed every few years; if you are under 40-years-old, your third-class medical certificate is valid for 5 years. If you are 40 or older, your third-class medical certificate is valid for 2 years. After that, it will need to be renewed. To become a **sport pilot**, where your interests are limited to the occasional recreational flying, a medical certificate is not required; you simply need a valid U.S. driver's license.

We mentioned vision and hearing as part of your medical requirements. Your vision must be 20/40 or better with or without corrective lenses, and you must be able to perceive those colors necessary for the safe performance. If you have any limitations identifying color, this might prohibit you from night flying, but sometimes waivers are issued in certain cases. You should also have reasonably good hearing, but there have been deaf pilots in the past. Even in cases of paralysis or missing limbs, you can get a certificate of demonstrated ability. There are several organizations that support wheelchair pilots and people with disabilities who want to fly.

Ground School

In **ground school**, you will cover things like weather, aerodynamics, navigation and regulations. Some people ask which should come first, flight training or ground training? Opinions differ, but most experts suggest a balanced approach to learning. It's not necessarily advantageous for you to complete ground school before beginning flight training, or vice versa. In fact, be skeptical of flight instructors who tell you to get in touch with them only after you've completed ground school.

What to Expect from your Flight Lessons

What is the minimum number of hours needed to get a license? Under Part 61 of the FAA, the minimums are 20 hours with an instructor, and 10 hours of solo flight time, though most students will actually have many more hours by the completion of their training.

You should also know the differences between a Part 61 and Part 141 flight schools, which are two different sets of regulations set by the Federal Aviation Administration (FAA) that govern flight training programs in the United States. They determine how flight schools operate, the requirements for pilots, and the way training is structured.

Part 61 offers more flexibility, is more self-paced, and is ideal for those who want less structure or who have irregular schedules. It also tends to be cheaper, though it may require more flight hours to complete training. **Part 141** is highly structured, provides more direct oversight by the FAA, offers a set curriculum, and typically reduces flight hours required to obtain a certificate. It's a good choice for students who want a more formal training environment and potentially quicker completion of their training. Either school will train you to pass the very same practical test.

What do flight lessons consist of? Early flight lessons are dedicated to familiarizing you with the basics of aircraft control. As you progress, you will explore the airplane handling and other areas of flight, such as the slow speed range during takeoff and landing and in steeper angles of bank. You will explore flight in different aircraft configurations such as when the wing flaps are extended.

Then you will learn to maneuver the aircraft with reference to objects on the ground. This will teach you how the aircraft's speed over the ground is affected by flying into the wind, downwind, at an angle to the prevailing flow, and how the pilot must adjust his course to maintain the desired track or direction of flying. Once you have mastered these concepts, it's time to practice takeoffs and landings, and learn airport traffic pattern operations, where all of the skills you've learned will come into play. Once you've logged several hours of practice, and your landings take on a consistently acceptable quality, the first solo is not that far down the road.

A pilot's first **solo flight**, when you actually take off and land completely on your own, is a moment that no pilot ever forgets. Once you are soloing in the local area, dual flights with your instructor will enter a new phase: **cross-country training**, or **point-to-point flying** within the air traffic control system. With your instructor, you will begin to plan and fly cross-country in preparation for completing at least five hours of cross-country solo flying en route to earning your private pilot's license.

At this stage, you'll learn to use **aeronautical charts** and your aircraft's performance manuals to plan your flights, thus applying your ground school knowledge of aircraft systems, aviation weather, navigation and the air traffic system. While hand-held **GPS**, or **Global Positioning Systems**, satellite-based navigation systems, have become commonplace in small private airplanes (just as they are in your cellphone), you still need to learn and understand aeronautical charts in the event of equipment failure.

That leads to **night-flying training**, which will include at least three hours of flight time, one cross-country flight at night of at least 100 miles total distance, and 10 takeoffs and landings at night.

Another training requirement is **instrument training**; learning how to keep the aircraft under control solely by referencing the flight instruments as an emergency-only method of handling unexpected encounters with clouds or bad weather.

As you close in on the required flight time minimums for each of the various flight operations, it's time to focus on your upcoming flight exam, which is a combined oral test and flight test.

The test preparation phase is where you'll put it all together. Using a practical test checklist, you and your instructor will spend some time putting the finishing touches on your flight planning skills and your knowledge of aircraft systems, aerodynamics, regulations, weather; all of the principles you have been studying. When you get a written recommendation from your flight instructor, you'll be ready for your flight test.

Of course the scariest question still on your mind is, *"How much will I have to spend to get a pilot's license?"*

The cost will certainly vary depending on what region of the country you live in, and how many hours it takes you, but the number that I keep coming up with is roughly the same. You should plan on investing between $5,000 and $9,000, depending on the certificate being sought. Of course, you don't need to pay all of your flight training up front; most training programs will let you pay over time, and as you go. In other words, that intimidating figure will mostly likely be spread over many months or years.

Scholarships & Grants

There are several scholarships and grants available to budding pilots who could use financial assistance. Many aviation organizations offer funding to aspiring pilots. The Aircraft Owners and Pilots Association (AOPA) provides flight training scholarships, while the Experimental Aircraft Association (EAA) also offers financial support for student pilots. Women looking to enter aviation can explore scholarships through Women in Aviation International (WAI) and The Ninety-Nines.

Airlines and aerospace companies also support future pilots through scholarship programs. Major carriers like Delta, Southwest, and United Airlines offer financial aid as part of their pilot pathway initiatives. Additionally, aviation manufacturers such as Boeing and Lockheed Martin have been known to provide grants for pilot training. Some state governments also offer aviation workforce development grants, and students enrolling in aviation college programs may qualify for financial aid through FAFSA (Federal Student Aid).

Local flight schools and community colleges often have scholarship opportunities, so it's worth inquiring about funding options directly through your chosen institution. The Civil Air Patrol (CAP) Cadet Wings Program offers scholarships to young pilots, and military-related programs such as ROTC flight training scholarships can also be an option for those considering a military aviation path. Additionally, online databases like Fastweb.com, Scholarships.com, and AviationScholarships.com provide comprehensive lists of available funding sources.

Researching and applying for these opportunities can reduce the financial burden of flight training and get one step closer to earning your wings.

Finding a Flight Instructor or Flight School

Unless you already know a pilot or a flight instructor you can obviously just do a Google search for flight instruction in your area.

The Aircraft Owners and Pilots Association (AOPA) has some great articles and links for flight training, finding a local flight school, and dozens of other aspects of learning to fly. Click on "Flight School Finder" and it will take you to their flight school database where you can find a flight school in your area.

PILOTS LOVE TO TALK AVIATION

Another option is to head down to a local airfield and just chat with some of the local pilots. Just tell anyone that you are interested in some flight training, and they will be more than happy to tell you all they know. Pilots love to talk aviation. This is their passion. Just show a little interest and they will give you a world of information. A few minutes with one of these guys and you will understand why they get so excited about what they do. Being behind the wheel of a plane is a thrill unlike any other.

Do this just one time and you will feel like a different person. Maybe you'll even feel a little bit more like James Bond.

Landing

Before we finish this chapter, we're going to have to land this plane. To start our descent, lower the RPM slightly, and you'll immediately notice that just by changing the speed of the airplane, the nose will start to dip, and you are now beginning to descend. You didn't have to push forward on the controls at all; just by changing the speed of the plane you've changed the ratio of weight to lift just enough to begin to lose altitude.

While you descend, you are going to look over your instruments; the altimeter is gently unwinding, showing that you are descending, the vertical speed indicator shows a steady rate of descent, and the attitude index shows that the nose is just below the horizon.

Take a look out the window and get a good feel of how that looks. The nose is now definitely under the horizon, and it will stay this way for most of the descent. Just like you did when you took off, you will check the ATIS at the local airport where we are going to land. Then you'll radio the tower for instructions. Look out for traffic, and begin your descent.

You go down your landing checklist. The mixture is correctly set to full forward, the electric fuel pump is on, and the tower has told you that you can approach. So you lower the RPM a little bit more, and the nose will dip into the descending angle or descending attitude. The tower then tells you that you are clear to land. You lower the flaps to create a little drag to decrease your airspeed, allowing you to go in nice and slow. You keep looking forward and keep looking at that horizon. You are going to keep the horizon steady for a nice, stable descent. You continue your approach, and once you're about ten or fifteen feet above the runway, you'll do what is called a **roundout**, or a **flare**. You pull back on the wheel just a little bit to hold the plane off the runway, until the nose comes up to about a climb attitude, right about the same attitude we had when you took off. Touch down very gently on the two main wheels, lowering the nose down onto the runway. Once you are safely on the ground, you will reduce speed by applying the brakes gently, and you'll raise the flaps back up, putting all the weight down on the ground. As you taxi to a complete stop, you have just completed your first flying lesson.

Right about now you can turn to the person next to you and say, "I know a great restaurant. We can just make dinner."

As we conclude this chapter, you should now have a solid understanding of the fundamentals of flying, how an airplane operates, and what it takes to earn a pilot's license. With this knowledge, you can decide whether pursuing aviation is a path you'd like to explore and potentially make a part of your life.

Further Reading

Right about now, I usually add a caveat by reminding the reader that nothing beats hands-on experience; needless to say, that's especially true when it comes to flying. But check out a few sources for further explanation, some of which come highly recommended.

'The Pilot's Handbook of Aeronautical Knowledge'

This is the official FAA book that covers all the basics of aeronautical knowledge, including aircraft systems, aerodynamics, weather, regulations, and flight planning. It is highly comprehensive and structured to provide you with the knowledge needed to pass your written exam.

'Stick and Rudder: An Explanation of the Art of Flying'

A classic in aviation literature, Wolfgang Langewiesche explains the fundamentals of flying with simplicity and clarity. It focuses on the mechanics of flying, helping you understand the forces involved in flight and how to control an aircraft. It's an essential read for grasping the practical aspects of piloting.

King Schools

A well-renowned aviation training institution serving aspiring pilots for decades, King Schools offers a variety of online courses that cover everything from private pilot certifications to more advanced ratings and endorsements. Founded by John and Martha King, the school is famous for its comprehensive, user-friendly flight training programs designed to suit pilots at all levels, from beginners to seasoned aviators.

www.kingschools.com

And don't forget the **AOPA** website, the Aircraft Owners and Pilots Association, found at www.aopa.org, or just go to Letsgoflying.com. It has great articles and resources, including information about flight training and finding flight schools.

Special thanks to my friend Chris Morales (That One Bond Guy), a licensed pilot and trainer for the Federal Aviation Administration, for checking my homework and offering suggestions to make this chapter complete.

That concludes this chapter on flying an airplane.

Good luck, and happy landings.

London

*"We are not now that strength which in old days
Moved earth and heaven…"*

James Bond burst out of the subterranean Westminster Station into the harsh daylight. The first responders and paramedics rushed past him, down into the Metro as the chaos on the street and the sound of the sirens made him pause briefly to get his bearings. Then, without hesitation, he broke into a sprint heading north along Parliament Street to get to the tribunal.

*"that which we are, we are;
One equal temper of heroic hearts,…"*

She sat resolute, like the Union Jack-adorned bulldog that guarded the paperwork on her desk for years. Olivia Mansfield – better known to this inquiry as M – served as the stalwart defender of the faith for decades. But today she was to be punished; put on display and shamed in order to repent for her perceived crimes. 'Standing in the stocks at midday.'

*"Made weak by time and fate,
but strong in will…"*

But it wasn't just M that was on trial, it was the entire Secret Service, and perhaps, even the Crown itself. For what was Britain's place in this modern world? For centuries, the United Kingdom had been called upon to defend liberty against the forces of tyranny, and M did the job that most would never dare; and that included the very accusers seated across from her. M was the one called upon to confront our darkest fears. She had to make the tough calls. She knew that the face of evil was always at the gate, always lurking in the shadows. And that was where she did battle; in the shadows.

"To strive, to seek, to find,
and not to yield."

Bond was gasping for breath. His heart was pounding violently in his chest; his quads and hamstrings were screaming as he continued to sprint towards the inquiry. His pulse was surging with a raw sense of genuine fear; for evil was no longer lurking in the shadows – it had just burst into the light.

Overview

When you embark on your mission of traveling the world of James Bond, why not start in the same place 007 always begins his missions. A city still bustling with big red buses and vintage black cabs, where centuries of royal tradition meets the ultra modern, and classic style still reigns. It's no wonder James Bond chooses to call London his home.

"When a man is tired of London he is tired of life, for there is in London all that life could afford."

– Samuel Johnson, Author of the First English Dictionary

London is one of the largest and most populated cities in Europe, covering an area of nearly 1,600 square kilometers (or over 600 square miles), and is overflowing with some of the world's most magnificent icons and attractions including Big Ben and the Houses of Parliament, Buckingham Palace, St. Paul's Cathedral, the Tower Bridge, Westminster Abbey, the British Museum, the London Eye, and the O2, just to name a few. If you are looking for history, culture, or clubs and nightlife, it's all here.

While it's nearly impossible to experience all that London has to offer in a single visit; for the James Bond fanatic, part of the allure of visiting London is that you can take in the best that this city has to offer, while secretly exploring familiar Bond locations, all at the same time – and this is true whether you're traveling solo or with a companion.

Also, so much has changed in the years since I first completed this humble chapter on the city of London. We lost Her Majesty, Queen Elizabeth II (1926–2022) a symbol of stability and the longest-reigning monarch in British history, who had ruled for 70 years, and worked with 15 Prime Ministers, and met with 13 US Presidents.

We also saw the release of three new James Bond films; *Skyfall, Spectre,* and *No Time To Die,* all of which prominently featured London as a setting, offering exciting new locations to visit. *Skyfall* in particular felt like a love letter to Great Britain, and to the city of London. So needless to say, it was time to update this edition to include many new locations.

Where to begin?
London is nothing if not 'bustling,' so it may seem slightly overwhelming at first, but take heart; a great way to get some perspective is to take a sightseeing tour. You're not an official Londoner until you've ridden on the top of a big, red, double decker bus, so you might as well make it a tour bus. A little touristy? Maybe. But it's really fun, and will help you get your bearings and assist you in planning out the rest of your sightseeing.

One of the most popular tour bus companies is **The Big Bus Company** (www.bigbustours.com), and if the bus has an open top, be sure to have your camera ready and your umbrella handy. These tours offer a wonderful overview of all the must-see attractions, landmarks, and bridges, in central London. The Big Bus tours offers a "Hop on, Hop off" feature, so you can get off the bus at whichever stop or landmark you wish to visit, and another bus will be along at regular intervals to pick you back up, taking a lot of the guesswork out of having to find your way around. Also, Big Bus offers packages that also include a river cruise on the Thames, along with several guided walking tours. A great way to get your bearings.

THE THAMES RIVER

It's almost impossible to see a James Bond film and not catch a glimpse of the Thames River. Establishing shots of the Thames, with its picturesque views of Big Ben and Parliament, have been featured in many films including *Dr. No, From Russia with Love,* and *Goldfinger.* Bond nearly nose-dived a helicopter into it in *For Your Eyes Only,* and he tore up the water in the high-powered Q-boat in *The World is Not Enough,* passing through, or crashing through, some well-known features of the Thames. But of course, the Thames was heavily featured in *Spectre,* as James Bond used a small speedboat to chase a helicopter up the Thames River, taking down the helicopter with a single bullet, causing it to crash land right onto the Westminster Bridge, taking out one of the most sinister masterminds of all time. Pretty impressive.

Whether you're boating on the water, or just taking a riverside stroll along side, the Thames provides plenty to do and see. It also seems to have a calming effect on anyone who happens to stop by for a chat. After a pretty intense and sometimes ugly disagreement on the wisdom of the Heracles project, James Bond and M have a much cooler exchange along the Thames, just outside the Furnivall Sculling Club.

FURNIVALL SCULLING CLUB

A rowing club based on the Thames in Hammersmith, London, the Furnivall Sculling Club welcomes new adult members of any age and all rowing, sculling and coxing abilities, including complete beginners. They offer a variety of groups catering for different levels of experience and commitment, and proudly proclaim a vibrant social life with events throughout the year. If you happen to live in London and want to give the sport of rowing a try, or prefer to walk past and check out a familiar Bond location, check them out. Big thanks to Pete Brooker and his amazing 'London Bond Map' for scoping out this location.

Furnivall Sculling Club
19 Lower Mall
W6 9DJ, UK

Along with the Big Bus River Cruise options, there are several boating companies that offer river cruises that will give you a more expanded view of the Thames, with many of them offering themed cruises, like the lunch or dinner cruises, afternoon tea, or sparkling wine and canapes. If you're looking to get the adrenaline going you could speed things up with a speedboat cruise with the London Thames RIB Experience. This group offers tours on high-powered RIBs (Rigid Inflatable Boats), and advertises an 'Ultimate Spy Experience' which promises spy-themed guided commentary followed by a high speed ride past iconic filming locations like MI6, Westminster Bridge, and the O2 Arena.

Culture

Even though we get asked the same question on a regular basis, it's never easy to answer, is it? It's tough to define the fascination we have with the world of James Bond. It's not one, or even a few, single ingredients; It's a perfect cocktail. It's a heavy dose of testosterone and adrenaline, with a healthy pour of sensuality and the good life. But, I would offer that this cocktail is not complete without a few dashes of culture.

Culture makes many surprise appearances in the Bond films. It may come in the form of a portrait of the Duke of Wellington by Francisco Goya, or in the delicate stanza; *"For thee, the ships are drawn down to the waves. For thee, the markets throng with myriad slaves."* It may come as a priceless Imperial Easter Egg by Carl Fabergé, or Mozart's 40th Symphony in G minor played by a perfectly tuned Stradivarius. It could be a performance of Giacomo Puccini's 'Tosca,' or it could be an 1838 oil painting by the English artist Joseph Mallord William Turner, known as 'The Fighting Temeraire,' currently hanging in the National Gallery in London.

THE NATIONAL GALLERY

Located in Trafalgar Square in Central London, the National Gallery was founded in 1824, and it houses a collection of more than 2,300 paintings dating as far back as the mid-13th century, by such masters as Turner, Leonardo, Velázquez, Titian, Constable, Botticelli, Monet, Caravaggio, Vermeer, and Cézanne. Some of the gallery's most popular works include 'The Arnolfini Portrait' by Jan van Eyck, Holbein's 'The Ambassadors,' and Van Gogh's 'Sunflowers.'

Skyfall wasn't subtle in its underlying themes of old versus new, out-dated versus modern, or just, the indignity of no longer being needed. No work of art might convey this notion quite as perfectly as 'The Fighting Temeraire.'

"It always makes me feel a little melancholy." This painting depicts the HMS Temeraire, one of the last ships to have played a role in the Battle of Trafalgar, being towed up the Thames by a paddle-wheel steam tug towards its final berth in Rotherhithe to be broken up. *"A grand old war-*

ship being ignominiously hauled away for scrap." The sun sets above the estuary symbolizing the end of a bygone era; as age of steam power was quickly replacing traditional sailing ships.

This oil-on-canvas painting was created by the English Romantic artist Joseph Mallord William Turner, who was celebrated for his ability to capture atmosphere, movement, and the interplay of light and color. It was painted in 1838, and it hangs on the wall of the National Gallery, just as it did in *Skyfall,* where you can see this and countless other works. The cost to enter is free, and don't forget to hit the gift shop and pick up a print of the 'Temeraire' to bring home.

Huge thanks to Ajay Chowdhury for being such a wonderful host, for bringing my wife and I to the museum, and for insisting that we pick up a print. It's currently hanging in a quiet corner of our living room.

The National Gallery
Trafalgar Square
WC2N 5DN, UK

SOTHEBY'S

James Bond was always an admirer of great beauty; whether it was a superb, green and gold Imperial Coronation Easter Egg created by the House of Fabergé, or the tall, absolutely stunning, golden-blonde with a statuesque figure with Swedish features and high cheekbones, who came to bid on the egg, and possibly distract the other bidders.

Located in the heart of London's Mayfair district, Sotheby's was founded in London in 1744, and established its location on New Bond Street in 1917. The exterior of Sotheby's looks identical to how it appears on screen; the front facade with its symmetrical design, characterized by tall sash windows framed by clean, classical lines and muted colors is a perfect example of understated luxury.

The one thing missing is The Bond Street Kiosk; Bond discreetly purchases a magazine from a nearby newsstand as he watches the buyers leave in a black Mercedes with the fake Fabergé egg in tow, and signals the tail to follow them to Heathrow. Much to my absolute shock, this newsstand was a real, functional newsstand located near the famous auction house on New Bond Street, offering newspapers and magazines to passersby. Like most traditional newsstands, the kiosk no longer exists. Come to think of it, that newsstand is awfully intrusive, blocking the front facade of Sotheby's almost completely.

Most auctions at Sotheby's are open to the public. These auctions are meticulously organized events that combine centuries-old traditions with modern technology. There's no cost to attend most auctions, but you may need to register in advance as space can be limited. You don't have to bid to attend; many people go simply to experience the atmosphere, see incredible pieces of art or antiques, or just to observe the auction process. Attendees are under no obligation to bid.

Sotheby's auctions offer an extraordinary variety of objects and works of art from impressionist and modern art, contemporary art to old master paintings, nineteenth century European and Islamic art, amongst many others. Sotheby's galleries host a wide variety of rotating exhibitions, with displays changing frequently.

The experience of attending an auction can be thrilling, blending the excitement of competition with the elegance of fine art and historical treasures, and it's a fascinating way to witness the art and auction world in action, even if you're not a buyer.

Sotheby's also has a restaurant set in the heart of the Bond Street auction house, which is touted as vibrant and contemporary. The restaurant is open for light breakfasts and delicious all day dining food choices. The menu is seasonal and changes weekly.

While Sotheby's doesn't have a strict dress code, auctions are generally formal or business casual events, so be sure to dress appropriately.

Sotheby's
34-35 New Bond Street
W1A 2AA, UK

Classic Bond

"It was eight o'clock as Bond followed M through the tall doors, across the well of the staircase from the card room, that opened into the beautiful white and gold Regency dining-room of Blades."

– Chapter Five, 'Moonraker,' 1955

Historically, London is well-known for private members' clubs, reserved for wealthy, high-society men. Gentlemen's clubs began around the 17th century, particularly around the area of St. James and Pall Mall, which became known as "Clubland."

In the novel *'Moonraker,'* M is a member of the private club Blades, where he often goes for lunch, usually eating a meal of grilled Dover sole and *"the ripest spoonful he could gouge from the club Stilton."* James Bond was not a member, but went to Blades often as M's guest.

First appearing prominently in *'Moonraker,'* Blades was subsequently featured in *'You Only Live Twice'* and *'The Man with the Golden Gun,'* and is mentioned in *'On Her Majesty's Secret Service.'* It also appeared in the comic strip adaptations which ran in *The Daily Express* newspapers.

In reality, Blades is a fictional place. It's generally acknowledged that Ian Fleming based his club on one or more of London's real-life private clubs. Some suggest it's based on Pratt's, as the fictitious Blades is situated on "Park Street" (actually Park Place) right off St. James's Street, which is the approximate location of the real-life club Pratt's. Others suggest it's based on Boodle's, possibly due to a depiction of Blades in *The Daily Express* comic strip, looking identical to the front facade of Boodle's.

However, when it came time to portray Blades on the big screen, the film-makers looked to the Reform Club.

THE REFORM CLUB

"Are you a gambling man, Mr. Bond?" In *Die Another Day,* James Bond provokes the mysterious Gustav Graves into a fencing competition, which explodes into an epic sword fight, wreaking havoc on the Blades Club. The Reform Club doubled as Blades.

The Reform Club first opened its doors to members in 1836. True to its name, the Reform Club was founded on the ideals and political activity which, in part, had found expression in the Great Reform Act of 1832. Having succeeded in securing the passing of the Reform Bill, Radicals and Whigs needed a central location for their political activities.

Today, the Reform Club is politically neutral, but pledges to remain true to its founding principles. As with all of London's original gentlemen's clubs, the Reform Club had a male-only membership for decades, but was one of the first to change its rules to include the admission of women in 1981. Indeed, The Reform Club is the real life setting of this epic duel. While the more destructive scenes were filmed in the studio at Pinewood, much of the struggle was filmed in the upper gallery of the club. When Bond and Graves 'settle up downstairs,' we're once again inside the Reform Club, in the main hall, just behind the entrance of the club.

But, that wasn't the last time the Reform Club would appear in a James Bond film. In *Quantum of Solace,* The Reform Club doubles as the Foreign Office, where M is summoned to meet the Foreign Secretary. We see her in the atrium of the Club, and sharp-eyed viewers will recognise the staircase and the same distinctively patterned floor from *Die Another Day.*

The Club does not hold tours for the general public, but organised groups can be arranged. Those taking part in tours are invited to contribute £15 per person to the Reform Club Conservation Charitable Trust. Visitors are required to adhere to the Club's dress code.

Each September, the Club participates in an Open House Festival, the world's largest architecture festival, when hundreds of buildings in London open their doors to the public. The Reform Club occasionally offers access to the public to view its unique historic and architectural features, art collection, furnishings and artefacts.

Special thanks to Remmert van Braam and his incredible website *Bond Lifestyle (www.jamesbondlifestyle.com),* for some great location spotting and supporting screenshots identifying many of these locations.

The Reform Club
104 Pall Mall
SW1Y 5EW, UK

LES AMBASSADEURS

"It happens to be 3:00am. When do you sleep, 007?" When James Bond has a little downtime, he might use it to play chemin de fer opposite a stunning brunette in a striking red dress with a one-shoulder neckline and a silver pin, at the **Le Cercle** casino in the **Les Ambassadeurs Club**.

Filmed on a set built at Pinewood Studios, Ken Adam's design for the casino was based on the real Les Ambassadeurs. Also known as "Les A," Les Ambassadeurs Club is a private club and casino located in the Mayfair area of London.

Les Ambassadeurs Club has a history that dates back to 1836 when it first opened its doors to members. The club moved to Hanover Square in 1941, and then to Hamilton Place in 1950, with the Le Cercle casino being established at the club in 1961.

The main gaming floor of the Le Cercle has sixteen tables, where roulette, baccarat, blackjack and three card poker can be played. Roulette and more discreet games of cards can be played in the club's Marble Room. The club also has a garden area where players can smoke while placing their bets. The club's Red Room has a separate entrance at 6 Hamilton Place.

Les Ambassadeurs Club is an exclusive private members' club, and membership is required to access the club. Anyone interested in visiting can contact the club in advance to inquire about membership, guest policies, or special events that might allow non-members to visit. Keep in mind that a formal dress code and strict entry policies are typically enforced.

Ambassadeurs Group
5 Hamilton Place
W1J 7ED, UK

MI6

Whether you're deciding on an appropriate starting point for your tour, or looking to follow the path of the infamous boat chase in *The World Is Not Enough,* a perfect place to kick off your adventure might be the same place that James Bond initiates his missions; real-life home to the Secret Intelligence Service or SIS; more commonly known as MI6.

A film staple since *GoldenEye,* the **MI6** building is truly breathtaking and very easy to get to. As you walk up the steps emerging from the Vauxhall tube station, the massive MI6 building emerges right there in front of you, and it is every bit as ominous as it looks in the films. You can walk right up to and around the building, along an attractive walkway adorned with benches and a gazebo; all of which can actually be seen in the opening of *The World is Not Enough.* As I walked around the building, I looked up and could see a few well-dressed people sitting and talking on the mezzanine, and I began to wonder what they might be talking about; some international terrorist plot, or where to go for happy hour?

Use the London Underground and take the Victoria Line to the Vauxhall Station. Once you emerge from the station, you'll see the massive, elaborate structure of tan concrete and blue-green glass, shaped like a Mayan temple. The best views of the building are gleaned from across the bridge over the Thames, and down the steps to the Albert Embankment.

While it should be fairly obvious, it's probably not a wise move to try to enter this government building where police officers with automatic weapons will frequently patrol.

MI6
85 Albert Embankment, Vauxhall
SE1 7TP, UK

THE O2 (THE MILLENNIUM DOME)

The boat chase sequence from *The World Is Not Enough* is rich with real-life London locations, from MI6 to Big Ben and the Houses of Parliament, past Waterloo Pier and the Tower Bridge, and tearing through the docks at the Isle of Dogs. To follow the chase all the way to its grand finale, you need to head over to the Greenwich Peninsula and check out **The O2**, formerly known as **The Millennium Dome**.

In conjunction with the Millennium Bridge and the London Eye, the Millennium Dome was a major exhibition created to celebrate the new millennium. It was constructed as part of London's millennium celebrations to house the Millennium Experience, which was intended to be a year-long exhibition. It officially opened on December 31, 1999, with a ceremony attended by Queen Elizabeth II. This was an incredibly ambitious project, and as such it also faced criticism for high costs, perceived lack of purpose, and an underwhelming number of visitors.

After the Millennium Experience ended in December 2000, the Dome closed, and there was debate about what to do with the massive structure. Even though it was a significant investment, it remained largely unused for several years.

In 2005, the site was redeveloped into a world-class entertainment venue. The original dome structure remains, but the interior was transformed to house a 20,000-seat arena for concerts, sports, and events, an entertainment district with restaurants, bars, and cinemas, and a roof walk experience known as The Up at The O2. It's since become one of the world's busiest arenas, hosting major concerts, sporting events, and cultural festivals, and remains a symbol of London's adaptability, transforming from a controversial exhibition space into a globally recognized hub for entertainment and culture.

The Dome is located on the Greenwich Peninsula, reachable by taking the Jubilee Line to the North Greenwich Station. For an in-depth look at this, and all the locations from the infamous boat chase, check out the masterful book, *'On the Tracks of 007'* by Martijn Mulder and Dirk Kloosterboer.

London's Traditional Bond Locations

London is so rich with Bond locations, that even as you're taking in some of London's most traditional landmarks – it's almost impossible not to find yourself in the footsteps of 007. Many are one in the same.

BUCKINGHAM PALACE

In *Die Another Day,* Gustav Graves makes a flashy entrance by parachuting out of an airplane and landing safely in front of an impressed crowd of journalists and press, at the gates of **Buckingham Palace**.

Buckingham Palace is the official residence of the monarch of the United Kingdom, and has been the royal residence since 1837, when Queen Victoria ascended the throne. The palace is also the venue for many significant state functions and ceremonies, including official events, receptions, and state visits. Buckingham Palace is a symbol of the British monarchy and a key part of the UK's national heritage.

The Changing of the Guard takes place regularly, occurring most days of the week. The exact schedule can vary depending on the time of year, but in generally held at 11:00am every day from May to August, and on alternate days the rest of the year. This area can become quite crowded, especially during tourist seasons, so get close to the railings by 10:30 am.

Buckingham Palace
London
SW1A 1AA, UK

THE COLLEGE OF ARMS

While you are taking in some traditional London landmarks, like St. Paul's Cathedral, this is another great opportunity to spot other real life Bond locations, including **The College of Arms**, which was first mentioned in Ian Fleming's 1963 novel, *'On Her Majesty's Secret Service,'* and made its cinematic debut in the 1969 film adaptation of the same name.

Founded in 1484, the College of Arms, or Heralds' College, serves the same real-life function it did in the film, regulating heraldry and granting new armorial bearings for England, Wales, and Northern Ireland.

In front of The College of Arms, you can see the familiar courtyard that Bond strolls across in *On Her Majesty's Secret Service.* Most of the interiors were shot in the studio even though, according to Peter Brooker of the London Bond Map, "It does seem nuts they shot the interiors at Pinewood when they modeled it so closely on the Earls Marshal's Court, which is free for the public to view."

Pete also adds, the closest Bond location to the College of Arms is the Castle Baynard Tunnel, where Bond gets kidnapped in *Spectre,* and the closest pint is at The Black Friar, a timeless British pub dating back to 1873, and supposedly haunted. *"Buy me a pint!"*

The College of Arms
130 Queen Victoria St.
EC4V 4BT, UK

IAN FLEMING'S LONDON HOME

In October 1936, Ian Fleming decided that flat No. 22B on Ebury Street was the perfect place to set up his "bachelor quarters," away from his domineering mother. Fleming entertained many of his lady friends here, as well as the members of his club Le Cercle, until the threat of German bombs forced his evacuation to safer quarters in 1940. After the war, Fleming briefly occupied several flats in Marylebone, Mayfair, and Chelsea, but it was this Victoria Square house that Fleming settled on, and would be his last London residence.

This building was designed by architect J. P. Gandy-Deering and completed in 1830. Its Doric columns and pediment suggest a kind of temple or chapel, for which it was used in the 19th century. After years as a school, a nightclub, and even a furniture store, it was eventually converted into four flats in the 1930s.

In 1966, Ian's brother Peter petitioned the Greater London Council to commemorate this location with its prestigious "blue plaque." To merit this award, a proposed recipient must be judged to be eminent by his or her peers; or have made an important positive contribution to human welfare or happiness; or have a name that the well-informed passer-by will immediately recognize; or deserve national recognition. Judged by any of these criteria, Ian Fleming seemed a sure bet. However, his nomination was initially rejected.

On April 15, 1996, with members of the Ian Fleming Foundation, Peter Fleming's daughters (Ian Fleming's granddaughters) Lucy Williams and Kate Grimond, along with actor Desmond Llewelyn all in attendance, English Heritage erected the prestigious plaque at No. 22B. It reads simply: "*Ian Fleming, 1908-1964, Creator of James Bond lived here.*"

It's currently occupied as a photo studio, so maybe you could pay them a visit and request a photoshoot? According to 'James Bond's London' by Gary Giblin, take the metro to Victoria Station, turn left out of the Station, cross Buckingham Palace Road to Lower Belgrave Street and follow this to Ebury Street; turn left onto Ebury and look for the house ahead on the right. Special thanks to Gary's extensive work in researching this location.

Ian Fleming's Home
22B Ebury Street
SW1W 8LW, UK

JAMES BOND'S LONDON HOME

There's an interesting debate over exactly where literary James Bond actually called home. In *'Casino Royale,'* Bond's home is referred to as a 'Chelsea flat.' In *'Moonraker,'* Fleming writes that James Bond has a small ground floor flat in a converted Regency house off the King's Road and is adorned with plane trees. In *'From Russia with Love,'* he tells us the sitting room has a bay window. It's important to note that neither the square, nor the flat number, is mentioned in any of the Fleming novels.

One possible location might be No. 30 Wellington Square, a location attributed to John Pearson in the 'James Bond: Authorized Biography.' But most disagree. Based on an article by David Salter on Literary 007. com, this was simply because Pearson had a friend who lived there. Several other details fail to support Pearson's theory, including the absence of a bay window, and not a plane tree to be seen.

Glimpses into the cinematic Bond's home life are rare. In *Dr. No,* James Bond returns to a handsome, but modest, flat to find a familiar ravishing brunette practicing her golf putts. In *Live and Let Die,* Bond gets a visit from M and Moneypenny and serves up some espresso while a missing Italian agent hides in his wardrobe.

"My place, nine o'clock." We get a much different perspective in *Spectre,* where Bond awaits Moneypenny to deliver *"personal effects they recovered from Skyfall."* Not only do we get to visit Bond's home, which looks like he's only recently moved in, (most likely due to Bond's absence while "enjoying death" in *Skyfall*), but this time, we also get a view from the outside as well, allowing us to narrow down its location to Stanley Gardens, in the Notting Hill section of London.

One of London's most vibrant and eclectic neighborhoods, Notting Hill is renowned for its charming streets lined with townhouses, boutique shops, and cafes. Located in the Royal Borough of Kensington and Chelsea, it has a unique blend of bohemian flair and upscale sophistication.

James Bond's London Home *(Spectre)*
1 Stanley Gardens
W11 2ND, UK

WESTMINSTER BRIDGE
Some locations are just too perfect! In the heart of central London, you'll find the most iconic, must-see attractions like Big Ben, the Houses of Parliament, the London Eye, and Westminster Abbey. As an added bonus, this area is also home to three incredible Bond locations; and all three are just a short walk from one another. These landmarks and locations are all walking distance from Westminster Bridge.

George Lazenby's Lamppost Photoshoot
Hard core fans of James Bond will be familiar with the promotional stills of George Lazenby hanging from a lamppost with Big Ben in the background in anticipation of *On Her Majesty's Secret Service.*

To check out the site of George Lazenby's famous shoot (and to get a few shots of yourself in the same iconic pose), head to the Westminster section of London. Get off the underground at the Westminster Station, the closest station to Big Ben and Parliament, and walk across the Westminster Bridge to the east side of the Thames River. At the end of the bridge, you'll walk down a stairway on the right side (facing south), leading down to the Albert Embankment River Walk, and right at the bottom you will find the famous lamp-post at the base of the steps. Just climb up, and you'll be standing in James Bond's footsteps. The lamppost was damaged and replaced recently, so it may look a little different then you remember.

Gary Giblin suggests that the best time to take photos on a sunny day is in the morning; the view is almost directly due west and the sun will be at the photographer's back.

Abandoned Station for Abandoned Agents

If you cross the street to the north-west corner, and descend the staircase walking in the direction of the London Eye, just down those steps and on your right, you will find yourself at another familiar Bond location.

Not only does this spot provide one of the most familiar and picturesque views of Big Ben, the Westminster Bridge and Parliament, but you may find another familiar view.

In *Die Another Day,* James Bond has just crossed Westminster Bridge, descends the staircase, and uses his key to unlock a familiar wooden door to rendezvous with M. *"Abandoned station for abandoned agents."* This door doesn't open to an underground MI6 rendezvous, so please don't try (in real life, this door houses a small office), but be sure to grab a few selfies near this iconic Bond spot.

Westminster Tube Station

Following a breathtaking scene in *Skyfall* where James Bond chases Raul Silva throughout the Underground Metro system, Bond emerges at the Westminster Station, to run north on Parliament Street towards the Whitehall section of London.

Walk back across the bridge heading west. As soon as you're across, continue one more block, passing Big Ben on your left. The first major intersection will be Parliament Street. Turn right onto Parliament Street, and you'll see the same Westminster Station where Bond appears.

Westminster Tube Station
SW1A 2JR

TEN TRINITY SQUARE

By the way, if you were planning to reenact Bond's sprint all the way to the hearing, you might be doing a lot more running than you planned. By way of a little movie magic, the actual location where Bond enters the hearing was in Ten Trinity Square, about 2.5 miles away. This is also where M arrives to meet Gareth Mallory to discuss *"retirement planning."*

Now a Four Seasons luxury hotel, **Ten Trinity Square** sits adjacent to Trinity Square Gardens, and occupies the former headquarters of the Port of London Authority. This is one of London's iconic historical landmarks; designed by famed architect Sir Edwin Cooper, and officially opened by Prime Minister David Lloyd George in 1922. The hotel offers a collection of elegant spaces that include a dining room, billiards room, bar lounge, the first Château Latour Discovery Room outside of France, taking its name from the French wine estate, and boasts the only indoor cigar lounge in the city.

To reenact Bond's arrival at Ten Trinity Square, you'd have to run south on Cooper's Row, and into Trinity Square. You'll see the familiar wrought-iron fence topped with the gold spikes, signaling for you to follow them to the right, where Ten Trinity Square will appear in front of you, easily recognizable by its magnificent towering columns.

According to Peter Brooker, you can feel free to enter the lobby area and visit the Rotunda Bar and Lounge where you can drink and eat, even if you're not a guest of the hotel.

Ten Trinity Square
10 Trinity Square
EC3N 4AJ, UK

London's 'Exotic' Bond Locations

As much as James Bond fans love the thrill of jet-setting and seeing exotic parts of the world on the big screen, film-budgets and just plain practicality often force the filmmakers to improvise; and sometimes the best stand-ins to portray far off locations are found right here in London.

SOMERSET HOUSE

In *GoldenEye,* James Bond travels to St. Petersburg, Russia, where he meets his contact, Jack Wade of the American CIA. *"Muffy?"* They don't get very far before Wade's car breaks down in the middle of a Russian courtyard, and Bond has to help Wade repair his 'ugly little bitch.' Somerset House was used to portray the Russian courtyard.

Somerset House also appeared in *Tomorrow Never Dies,* as Bond's Aston Martin DB5 travels down the Strand, turning left into the courtyard of Somerset House, to arrive at his briefing.

Somerset House is a London landmark, built in the late 18th century by architect Sir William Chambers, replacing a Tudor palace that previously stood on the site. For much of its early history, Somerset House served as a government building, housing offices like the Navy Board and later the Inland Revenue. Its symmetrical design, sweeping courtyards, and classical details make it a masterpiece of Neoclassical architecture.

Today, Somerset House is a major center for the arts and culture, hosting exhibitions, performances, and events all-year-round. It features contemporary art and design exhibitions, including works by emerging and established artists. In the summer, the courtyard transforms into an outdoor cinema, and during the winter the courtyard becomes an ice-skating rink. It's home to a thriving creative community, including the Courtauld Gallery and Institute, which houses an impressive art collection.

Somerset House
Strand
WC2R 1LA, UK

'OUR LADY OF SMOLENSK'

In *GoldenEye,* having escaped the attack on Severnaya, Natalya tracks down Boris online, who responds with: *"You aren't safe. Trust no-one. Meet me at the Church of Our Lady of Smolensk in one hour."*

The Church of Our Lady of Smolensk was filmed in two locations; both in London. The exterior shot of Natalya running into the church was filmed at one of the chapels in the Brompton Cemetery. Listed as one of the Royals Parks, the **Brompton Cemetery** has over 200,000 people lie in peace here, their lives commemorated with scores of spectacular memorials, from grieving angels and ivy-clad crosses to ornate mausoleums and imposing columns.

The interior of Our Lady of Smolensk was filmed inside the **Saint Sofia's Greek Cathedral** (or the Greek Orthodox Cathedral of the Divine Wisdom) in the Bayswater section of London. Established as the first Greek Orthodox Church in London, its origins date back to the late 17th century, and was founded as a result of the growing expansion and the establishment of the Greek community in London.

This cathedral's interior may be tricky to access, as its doors are only open during certain times. The Cathedral is open for private prayer on Tuesdays, Wednesdays and Fridays between 10:00am and 2:00pm. Thanks again to Ajay Chowdhury for bringing us to this gorgeous location.

Brompton Cemetery
Fulham Road
SW10 9UG, UK

St. Sofia's Greek Orthodox Cathedral
Moscow Road
W2 4LQ, UK

BROADGATE TOWER

So, London can portray Eastern Europe, but what about the Far East? No problem. In *Skyfall,* James Bond is in pursuit of Patrice, the assassin who got hold of a highly-classified list of undercover MI6 operatives. The trail leads Bond to Shanghai, China, where he tails Patrice from the Shanghai Pudong Airport through downtown Shanghai, to a particularly modern-looking skyscraper; notable for its sharp, angled facades, and vibrant neon lights tracing its contours and illuminating the sleek glass and steel surfaces, creating a striking fusion of cutting-edge design and futuristic aesthetics. This skyscraper is not in Shanghai, but in London.

This is **Broadgate Tower**, located in the financial district in the heart of London. It is directly above the train station 'Liverpool Street' at Broadgate Plaza. Filming took place at the entry to the building, but not on the upper floors. Look out for the characteristic criss-cross style steel columns and the lobby!

According to huntingbond.com: The [surrounding] area is home to one of London's most vital creative scenes. You'll find Banksy graffiti at the walls, hip fashion outlets and rough vendors who sell their Fish & Chips at the street market. Always a good choice is the Ten Bells, one of the oldest pubs in London. Legend has it that Jack the Ripper cruised this pub back in the old days to hunt down his victims. It still looks like it is stuck in the Victorian age, but now with great craft beer from the 21st century.

Broadgate Tower
20 Primrose Street
EC2A 2ES, UK

Navigating the Tourist Traps

I'm not going to lament the passing of the once-explosive surge of celebrity chain restaurants, but at one time, the **Planet Hollywood** in Piccadilly Circus had offered a look at some terrific Bond memorabilia, including a full-scale replica of Little Nellie from *You Only Live Twice* which hung high above the dining room.

First opened on May 17, 1993, near Piccadilly Circus, and relocating to Haymarket in 2009, Planet Hollywood remained a popular spot for tourists and movie enthusiasts. But as of 2024, the brand appears to have been facing a decline globally, and it remains unclear whether this once-popular attraction will have survived the ravages of the pandemic.

Now that the kitschy appeal of Planet Hollywood is no longer an option, you might do well to avoid the standard tourist traps altogether and stick to a 007-inspired experience. But if that itch for kitsch just needs to be scratched, there's the ever-popular Madame Tussauds Wax Museum.

MADAME TUSSAUDS WAX MUSEUM

In 2021, Madame Tussauds announced that all six of the actors who played the legendary British spy on film would see their figures return to **Madame Tussauds Wax Museum** and take up permanent residence.

If you're in the mood for a little cheesy fun, the price of admission ranges from the £25 standard ticket to the £40 Fast Track, as well as additional combo price options which include access to the Big Bus Tours, and/or attractions like the London Eye, the Aquarium, and others.

This overpriced, overcrowded, and overhyped theme park attraction can definitely be a lot of fun, but let's get back to some better ways to spend your time in 007's London.

Madame Tussauds Wax Museum
Marylebone Road
NW1 5LR, UK

Shopping in London

No trip to London is complete without doing a little shopping. Even if shopping isn't your thing, London offers a shopping experience that's more about exploration and culture than just buying things. Shopping in London isn't just about the act of buying; it's a window into the city's culture. From the high-end luxury of Mayfair to the quirky, bohemian vibes of Shoreditch, every area has a story to tell.

London has plenty of iconic shopping districts, like Oxford Street, Regent Street, and Knightsbridge; and particularly for the James Bond fan, there are a few areas and shops that are not to be missed.

HARRODS

"The brand on the list was questionable, sir. So I took the liberty of choosing something else." If M should call upon you to pick up a parcel, you'd better stop by Harrods department store. More than just a shopping destination, and more than just a magnificent building, **Harrods** began trading here in 1849 as a small family run grocery shop, and has since become a London institution. Harrod's attracts millions of visitors each year, making it more than a store, but a tourist destination. People visit not only to shop, but also to experience its grandeur and iconic status.

It features grand architectural features, such as their Egyptian escalator, epitomizing Harrods' blend of elegance and extravagance. Harrods is also famous for its over-the-top seasonal displays, particularly at Christmas, drawing visitors from around the globe.

While you are at Harrods you definitely want to check out the magnificent food halls. Known for their exquisite displays and a wide range of delicacies, they are a must-see for food lovers. You have truly never seen anything quite like it. With the selections they have, you can understand how Bond was able to put together a parcel that was so expensive, it made M frown.

SAVILE ROW

In *Dr. No,* Felix Leiter holds Bond's PPK, and asks, *"Where were you fitted for this?"* James Bond fixes the lapels of his jacket and replies, *"My tailor, Savile Row."* You can't visit London without visiting the classic clothing shops. Located in the Mayfair section of London, **Savile Row** is well known for centuries of men's custom tailoring, featuring stores that include **Hardy Amies**, **Henry Poole & Co**, and **Norton & Sons**. Also, be sure to visit **Anthony Sinclair**, the real-life tailor who fitted Sean Connery for his iconic role as James Bond in *Dr. No*. While Anthony Sinclair had enjoyed an address only two blocks from Savile Row for decades, Sinclair now exists under the umbrella of **Mason and Sons**, and enjoys a posh address at 34 Montagu Square, easily identifiable by a blue plaque dedicated to the late John Lennon.

JERMYN STREET

Just a few blocks from Savile Row is another street which should attract many James Bond fans. **Jermyn Street** is located in the Westminster area of London, and offers several shops that have connections to James Bond. If you are interested in the shoes that Bond wore, be sure to stop at the **John Lobb** and **Church's store**. In the novels, Ian Fleming's James Bond always wore Floris No. 89, so be sure to visit **Floris of London**.

One must-visit shop in London is **Turnbull & Asser**, known world-wide for their custom men's clothing since 1885. T&A provided many of the shirts and ties worn by Pierce Brosnan and Daniel Craig. On my last visit, they were offering the brown and blue-diamond pattern that Brosnan wore in the Hamburg scenes in *Tomorrow Never Dies,* the Mondrian-patterned tie worn in *The World Is Not Enough* during the Thames River boat chase, as well as the blue polka-dot tie James Bond wore as Gustav Graves parachuted down to Buckingham Palace in *Die Another Day.*

In 2002, Turnbull & Asser expanded this collection. From Matt Spaiser over at bondsuits.com: 'Turnbull & Asser Launches an Extended and Revised James Bond Collection: For a number of years now they have sold the *Casino Royale* waffle-weave dress shirt, three ties from Pierce Brosnan's series, and a *Dr. No* cocktail cuff shirt as part of their Bond line. They also have consistently sold the grenadine and knit ties as well as black bow ties they originally provided for Bond. Now Turnbull & Asser have added a number of ties, shirts and a pocket square to their James Bond Collection.'

Turnbull & Asser has also added a new blue *Dr. No* shirt with a cocktail cuff, more Pierce Brosnan ties, and the *Casino Royale* bow tie to their collection, among others.

Also, just a few blocks from Jermyn Street, be sure to stop at **Lock & Co.** and check out their 007 Hat Collection, which offers several hats inspired by the hats worn in the films, for both men and women, including the original Lock & Co. felt trilby hat first seen in the opening gun-barrel from *Dr. No,* updated for the 21st century, the stealthy black Panama hat with a new striped ribbon worn by James Bond in *Goldfinger,* as well as an exact replica of the Lock & Co. trilby originally created for Eva Green's Vesper Lynd in *Casino Royale* that she wears as she sets out on her journey to Montenegro's Hotel Splendide.

Rest & Recreation

After so much sightseeing and shopping, it might be time for a little recuperation. Maybe a few laps in the pool at a gorgeous spa with wonderful views of the surrounding city might be just a thing. When James Bond was visiting Shanghai in *Skyfall,* he decided to take a few laps in the beautiful rooftop pool overlooking the city, giving us another London location that doubled for the Far East; the Virgin Active Canary Riverside Spa.

A luxury five-star independent hotel, the Canary Riverside Plaza is set within the historic wharves and quays of East London, and is the only five-star independent hotel in Canary Wharf. **The Virgin Active Spa** is based inside the Canary Riverside Plaza Hotel, facing the Thames. The Health Club, located adjacent to the hotel and open to all guests free of charge, offers an unparalleled wellness experience. This luxurious facility includes three floors dedicated to fitness and relaxation, and guests can enjoy expansive fitness areas outfitted with cutting-edge technology, hydrotherapy pools, saunas, and steam rooms, and of course, the 20-metre infinity-edge lap pool.

While this pool is the same one Daniel Craig used to relax and rebuild his muscles in *Skyfall,* the large window view had been digitally altered to create the views of the Shanghai skyline. Keep in mind, the Virgin Active Spa is for hotel guests and members only, so plan accordingly.

Virgin Active Canary Riverside Spa
46 Westferry Circus
E14 8RS, UK

Cocktails

"I never have more than one drink before dinner. But I do like that one to be large and very strong and very cold and very well-made."

– Ian Fleming, 'Casino Royale,' 1953

Once you've had some rest and recovery, it's time for cocktails before dinner, and there's one place for drinks in London that all James Bond fans seem to agree on.

DUKES

Nestled in the heart of London's upscale St. James's district, Dukes London is not just a hotel – it's a sanctuary for cocktail connoisseurs. Renowned for its intimate bar and impeccable service, **Dukes Bar** has become a pilgrimage site, not only for James Bond fans, but for anyone who appreciates expertly crafted drinks in an atmosphere of timeless elegance. The bar's dim lighting, leather seating, and old-world charm provide the perfect setting for sipping world-class cocktails and soaking in a bit of London's aristocratic spirit.

At the center of Dukes Bar's acclaim is its legendary martini, and head bartender Alessandro Palazzi has elevated this cocktail to an art form, serving it tableside with precision and flair. Using frozen glasses, premium spirits, and a whisper of vermouth, the martinis at Dukes are known for their strength and smoothness. If martinis aren't your drink of choice, the bar offers a curated selection of classic cocktails, including the Vesper, each prepared with the same dedication to quality and tradition.

Dukes Bar isn't just about the drinks, it's an experience. An intimate setting, where conversations flow as smoothly as the cocktails, and the attentive staff ensures every guest feels like royalty. Whether you're a cocktail aficionado or simply seeking a quintessential London experience, Dukes London offers a masterclass in elegance, sophistication, and mixology that's hard to match anywhere else in the world.

Side note; I'd love to claim that I can write about Dukes Bar from personal experience, but unfortunately my last visit fell on a warm summer afternoon, and I learned that Dukes' dress code does not allow for shorts inside the establishment. So I missed out on martinis, but the tradeoff was a wonderful photo taken outside, alongside Calvin Dyson (also in shorts), Murray Gillespie ('James Bond Canada'), and Mark O'Connell (author of *'Catching Bullets: Memoirs of a Bond Fan'*). You can tell it was a spectacular afternoon!

Dukes
35 St. James's Place
SW1A 1NY, UK

Dining Out

"I take a ridiculous pleasure in what I eat and drink."

– Ian Fleming, 'Casino Royale,' 1953

After a day packed with the wonders of London, from iconic landmarks to a rejuvenating spa session, and a perfectly crafted martini at Duke's, it's time to indulge in the city's culinary scene. London's dining options are as diverse and vibrant as the city itself, offering everything from historic institutions to modern gastronomic marvels. Whether it's traditional British fare or a contemporary twist, a James Bond themed meal will be the perfect finale to an extraordinary day.

RULES

Founded in 1798, **Rules Restaurant** is the oldest restaurant in London, steeped in history and tradition; this iconic establishment has been serving classic British cuisine for over two centuries. From its wood-paneled interiors to its eclectic collection of artwork and memorabilia adorning the walls, Rules exudes an atmosphere of timeless elegance and charm. Its rich history includes famous patrons such as Charles Dickens, Laurence Olivier, and even members of the Royal Family, making it a destination for those seeking both heritage and fine dining.

Rules is renowned for its dedication to traditional British cuisine, with a menu that highlights seasonal game, oysters, pies, and puddings. Sourcing ingredients from its own estate in the High Pennines, the restaurant prides itself on authenticity and quality. Signature dishes include the steak and kidney pie, roast grouse, and sticky toffee pudding, all expertly prepared to honor Britain's culinary heritage. The bar serves an extensive selection of classic cocktails, fine wines, and traditional ales, offering the perfect complement to the hearty dishes.

Dining at Rules is an experience steeped in history and tradition. The cozy, intimate atmosphere, complete with attentive service and period decor, transports guests to a bygone era. Whether you're visiting for a special occasion, a pre-theatre dinner, or simply to savor the best of British cuisine, Rules promises an unforgettable journey into the heart of London's culinary and cultural legacy. Its enduring charm and commitment to excellence make it a must-visit for locals and tourists alike. It's no wonder this was Gareth Mallory's favorite restaurant.

Rules Restaurant
35 Maiden Lane
WC2E 7LB, UK

SCOTT'S

If fine seafood is more to your taste, you may want to dine at literary Bond's favorite London restaurant, Scott's. Nestled in the heart of Mayfair, **Scott's Restaurant** is a London institution, renowned for its refined ambiance and exceptional seafood. Originally founded as an oyster warehouse in the 1850s, Scott's has evolved into one of London's most elegant dining destinations, blending classic charm with contemporary sophistication. Its striking Art Deco interiors, complete with dark wood paneling, mirrored walls, and plush banquettes, create an atmosphere that is both luxurious and inviting, making it a favorite among locals, tourists, and celebrities alike.

As *The New York Times* put it, "Once you walk past the liveried doorman and set foot in Scott's, the venerable seafood restaurant where even clarified butter is raised to an art, the world ceases to exist." Scott's truly takes fine dining to the next level, and is celebrated for its impeccable seafood, with its menu offering everything from fresh oysters and lobster to expertly prepared Dover sole and Scottish salmon. The restaurant also boasts a striking crustacean bar, where diners can watch the chefs artfully assemble seafood platters.

After a martini, I ordered a dozen mixed oysters with wild boar sausages, and then for my entree, I went with the filet of cod with padron peppers and chorizo, accompanied by a California Chardonnay. Of course, if you want to really recreate a Bond moment, you could try the dressed crab with a Black Velvet, as Bond suggests to chief of staff, Bill Tanner, in chapter three of *'Diamonds are Forever.'*

While seafood is its specialty, Scott's also caters to diverse tastes, offering meat and vegetarian options of the highest quality. Pairing perfectly with its menu, the extensive wine list features curated selections from around the world, ensuring every meal is a culinary experience to remember.

Beyond its exquisite food and drink, Scott's is renowned for its impeccable service and attention to detail, which make every visit feel special. Whether you're visiting for a leisurely lunch, a romantic dinner, or a celebratory occasion, Scott's combines heritage, elegance, and exceptional dining into a single unforgettable experience.

Scott's
20 Mount Street
W1K 2HE, UK

THE RITZ RESTAURANT

In *'Diamonds Are Forever,'* James Bond paid a visit to the iconic Ritz Hotel in London – a venue synonymous with elegance and old-world charm. The hotel also earned mentions in *'Moonraker'* and *'The Man with the Golden Gun,'* further cementing its place in Bond's glamorous world.

The restaurant at The Ritz London, aptly named **The Ritz Restaurant**, is a masterpiece of luxury dining, celebrated for its opulent setting and exceptional cuisine. Located on the ground floor of the iconic Piccadilly hotel, the restaurant boasts an awe-inspiring Louis XVI-style dining room adorned with ornate chandeliers, towering mirrors, and gilded detailing, all overlooking the lush greenery of Green Park.

The menu, crafted by Chef John Williams, is a testament to classic French culinary techniques infused with British seasonal ingredients, offering dishes that are as visually stunning as they are delicious. Whether you're savoring their afternoon tea or indulging in the Michelin-starred tasting menu, dining at The Ritz is an experience of timeless elegance and impeccable service; truly one of London's most iconic institutions.

THE DORCHESTER

In 1792, the Earl of Dorchester bought a house on Park Lane overlooking Hyde Park, in the Mayfair section of London. His house became known as 'Dorchester House.' In 1853, the home was rebuilt to resemble a grand Italian palazzo. By 1910, Dorchester House had served as the American Embassy, and later a hospital during World War I. The house was demolished in 1929, but the newly rebuilt and redesigned Dorchester Hotel opened its doors on April 20, 1931, and has served as a London institution ever since, serving as the epicenter of high society.

Defined by grandeur and wonder, strength and elegance, **The Dorchester Hotel** seamlessly blends luxury, history, and a touch of espionage and intrigue – in 1944, during World War II, Dwight D. Eisenhower stayed here while planning the Normandy Invasion.

Known for its majestic interiors, impeccable service, and a storied roster of guests that includes royalty, world leaders, and icons of cinema, the

Dorchester resonates with sophistication and exclusivity, and has been a symbol of opulence since it first opened.

It's tough to separate fact from fiction, and legends about where Ian Fleming actually spent his time may vary, but it's well-documented that Fleming was a frequent visitor to The Dorchester Hotel. A popular gathering spot for influential figures during Fleming's time, it's said that the hotel's ambiance may have influenced some of the luxurious settings described in his novels. Fleming's association with the hotel is part of its rich cultural history.

According to Ajay Chowdhury, Ian Fleming had his very first meeting with Harry Saltman at The Dorchester Hotel. Both Albert R. "Cubby" Broccoli and Harry Saltzman were known to have used The Dorchester Hotel as a venue for business meetings and entertainment. The hotel's luxurious setting made it the perfect place for discussions and negotiations related to the James Bond films. It was the perfect hub for creative collaborations and high-profile deals.

Additionally, two James Bond actors were introduced here, as the press conferences announcing George Lazenby (on October 7, 1968) and Roger Moore (on August 1, 1972) were both held in the Dorchester.

Dining at The Dorchester is an art form – an exquisite, yet diverse experience, offering a wide range of world-class culinary options within its luxurious surroundings. The Grill by Tom Booton offers visitors modern British cuisine with a creative flair, served in a vibrant yet elegant setting. For a taste of authentic French gastronomy, Alain Ducasse at The Dorchester, is a three-Michelin-starred restaurant, which offers an unforgettable fine-dining experience with exceptional precision and artistry. China Tang at The Dorchester brings the flavors of 1930s Shanghai with its exceptional Cantonese cuisine served in a richly designed interior. Meanwhile, those seeking traditional afternoon tea can visit The Promenade, a stunning space adorned with opulent decor. Each venue within The Dorchester delivers impeccable service and culinary craftsmanship, ensuring an unforgettable dining experience for every guest.

In December 2022, the Dorchester launched a new bar concept honoring the hotel's long-standing connection to James Bond, to be called the Vesper Bar.

The newly unveiled **Vesper Bar** pays homage to the timeless sophistication of James Bond, taking its name from James Bond's first love, the iconic Martini bearing her name, first introduced in '*Casino Royale.*' Designed with sleek Art Deco-inspired interiors, the bar exudes glamour, featuring plush seating, rich gold and green accents, and an intimate ambiance perfect for indulging in expertly crafted cocktails.

Headed by renowned bar director Lucia Montanelli, Vesper Bar showcases an innovative menu of signature drinks alongside refined classics, celebrating both tradition and creativity. Whether savoring the famous martini or a bespoke creation, guests are transported to a world of elegance and intrigue that perfectly aligns with the legacy of Bond himself.

Montanelli has put her personal spin on the Vesper – Elit Vodka, Old Tom gin, redistilled Forbidden Fruit liqueur, and Del Duque 30 Year Sherry – served in a slender-stemmed glass and under a mist of 'Vesper Scent' standing in for a twist.

Whether you're looking for a world-class culinary experience, a luxurious hotel stay, an indulgent Vesper martini, posh afternoon tea, or just to soak in its iconic ambiance, the Dorchester Hotel offers a taste of the world that inspired one of literature and cinema's most enduring heroes. Its time-less elegance, and significance in London's social and cultural history, make it a worthy pilgrimage for any Bond aficionado.

Afternoon Tea

Although Fleming's James Bond was known to scorn tea, calling it a *"flat, soft, time-wasting opium of the masses,"* afternoon tea is still a London institution to this day, and tea at the Ritz is an institution in itself. **The Ritz London** is renowned for its world-famous afternoon tea, which is considered one of the most iconic and luxurious experiences in the city. Served in the stunning Palm Court, the setting is as elegant as the experience, with gilded interiors, chandeliers, and soft live piano music creating an atmosphere of timeless sophistication.

The traditional menu includes a selection of finely cut sandwiches, freshly baked scones with clotted cream and strawberry preserve, and a variety of exquisitely crafted pastries and cakes. Guests can choose from an extensive tea menu featuring over 18 varieties or enhance their experience with a glass of Champagne. Afternoon tea at The Ritz is an immensely popular event and requires advance booking, often weeks or months ahead, to secure a table. It's a quintessentially British indulgence, perfect for special occasions or simply to savor the elegance of this iconic hotel.

Other hotels for taking afternoon tea include the Savoy London, the Lanes-borough, the Waldorf Hilton, Browns Hotel, Claridges, and of course, the Dorchester, among others. Each of these establishments provides a unique and elegant setting for this quintessentially British tradition.

In addition to these Bond-like places to eat, London has over 15,000 restaurants, including 74 with Michelin Star status, and 3,500 pubs, serving a diverse population of nearly 9 million residents, so you will never go hungry at any price range. The number of restaurants fluctuates over the years, with a notable increase in new openings in recent times, indicating a resilient and dynamic food industry.

Seven tips to prepare you for London

HAVE ENOUGH CASH
Don't get caught short. While it's well worth the cost, London can be one of the most expensive cities in the world. A drink in a London pub can be nearly double what you might normally spend. So as Paul Kyriazi might say, make a budget for your trip, and then double it, in case of any unforeseen expenses.

ALWAYS CARRY MAPS
Thanks to GPS and apps like Waze or Google Maps, there's little need these days to carry around a physical map (unless it's the 'London Bond Map' of course). But being able to quickly see both a map of the city, as well as an Underground map, will be essential, so keep these handy. If you want, study them before leaving home to get a feel for the area to ease the learning curve a little bit.

DRESS APPROPRIATELY
They say, if you don't like the weather in England, wait ten minutes. There is no bad weather in London, only inappropriate clothing. So prepare for London's notorious wet, dreary weather, especially from September all the way through to April, but this can change to warm sunny weather in a matter of minutes. Be sure and check ahead and dress for the weather.

BE PREPARED FOR THE CROWDS
London gets millions of visitors year round, and not just in the summer months. The area of South Bank where the London Eye is located, and across the Westminster Bridge headed towards Big Ben, can be so con-

gested with pedestrian traffic that it's difficult to take a full step. Keep this in mind if you or a traveling companion gets nervous in large crowds. Expect tourists to be out in full force.

DON'T DRIVE

Even though I do have some experience driving on the left side of the road, I still wouldn't even think about renting a car within the city. The London streets are always congested, drivers are aggressive, and parking is virtually nonexistent. If you're an American, or anyone used to driving on the right-hand side of the road, this is not the place for a beginner to learn to drive on the 'other' side of the road. Taxis and the Underground are so convenient that it's silly to rent a car.

USE THE UNDERGROUND

"He's keen to get home." The London Underground (often called "The Tube") is easy to navigate and the trains run very regularly, so try to be sure that your hotel is only a short walk from the nearest Underground station. Purchase all day Underground passes which allow speedy entrance and exits to the underground. Buying individual tickets will slow you down and cost you more over the long run.

WEAR COMFORTABLE SHOES

Even with the help of the Metro system, you can expect to do a great deal of walking in London, so a pair of comfortable walking shoes will be your best friend, and be ready to get your steps in.

Conclusion

Returning from my trip to London, I watched a fairly obscure film called *84 Charing Cross Road.* One of the quotes in that movie stuck in my mind. "Tourists go to London with preconceived notions, so they always find exactly what they are looking for." I went to London looking for a place that blends centuries of culture with modern cosmopolitan living, drawing from a diverse range of peoples and cultures, and I seemed to find it all. So hop on a red bus or a black cab, or just hop on the tube, and I'll meet you at Dukes for a martini. Mind the Gap.

Special thanks to Peter Brooker for the helpful hand in double-checking my facts and providing some much needed guidance and suggestions.

Further Reading

Believe it or not, as many places as I've touched on, this is still just scratching the surface of all the infamous Bond locations that are scattered around London. As always, I stand on the shoulders of giants – the many people who've written so extensively on the many Bond connections throughout London. So please be sure you check out these other wonderful sources before any trip to the UK.

'On the Tracks of 007'

You know it, you love it. The quintessential work on James Bond locations, and Martijn's location spotting in London and all of England, going all the way back to *Dr. No*, it is unmatched. If it's not there already, get this one on your bookshelf.

www.onthetracksof007.com

'London Bond Map'

Peter Brooker has absolutely outdone himself, creating the definitive map of James Bond locations. The physical map is so attractive in its graphic design that I'm tempted to purchase a second one just to frame and hang in my office. I referred to it many times in the updating of this chapter; both the physical map and his companion website. I highly recommend picking one up, and check out his YouTube channel!

www.londonbondmap.co.uk/

'Hunting Bond'

This is a new one on my radar. Marc and Julia, the couple who research and curate the website huntingbond.com, have done an amazing job location-spotting in a few hundred locations, from at least 22 individual countries. It came up often in my research and was a delight to peruse through. Their website is well-organized and gorgeous to look at! Check it out!

www.huntingbond.com

'James Bond's London'

While it's become something of a collector's item lately, 'James Bond's London' by Gary Giblin is perfect for any Bond fan visiting London. It explores all the spots in London related to James Bond, and it's extremely thorough. Whether it's real life Ian Fleming hangouts, filming locations, locations mentioned in the novels, or even real life espionage and defense locations, this book has it all.

EXTREME 007

Bungee Jumping

In the trade Bond knew too well, death was a reliable tool, but an ugly one; cold-blooded murder was a filthy business. But this mission didn't call for the sudden bark of a gun or the sharp twist of a knife. Bond's orders were clear: no alarms, no bodies, no attention. He was to infiltrate the chemical weapons facility in a wretched, frozen outpost in the far north of the Soviet empire. This mission was about subversion, and there would be no second chance if he stumbled. Bond adjusted his breathing, felt the old instinct settle into him, and moved forward into the darkness.

Bond observed his true objective: the colossal wall of concrete stretching across the narrow mouth of the valley. Sheer, smooth, and cold, the dam presented an unnerving vertical face to the valley below. Towering at over 220 meters high and nearly 380 meters across at its crest, it was one of the tallest dams ever constructed; its stark, curving façade seemed almost to defy nature itself.

The guard house was a squat relic of poured concrete and rusted steel, its windows darkened by years of cigarette smoke and suspicion, and it was currently manned by a handful of weary Russian soldiers, lulled into complacency by routine and vodka. Yet even here, where apathy had long since replaced discipline, death could awaken at the smallest noise.

In the distance, Bond watched a Pilatus PC-6 single-prop reconnaissance airplane making periodic passes across the valley and over the cracked bunker. Bond waited patiently.

Beyond the wire fence, a pair of Rottweilers barked at a phantom beyond the perimeter, straining at their chains. Something was out there. Muttering a curse, one of the guards rose, slinging on his overcoat as he stepped out to calm the animals, leaving his comrade alone to argue with the static of the tiny television monitor; their only source of distraction.

Just then, the patrol plane roared overhead, rattling the window glass. Bond moved.

In one motion, Bond slipped through an open door into the hallway to the gate control panel set flush into the wall – he pressed the release, and vanished before the soldier could turn his head. Outside, iron groaned against iron as the heavy locks disengaged and the heavy gate at the top of the dam began to creak open, dragged across concrete.

Bond raced through the breach, sprinting into the morning light. He felt the exposed vulnerability of open ground; his breath steady, his mind calculating. Every second counted. At the center of the dam, he dropped the heavy bungee cord. With no room for error, Bond worked swiftly and without wasted movement. He clipped the first carabiner to the waist-high steel rail, tugged it once to test the anchor point, and snapped the second to the reinforced loops on his boots. He had done the calculations. He knew the odds. Industrial elastic. Military grade. Enough to save him – as long as everything held.

Bond stepped onto the lip of the dam. The height loomed before him, a sheer wall of stone and silence. The wind rose from the ravine and pulled at him. For a brief moment he allowed himself a single thought; not of death, but of weightlessness, of the instant where control surrendered to gravity and skill alone decided the rest. For a heartbeat, time itself seemed to hold its breath. Bond centered his weight, feeling the tug of the cord at his ankles and the harness on his legs. He leaned forward, and for an instant, he hung there, suspended between decision and death.

Then, he dove forward into the emptiness. His body slicing through the void; the wind howling past his ears in a deafening rush. His heart pounded against his ribs as the earth raced up to meet him with murderous speed. There was only instinct, cold and ruthless, holding the panic at bay. Gravity seized him in its brutal grip, but the thrill was undeniable – sharp, raw, and blindingly alive.

James Bond was no stranger to finding inventive ways to breach an enemy's stronghold, but this time, the stakes demanded something far beyond even his usual audacity – this time, he would have to take infiltration to the extreme. When *GoldenEye* was released in 1995, after a five-year hiatus, the filmmakers knew they had to bring it up a notch. Having tackled just about every traditional stunt known to man, it was time to venture into the world of extreme sports. The challenge would be bungee jumping.

James Bond would therefore tackle the Verzasca Dam in Locarno, Switzerland, which still holds the record for the highest stationary jump in the world. And fortunately for adrenaline junkies and James Bond fans everywhere, the Trekking Team still supervises bungee jumps off the Verzasca Dam. So you can do more than just walk in the footsteps of James Bond, you can fly in his footsteps!

If you read the first chapter, then you know that I attempted to brave the *GoldenEye* jump; attempted and failed. The first time around, I spent fifteen grueling hours in a rental car. The entire trip consisted of two hundred miles of driving, fifteen thousand feet of Swiss Alps, and one destroyed passenger-side mirror. One year later, I was back, and this time I would do it right. Determined to follow in Bond's footsteps, I had to tackle this stunt for myself.

Let me confess right up front, this chapter was a struggle. Let's face it; what does it really take to learn how to bungee jump? You just need to show up, hand your money over, and then kiss your ass good-bye. Pure and simple!

So, then what are we going to talk about in this chapter? We'll give you a brief history of bungee jumping. We'll give you an introduction to the different types of jumps, including crane and tower jumps, bridge jumps, and balloon jumps. We'll talk about the equipment; the bungee cord and the harnesses. We'll review the safety factor of bungee jumping, and a little bit about skills that can be applied, and tricks that have been done. And of course before we finish, we're going to visit the *GoldenEye* bungee jump in Locarno, Switzerland. We'll give you all the details you will need to scratch this amazing James Bond experience off your bucket list. We'll tell you where it's located, when you can go, how much it costs, what the requirements are, the training that's involved, and finally, where to sign up.

What is Bungee Jumping?

Bungee jumping is the sport of jumping from extreme heights while attached to an elastic cord from a high platform. The bungee cord allows the jumper to free-fall toward the Earth, and then snap the jumper back up before he hits the ground. It's the modern-day answer to the primal urge to experience the intense rush of adrenaline. There's something about forcing your body to do what's against gut-level human nature, and something stimulating about walking away from a near-death experience. The intense feeling of being invincible.

The History of Bungee Jumping

According to legend, bungee jumping was born from a woman's ingenuity in the South Pacific. After enduring mistreatment, she fled her husband by climbing a tall banyan tree. When he found her, he climbed up after her. While he climbed, she tied some vines around her ankles, so when he reached the top and tried to grab her, she jumped–and he jumped with her. The vines saved her from reaching the ground, as he fell to his death. Deciding that no woman should ever get the best of a man again, the men in the village began practicing diving out of the trees with vines attached to their feet.

Years later, people would adopt this concept and add a few high-tech features. On April Fool's Day in 1979, the Oxford 'Dangerous Sports Club' attached themselves to elastic bungee cords and jumped off the 245 ft. Clifton Bridge in Bristol, England. The same group would later jump off the Golden Gate Bridge in California, and then in 1980, would jump from the Royal Gorge Bridge in Colorado. Throughout the '80s and into the early '90s, bungee jumping had moved more and more into the mainstream, right up until 1995 with the record-breaking bungee jump in the film *GoldenEye*. Today, commercial bungee jumping sites can be found all over the world.

Types of Bungee Jumps

There are four basic types of bungee jumping, or rather, bungee platforms that you can jump off of. Those four include cranes, towers, bridges, and even hot-air balloons.

A **crane jump** is probably the most common type of bungee jump. A cage is suspended from the cable attached to the boom of the crane. The jumper enters the cage as it sits on the ground, is hooked into his harness and safety hooks, and then the crane lifts the cage and the jumper into the air to the desired height. With the cage at the proper height, the jumper jumps. Once the jump is completed, the crane lowers the jumper to the ground, where the ground crew unhooks him. The cage is then lowered to the ground, ready for the next jumper. Since this type of jump is the simplest and easiest to set up, it's become relatively common to find a crane jump in highly populated or touristy areas in the last ten years.

The next type of a jump is off a tower. A **tower jump** simply refers to jumping from any man-made stationary platform, varying in height, structure, and the jumping methods that can be used. Next is the **bridge jump**. Since bridges can be found most anywhere, this would make them the most readily available platforms. However, bungee jumping off bridges is illegal in most parts of the United States, unless the operators have secured special permits or own the bridge themselves.

The common question asked of tower and bridge jumping is, "How do you get the jumper off of the cord after the jump?" There are essentially two ways to free the jumper: you can raise him back up, or you can lower him all the way down. Considerable manpower is required to raise the jumper back up to the platform, so this is done either a pulley system with several people pulling, or a motorized pulley system. Otherwise, the jumper has to be lowered to the ground, and the bungee cord is then disconnected from either the jumper or the bridge.

The last type of jump is from a hot-air balloon. **Balloons** became popular as bungee platforms as authorities began to ban the use of bridges. Of course, it wasn't long until the FAA stepped in and began to regulate the use of balloons for bungee jumping as well. So, in the interest of safety and trying to work within FAA regulations, you can bungee jump off a tethered balloon.

A tethered hot-air balloon refers to a balloon that is attached to the ground by cables so the wind can't carry the balloon away, making this a good option for the jumper. A hot air balloon, by its nature, will travel with the wind, so even as the balloon lands, it's still moving forward, giving the jumper a pretty rough landing. Stabilizing the balloon solves this problem. Once the jump is completed, pulling down on the cable will lower the balloon, thereby lowering the jumper to the ground so the ground crew can safely unhook him. When the balloon settles to the ground, the next jumper is hooked in and off they go.

Equipment

Since we already have gravity and courage, and something high to jump off of, the only other components needed for bungee jumping are a bungee cord and harness. **Bungee cords** are made from multiple strands of rubber that are bound tightly together. They are manufactured in many diameters and strengths, with most cords ranging between 3/8-inch to 1- inch in diameter. Some bungee sites use only one cord, whereas some will use up to five or six cords bundled together. Military specifications will require the site to use one cord per every 50 lbs. of the jumper's body weight to achieve the desired stretch. At the *GoldenFye* site, the Trekking Team will give you a 2-foot length of old bungee cord as a souvenir. It's thick enough that you could just about get your fingers around it.

The next thing you need is a **harness**. There are basically two types of harnesses: the full-body harness or an ankle harness. The full-body harness comes in a one-piece system, or a two-piece system, which is connected by short straps that hold the two pieces together. The top piece is worn around the armpits and shoulders and around the back like you're wearing a vest, while the bottom piece is worn around the waist and crotch area as if you were wearing a pair of shorts. The bungee cord is then attached in the front to both harnesses. The ankle harness simply fits around your ankles, and can cover as little as a few inches of the ankle, or as much as the entire area between the ankle and knee.

Safety

The next question is, "How safe is bungee jumping?" Of the millions of jumps that have been done worldwide, there have been relatively few injuries or deaths, and these are usually not attributed to professional, commercial bungee operations, but to renegade adrenaline junkies trying out new stunts. Even minor injuries are very rare as well. These types of injuries would include getting your fingers and skin between metal links or solid parts of the equipment, or a jumper getting hit with the cord, rope, or other hardware. There are usually protective coverings and padding over any joints that are close to the jumper and will protect you from any injury. By using common sense, listening to your instructor and following the instructions carefully, minor injuries will be rare or nonexistent.

Tricks and Stunts

Many of the injuries that do occur, happen while doing the types of stunts that are generally frowned upon by commercial operators. Here are a few examples: One type of jump that's generally regarded as dangerous is the **water dunk**. You've probably seen this one before. Usually from a suspension bridge, the jumper leaps off the bridge, and the length of the bungee cord is just long enough so that the jumper is able to submerge his head briefly before he is snapped back. The problem with this stunt is that the margin for error can be very small, depending on the jumper's weight and the depth of the water. You will see very few commercial sites offering these types of jumps.

In a **negative jump**, instead of the jumper jumping out of the crane to the ground, the jumper starts at the ground with the bungee cord stretched tight, then the jumper is released and hurdled upward. The problem with this jump is that it's very difficult to judge how much energy is being stored in the cords, so it's tough to know for sure how far the jumper will be hurdled. If he's hurled too far, that means he's going straight into the cage headfirst.

The **sandbag** involves a jumper who jumps while hugging a large bag of sand. The jumper leaps from the platform with the sandbag in hand, and with the added weight of the sandbag, he's pulled down even further. When the cord has reached full extension, the jumper drops the sandbag, causing him to rebound higher than the original platform. This is another kind of a jump that really isn't recommended, because the path of the jumper is difficult to predict, and the jumper could come back up and hit the platform.

So, is there any skill involved in bungee jumping? Do you just close your eyes and jump, or is there some style that you can bring to your jump? Each commercial site is different, and depending on the platform and the equipment, each site may have a preference as to the style of the jump a first-timer should use. Some sites will tell you to jump face forward, others might tell you to go backwards. Some will say to jump feetfirst, and others will say head first. The instructor will always tell you what style is best for that site, but if there's something you have in mind, feel free to ask.

FLIPPING OUT

Of course you can always try a flip. When doing flips, you will find that the placement of the cord is very important depending on what style of jump you're going to do. You need to hold the cord to the side so that you're clear of the cord while doing your turns. If you're jumping for the first time, it's probably not the time to try flips, as these take a little practice. But again, save the flips until you've done at least one successful jump.

Another type of jump that is considered safe and done at many commercial sites, is the tandem jump. This is when two people are harnessed together and attached to the bungee cords as if they were one person. Because the equipment has been set up to handle an additional load, the risk in doing a tandem jump is minimal.

That's bungee jumping in a nutshell; everything from its origins, to the platforms, to the equipment, and the stunts. What's left? It's time to head over to the *GoldenEye* bungee jump and sign up.

The *GoldenEye* Bungee Jump

The Trekking Team is one of the oldest and safety-certified outdoor companies in Switzerland, and the *GoldenEye* jump is one of the safest and most professional bungee sites in the world.

As you drive up the winding ridge approaching the Verzasca dam, you can just start to make out patches of a sleek blue-gray that make up the face of the dam. It's when you come around the last bend to the clearing that you can finally see the dam for the first time, and you start to comprehend just how massive the dam is. At 722 ft. high, the Verzasca Dam is just shy of the Chrysler Building in New York City. It's almost hard to imagine anybody voluntarily jumping off of it. But, there was no backing out this time.

GETTING THERE

The *GoldenEye* bungee jump is located at the Verzasca Dam at the beginning of Verzasca Valley, in Tessin, Switzerland, overlooking the Lake of Vogorno (Lago di Vogorno). The nearest city is Locarno, which is a gorgeous Swiss city overlooking Lake Maggiore (Lago Maggiore). From the village of Gordola, you would drive up the Via Valle Verzasca into the Verzasca Valley for about five minutes (roughly 3.5 km.), until you are face to face with the massive Verzasca Dam wall. Needless to say, you can't miss it. The jumping platform and sign-up area is located at the center of the wall.

According to the Trekking team website, the season begins the week of Easter and lasts until the end of October. Generally, jumps are done only on the weekends, but are done Wednesday through Friday from July 14th to August 22nd. Also, the operation generally runs in the afternoons, but the schedule may vary, so be sure to phone or e-mail the Trekking team. Be sure to check the Trekking website for any updates or changes, and contact them to confirm before you make your arrangements. Bookings are required.

COST AND REQUIREMENTS

As of this writing, the price of the *GoldenEye* bungee jump is 255 Swiss Francs for adults, (roughly 190 Euros or 240 dollars), and 195 Swiss Francs if you're 18 or younger. They also offer discounted rates for the second jump, and they offer group rates as well. If you're under 18, you need the signature of your parents, and if you're over 65, you need written permission from your doctor. The minimum weight for jumping is 45 kilograms (about 99 lbs.), and the maximum weight is 110 kilograms (or about 242 pounds). The minimum age for jumping is 10 years old, and the maximum age is 70 years old. Check the website to confirm.

SIGNING UP AND TRAINING

The sign-up booth is out in the middle of the dam, right near the platform. You'll sign up, pay your fee, clear out your pockets, and then you'll be weighed in. Next, you'll be geared up, and you'll go through a short training session. The *GoldenEye* jump uses the two-part body harness, with a third section for your ankles; the top part fits around your armpits and shoulders, while the bottom fits snugly around the top of your legs, crotch, and waist, and the third part fitting tightly around your ankles.

Once you have been harnessed, you'll notice a knotted rope connecting the bottom of your harness: Once you've done the jump, you don't want to hang too long upside-down, so you will use the knotted rope to climb up into a vertical position, and then hook the upper part of your harness to the bottom of the bungee cord, allowing you to relax in a kneeling position. The Trekking team has a complete set-up where they can actually hook you into a large contraption to train in, and walk you step by step through how to do this. It's very simple.

Once your training is complete, it's your turn to jump.

The team will double-check that you have been adequately trained, and they'll do all the last-minute checking of your harnesses. All of this checking and re-checking will make you feel like you are in safe hands. Then, finally, the instructor will walk you to the end of the platform and let you know when it's time to jump. The rest is up to you. You look out at 722 ft. of nothing but air. Then, when you feel the tap on your shoulder, you shake out the last bit of doubt, and you leap into the air.

You will freefall for more than seven seconds.

Once your jump is complete, follow the training from your instructor. You'll grab the knotted rope, pull yourself up into a vertical position, and hook yourself into the top of the harness; now you can relax in a vertical, kneeling position. Next, you will hold your arms out-stretched to signal to the team above that you are properly strapped in, and the bungee team will lower a cable down to you. Once the cable has been lowered to your level, you'll wave your arm to signal the team to stop the cable.

As you're dangling several hundred feet below, the gentle swing back and forth is greatly exaggerated, so you will have to be patient as the cable comes over toward you. Once you've got it, you're going to hook it into your harness, and then wave a signal to the team above. With the mechanical pulley system, they will pull you back up. Then, it's a smooth ride back up to the platform, while you enjoy an amazing view of the mountaintops of Switzerland. Once you reach the top, you'll step back onto the platform, and unhook. You'll feel completely invincible.

Conclusion

If there was ever a James Bond experience that you and I can relive, this must be one of the most adrenaline-inducing of all. And once you've conquered the world of bungee jumping for yourself, you'll feel one step closer to feeling that there's nothing James Bond can do that you can't do.

For more information on the Trekking Team and the *GoldenEye* bungee jump, go to www.trekking.ch.

Good luck, and hold on for your life!

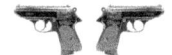

REST & RECREATION
Horseback Riding

James Bond could still hear the feverish excitement of the tourada behind him as he ran down the steps of the praça de touros towards a familiar red Mercury Cougar convertible; the cheers only growing louder as the fearless forcado de cara faced down the raging bull in a daring test of skill and bravery.

The 'pega de cara' was a traditional demonstration of courage in Portuguese bullfighting, in which eight forcados subdue a charging bull with their bare hands, without the use of weapons or capes. The bravest and most skilled (the forcado da cara) stared down the angry bull, taunting and provoking it to attack. As the beast lunges forward, the forcado braces for the impact and leaps forward at the bull's head, wrapping his arms tightly around the neck and horns and holding on tight. The rest of the forcados rush in to grab the bull's body and pile on, forcing the mighty animal into submission.

Bond called out, "Tracy!"

She stood frozen with her arms at her side, stopping short of getting into the car and escaping. Her chestnut hair was tied and fell down a traditional black riding jacket, and the red sash at her waist suggested defiance; not unlike the capes of the banderilleros used to taunt and provoke danger.

James Bond was no stranger to intrigue; seduction was just another tool for gaining information and extracting secrets. But this was different; he genuinely cared for Tracy and wanted to protect her, and now he had hurt her.

He approached her gently and took her shoulders. "Tracy, I was always taught that mistakes should be remedied, especially between friends…" She turned to face him, revealing the pearls of tears glistening in the sunlight. Bond gently brushed them from her cheeks. "...or lovers."

The musky scent of the mink oil still lingered on the leather saddles as Tracy ran a brush down the beautiful brown mane of the proud mare before her. The cavalieros had placed blankets over two of the horses and began to saddle them, but Tracy was no stranger to the ranch, and she couldn't resist helping the stable hands.

Lusitano saddles were placed on the two horses – Baroque-style saddles common in Portugal for classical dressage, bullfighting, and traditional working equitation, similar to a Spanish Vaquero saddle but adapted for Lusitano horses. The young ranch hand reached under the horse's belly and grabbed the girth, pulling the latigo strap through the cinch ring and tightened it firmly. He checked the saddle's position and adjusted the stirrups.

The cavaliero was still making final adjustments when Tracy grabbed the reins in her left hand, resting her hand on the horse's neck, and put her left foot in the stirrup, and in one movement, she leapt up, swinging her right leg over the horse's back and lowered herself into the saddle, smiling at James Bond in a subtle act of playful bravado.

Bond smiled back accepting the challenge and mounted his stallion. His Lusitano, a black steed with a proud arch to its neck, shifted beneath him, eager to move. Tracy's mare flicked an ear, sensing the quiet anticipation of the riders.

Adjusting the reins in her hands, Tracy glanced at her new companion with a knowing smile. With a gentle flick of her wrist, and an instinctive nudge with her right heel, she nudged her horse forward. With a half-grin, Bond followed suit.

The late afternoon sun was casting a golden glow over the rolling hills and the sunlight danced through the weeping willows. James Bond and Contessa Teresa "Tracy" di Vicenzo set out to explore the grounds.

As the riders passed through the sunlight cutting through the willows, and with each proud step of the horse, the cares of the world seemed to fall away, far behind. It wasn't long ago that Tracy seemed completely lost, desperate, and alone. She seemed out of time. But now, Bond could sense healing and hope, and there was now time for life to unfold, and to uncover all the precious things love had in store. They had time; nothing more, nothing less.

And they needed nothing more. There was no hurry you see; they had all the time in the world.

The Art of Good Horsemanship

Your equestrian needs may be romantic or purely practical. Perhaps a rival has challenged you to a traditional and gallant form of horse racing known as steeplechase. Maybe you need a quick and reliable way to chase an enemy's plane down a rugged dirt runway. Or just maybe, a breathtaking woman in a green sequined bikini has been spotted riding along the shore with the sea at her side and the wind in her hair. Whatever the reason, one thing is certain, mastering the art of horseback riding will serve you well and make life a little more interesting, so you'd better be ready.

Horseback riding is one of the most unique and rewarding experiences you'll ever have. Unlike many activities, it's never a solo endeavor – it's a partnership between you and a very powerful, living, thinking creature.

Unlike skills that depend solely on your own abilities, riding requires trust, communication, and cooperation. The horse has instincts, emotions, and a will of its own, therefore the outcome depends just as much on its responses as on yours. You don't just ride a horse; you work together.

Additionally, horseback riding blends athleticism, balance, and coordination with a strong mental component – you must be aware of your horse's mood, body language, and energy at all times. Lastly, whether you're galloping across open fields or enjoying a peaceful trail ride, riding also offers a rare combination of adventure and serenity. It's an activity that you can do anywhere; at home, on vacation, and anywhere around the world.

As you're beginning to realize, one of the key aspects of horseback riding is building a strong bond with your horse.

Unlike the simple mechanics of driving a car, riding a horse is very different because it requires much more than physical skill – it's about communication. Your ability to ride effectively hinges on how well you convey commands through subtle body movements. It's essential to ensure that your cues are clear, so that the horse can respond in the way you intend. Mastering this communication will not only make your ride smoother, but also elevate your overall experience, turning each ride into a thrilling and harmonious partnership.

In this chapter, we'll provide a good overview of horseback riding, and provide you with some tips and techniques that will separate you from the absolute beginners. Let's help you get a leg up – figuratively and literally – for your first day on horseback. We'll discuss the physical training that will help you to be prepared for your first day on the horse, we'll talk about clothing and how you should show up on your first day of riding, and we'll suggest ways to help you find a stable offering horseback riding lessons. We'll address the different styles of horseback riding, specifically Western and English styles. We'll explain how you should approach the horse, and how to avoid the common mistakes that most beginners make. We will talk about the saddles, and how to climb up into the saddle. Then we'll get into basic horseback riding; how to grip the reins, the different riding styles such as walking, trotting and canter. Lastly, of course, how to stop. So grab your riding boots and let's go horseback riding.

Expectations

When I first began working on this chapter, I thought a discussion of horseback riding would be a walk in the park. After all, I had been horseback riding before, and I knew pretty well how to ride – or did I?

The truth is, I had a good basic idea. Even though I have been on horseback many times before, what I had really done was 'trail rides,' but I assumed that was all I really needed to know. But, the more I explored horseback riding for myself, the more I realized there was a big distinction. Horses that are trained to give trail rides have done it over and over and will follow the trail from memory. The last time I was on a horse was with a large group, everyone mounted up, and when it was tIme to head out there was one rider who took the lead. The other riders followed along and when it was my turn to start walking, my horse just began to walk on his own. I really didn't do anything to get him moving. I did get to exercise some control at certain parts of the ride, but aside from that it was pretty clear; the trail ride was a little bit more than a glorified pony ride.

Now of course there is nothing wrong with trail rides; I've done trail rides many times before and I will do them again. But the simple fact is, I still had a lot to learn about horseback riding, and we're going to share those things with you here. Once you've made the choice to take a horseback riding lesson, what can you do to prepare yourself?

Training

Beginning riders might not consider physical conditioning before riding, as horseback riding can be deceptively simple. You just hop on, go for a ride, and you get off. Right? However, the next day you can't even walk upright, because you've been using muscles you didn't even know you had, so you're better off getting prepared physically. As with any physical activity, you need to focus on your endurance, strength, and flexibility.

ENDURANCE

While riding is not exactly a high-performance event, being in relatively good shape with a good level of stamina will just make the experience more enjoyable. Any exercise that improves endurance will allow you to ride longer without getting fatigued. Walking, jogging, bicycling and swimming are all good aerobic exercises that will help endurance.

STRENGTH TRAINING

As you might imagine, horseback riding relies on good core and lower body strength, but after a day of riding, you might be surprised to feel some soreness in your upper body, specifically your upper back and shoulder area. When you ride, you are using your entire body to stay upright, and to communicate with the horse in ways you might not have considered. Good overall physical condition is going to be very helpful. Not to mention, you probably want to be looking your best when you're squeezing into tight-fitting riding pants.

FLEXIBILITY

This is the big one. When you wake up the morning after your first day of riding, you might notice particular soreness in your inner thigh and groin area, particularly because you've stretched these muscles over the saddle for an extended period of time, and these are muscles that rarely get put to use. So when you're doing your stretches, focus on the 'saddle' area.

One of the most effective ways to stretch these muscles is to get on all fours, spread your knees out to the sides as far as they'll go (as if you were on a horse), but holding yourself up with your hands. If you can handle it, take your hands off the floor once you've gotten your knees as far out as you can, and then sit up so that your torso is vertical. Don't do this until you've pushed your knees out as far as they can, because once you are up you can't get them out any farther. Hold this stretch for as long as you can, and then lower yourself back down on all fours to lift yourself out of this position. Watch the pressure on the inside corners of your knees, and don't push beyond your ability. Don't strain or risk pulling a muscle. Try this on something soft, like a yoga mat or a folded-over blanket.

In addition to this exercise, you should continue to focus on overall flexibility. As you learn to ride, you will begin to realize how important it is to move your body in certain ways and maintain good independent movement. Stretching regularly and doing exercise like yoga will help to maintain a full range of movement in your joints and improve overall coordination.

It's also a good idea to do some warm up exercises right before each lesson. Take a good walk or maybe a jog, and spend a few minutes doing some bending and stretching. You'll feel better and will reduce the risk of any injuries.

Incidentally, it's never a bad idea to do a few exercises while you are actually sitting on the horse – a few stretches, twisting your torso, touching your toes, and doing a few arm circles will help to ensure your overall comfort on the horse.

Another interesting way to prepare for horseback riding is by incorporating an exercise ball or yoga ball into your daily routine. One experienced rider shared that she swaps out her desk chair for an exercise ball while at work – turning office hours into an opportunity for training. Simply sitting on the ball engages your core, strengthens your lower body, improves balance, and builds endurance, all without interrupting your day. It's a clever way to sneak in some conditioning, and a perfect solution when you're pressed for time. Keep that little tip in your back pocket the next time you're struggling to fit in a workout.

Clothing

What to wear for your first riding lesson? If you're planning to wear jeans and a pair of boots – you're on the right track. But, experienced riders will tell you that wearing jeans in the saddle can get pretty old, pretty fast. True equestrians will always point you toward a good pair of riding pants.

PANTS

When it comes to riding, jeans have seams and rivets in all the wrong places, and they tend to get particularly uncomfortable while you are in the riding position for an extended period of time. Specialty riding jeans without those seams and rivets in awkward places are available, but if you're seriously considering riding, you might want to consider riding pants, 'jodhpurs,' or 'breeches.'

Jodhpurs are a type of riding pants designed particularly in English disciplines like dressage, show jumping, and eventing, which is why James Bond opts for a pair of dark brown jodhpurs, which tuck inside his tall black leather riding boots in *A View to a Kill.*

Jodhpurs *(pronounced "JOD-purz")* are tight-fitting from the knee to the ankle, allowing a close contact with the horse and a smooth fit under tall riding boots or paddock boots. Many jodhpurs have extra patches or reinforced fabric on the inside of the knees (sometimes the seat too) to prevent wear and provide grip in the saddle. They're usually made from a stretchy, breathable material like cotton, with elastane, offering flexibility and comfort while riding.

Jodhpurs are recommended for beginners, and remain the classic choice for riding schools; they're designed to be worn with shorter boots which are more comfortable for new riders than tall boots, they're durable, easy to move in, and they work well with entry-level gear.

Riding breeches are specifically designed for equestrian activities. Traditionally, breeches *(pronounced "BREE-chuhz," just as it looks)* are tight in the legs, stopping about halfway down the calf, with buttons or laces in the calf section, and with a pronounced flare through the thighs that allows freedom of movement for the rider. They come in different materials such as nylon, cotton, twill, corduroy, and fleece. Whether you choose jeans or breeches, the point is to make sure that you are comfortable so that you can focus on riding, and not squirming around in the saddle trying to get comfortable.

With all that said, stick with a comfortable pair of jeans and boots for your first lesson, and leave the shopping until you get serious about riding.

FOOTWEAR

Even if it's only your first lesson and you haven't yet committed to riding lessons, you will want to show up wearing a pair of sturdy boots to protect your toes. Chances are you will be out in some rugged terrain, so you need to keep your feet protected. You also want to be protected in the unlikely event that your foot gets stepped on. A traditional pair of 'work boots' should do the trick.

If you're a little more serious about taking up riding, consider a good pair of riding boots. As we briefly mentioned earlier, there are two styles of riding; Western and English (more on each style to come). Before you make a purchase, be clear on which style you'll be studying, as the characteristics of each will vary according to style. Western riding boots, like cowboy boots, feature a higher heel for stability in stirrups, a wider shape for comfort, and often have pull straps for easy entry. English riding boots are slimmer, have a lower heel for better stirrup placement, and are often made of softer leather for a closer feel to the horse.

Whichever style you go with, your boots should fit well. This is not one of the sports that requires tight fitting footwear, so don't buy them too snug planning to break them in – buy comfortably.

HELMET

Last but not least is your headgear. Most stables will almost certainly provide you with a helmet for your first lesson, but just to be safe, call or check the website and make sure before you go. If you are planning to pursue riding, purchase a good quality helmet that fits well. It should be slightly snug, and if it fits correctly, your eyebrows will be able to move up and down in the helmet.

GLOVES

While they're not required, it might be a smart idea to consider a pair of gloves for comfort, safety, and control. Some schools suggest that gloves are highly recommended.

Gloves help you maintain a secure grip, especially if your hands get sweaty or the reins are slick (from rain or horse slobber). Reins can rub against your fingers and palms, especially during your first few lessons when you're still learning proper rein contact, so gloves will protect your hands from blisters. Even mild cold can make your hands stiff, but gloves can help keep them warm and responsive in cold weather. As an added bonus, wearing gloves will give a more polished look, and many instructors appreciate students dressing with care. Lastly, if a horse pulls hard or misbehaves, gloves can prevent rope burn from the reins.

Riding gloves are made with thin, grippy material that allows flexibility and feel. Look for leather or synthetic with reinforced areas between fingers (where the reins sit). If you're not ready to purchase riding gloves, any snug-fitting gloves with grip (like gardening or sports gloves) can work as a temporary option.

STYLE

Beyond the basics, the rest is up to you, and your sense of personal style. While my natural instinct is to suggest following James Bond's style when it comes to equestrian clothing, your opportunities for formal or even semi-formal wear will probably be few and far between.

If you do find the opportunity to step up your game, look to Bond. You might complete your look with an English riding jacket, designed to make the rider look formal and elegant. *On Her Majesty's Secret Service* and *A View to a Kill* offer some great insights into James Bond's choices for riding clothes.

In *On Her Majesty's Secret Service,* James Bond arrives at the bullring to meet Draco and Tracy wearing a hacking jacket, which is a type of tailored riding jacket traditionally worn for informal horseback riding, specifically '**hacking**,' which is a relaxed form of riding outside the arena, often on trails or country roads. In *A View to a Kill,* Bond wears a similar hacking jacket when he's challenged to a steeplechase riding the horse, 'Inferno.'

The **hacking jacket** is usually recognized by its subtle earth tones with understated plaid or check patterns, and is characterized by its slightly longer cut than a traditional blazer for comfort and coverage while riding and back vents to allow ease of movement in the saddle. They usually feature slanted (or "hacking") pockets, designed for easier access while mounted, and are typically made from a durable wool tweed, ideal for countryside conditions. It's a staple in British equestrian and country fashion and can also be worn as a stylish casual jacket off the horse. *(Thank you Matt Spaiser at Bondsuits.com.)*

Western versus English

When it comes time to take your lesson, you might be asked which style of riding you are interested in, Western or English style. It's not critical that you choose correctly, as you can always change styles later, and the basics of horseback riding are universal. But, here are some factors you can think about when making your decision.

Western style evolved as a practical means of getting work done on a ranch. You won't find very many cowboys around these days, but you will still see western riders at the show ring, the rodeo, and on ranches. **English style** also has a long history; part transportation, part sport, part pleasure, and part art-form. It is the kind of riding that the cavalry and the fox hunters still do, and you can still see English riding in the Olympics. While the basics of horseback riding are still the same no matter which style you choose, there are a few distinct differences, such as the gait.

Gait refers to the foot movement naturally employed by the horse at different speeds. In other words, walking, trotting, and galloping, are all examples of gaits. While walking is very similar in both English and Western style riding, the trot and the canters can be slightly different. *(More on gaits shortly.)*

The standard attire is also different; for Western riding you might wear a traditional western hat, shirt, jeans, western style boots, etc., whereas for English riding you would wear a traditional style hunt cap, a fitted jacket, breeches, tall boots, etc.

But the real difference between Western and English style riding are in the different activities and sports related to both styles. For example, in Western you could do more rodeo style activities, such as penning, cutting, reining, trail riding, roping, etc., while in English style you would do more jumping, hunting, dressage competitions, and even polo. Of course, this comes later in the game if you decide to get serious and really pursue horseback riding as a devotion.

At this point you might be asking, *"Ok but, which style of riding would James Bond use?"* The semi-obvious answer is English style riding. How do we know this for sure? Any time I've observed James Bond on horseback, he's riding English style. The most obvious way to know for sure is by checking out the saddle.

The saddle is different for Western and English style riding, and you can spot a Western saddle pretty easily by its parts. One of the easiest giveaways is the saddle horn at the front, which was originally used for tying off ropes when roping cattle. Western saddles are typically larger and heavier than English saddles, and built for long hours of riding and ranch work. The seat is deeper and more curved, giving the rider support and stability. Also, the stirrups hang from wide leather fenders that protect the rider's legs, unlike the more narrow leathers on English saddles.

The English saddle is a little bit different. The most obvious difference is that English saddles don't have a horn at the front. English saddles are generally more compact and lightweight, and designed for close contact between horse and rider. The seat tends to be flatter and less deep than a Western saddle, with a more forward-leaning position depending on the discipline. Instead of wide leather fenders, English saddles have narrow stirrup leathers that hang more vertically beneath the rider. The skirt is minimal or absent, allowing for a closer feel of the horse, and is more suited for activities like jumping, fox hunting, and racing. Lastly, typical English saddles include knee rolls or padded flaps to support the rider's leg position.

It's almost time to ride! But before we climb into the saddle, there are two more essential parts of the horseback riding experience; not just for the horse's well-being, but also for building trust with the horse and ensuring a safe and enjoyable ride. Those things are grooming and tacking up.

Grooming

Even though this isn't something you'll deal with during your first few lessons, it's definitely a big part of equestrian life and good horsemanship. **Grooming** refers to the process of brushing and cleaning the horse, which serves several important purposes. First, it helps remove dirt, sweat, and debris from the horse's coat, mane, tail, and especially the hooves. This is about more than just appearances; cleaning the horse before riding prevents discomfort and irritation that can be caused by grit or dried mud beneath the tack. It also gives you a chance to check for any cuts, bumps, or swelling that might need attention before riding.

The act of grooming is also an important part of bonding time. Horses are sensitive animals, and they quickly learn to associate this routine with care and trust. Spending those few extra minutes brushing your horse and speaking to them calmly helps develop a connection and sets a positive tone for the ride ahead.

Tacking Up

Once the horse is clean and calm, there's one more step before mounting up – it's time to tack up. **Tacking up** refers to putting on the riding equipment; specifically, the saddle and the bridle. The saddle is secured with a girth or cinch around the horse's belly, and a saddle pad is placed underneath to cushion and protect the horse's back. The bridle, which includes the bit and reins, is gently placed over the horse's head, and allows the rider to communicate with subtle signals during the ride. Each piece of tack needs to be fitted correctly to avoid discomfort or injury.

The importance of this process can't be overstated. Proper grooming and tacking ensure that the horse is comfortable, calm, and ready to work. For the rider, these routines also offer a moment to slow down, focus, and prepare mentally for the ride. In essence, grooming and tacking up are as much about care and connection as they are about preparation and safety.

Let's Ride!

This is it! Now that we've covered the essentials of physical conditioning, proper clothing, and an overview of riding styles, and we've looked at the processes of grooming and tacking, it's time to actually begin your riding lesson. So before we mount up, let's get familiar with our new companion, and establish a good relationship.

Getting To Know the Horse

Building a strong relationship with your horse from the beginning is essential. Horses are highly intuitive animals, and they can sense when someone is inexperienced; they can smell a beginner. If you're unsure or uneasy around them, they might pick up on that and respond in turn with hesitation or discomfort themselves. In other words, if you're not comfortable with the horse, the horse might not be comfortable with you. So let's make a good first impression.

THE CORRECT WAY TO APPROACH A HORSE

When approaching a horse, walk calmly and confidently toward it. Then, take a moment to pat the horse gently and get acquainted. Keep in mind, like most herbivores, horses have eyes on the sides of their heads rather than the front. Because of this, a horse may move its head slightly back and forth to get a better look at what's ahead. Understanding this is useful, not only when approaching a horse, but also later as your riding skills advance, and you begin to learn the limits of a horse's field of vision.

For example, keeping in mind its field of vision, you'll eventually discover that jumping is a particularly challenging skill, mainly because the horse can't clearly see the obstacle directly in front of it. This means the rider can't simply sit back and expect the horse to take over. Since the horse relies on the rider's guidance to time the jump correctly, the two must work closely as a team.

For now, just keep in mind that a horse sees best from the sides, so as you move around it, be aware of your position. Horses feel more at ease when they know exactly where you are.

Also, keep in mind that horses can and do sometimes kick, especially if they're startled or feel threatened. While you may be eager to connect with the horse, it's important to respect its space and signals. Sometimes, the horse just isn't in the mood to engage. Approach calmly, stay visible, and avoid standing directly behind the horse. Always let the horse know where you are and give it time to warm up to you. Building trust takes patience, and not every horse is immediately receptive, and that's okay.

HOW TO AVOID GETTING KICKED

If you need to walk behind a horse, always keep one hand gently on its hindquarters and stay very close – no more than six inches away. This may feel counterintuitive, but staying close actually reduces the risk of injury. By doing this, the horse knows where you are at all times and is less likely to get spooked. Also, if the horse does kick, it won't have the space to generate full force – it doesn't have a lot of room to wind up. Getting kicked by a horse feels like – well, getting kicked by a horse. But, if you stay close to the horse, he won't have room to build up thrust, and you will get pushed or bumped, rather than getting a good solid kick. It's best to avoid walking behind a horse when possible–but when you must, staying close and maintaining contact is the safest way to do it.

Mount Up!

When it's time to get in the saddle, tradition and practicality suggests that you should mount from the horse's left side. Why the left? This custom dates back to the days of knights and soldiers, who wore swords on their left hips. Mounting from the left kept the sword away from the horse's back and made for a smoother, safer transition into the saddle. Even though the swords are long gone, the tradition remains, and horses have been trained with this expectation for generations.

Again, confidence matters. Moving with purpose and familiarity helps the horse feel at ease and trust that you know what you're doing.

Hopping up into the saddle can feel a bit intimidating at first, as it's got the potential for a very embarrassing situation. But like anything else, once you know what you're doing, you'll find there's really nothing to it. With a little confidence and know-how, it will quickly become second nature.

HOW TO MOUNT THE HORSE CORRECTLY

Your first instinct might be to grab the saddle and hoist yourself up, but there's a better way. The proper technique is to grab the horse's mane – that's right, the hair on the back of its neck. Don't worry, it doesn't hurt the horse. In fact, it helps the horse feel where you are and understand that you're about to mount.

Start by placing your left foot firmly into the left stirrup. With your left hand, grab a handful of mane near the base of the neck. Then, with your right hand, reach over and hold the back of the saddle on the right side. Give yourself a couple of light bounces on your right leg, then spring upward, swing your right leg over the horse's back, and settle into the saddle. Slip your right foot into the right stirrup, make sure your weight is centered, and adjust until you feel balanced and comfortable.

And just like that, you've mounted the horse correctly.

If you anticipate having trouble getting onto the horse, you can always use something called a mounting block. A **mounting block** is essentially a small wooden step (or steps) that will help you get onto the horse. Most stables will have several mounting blocks scattered around which can make life easier for both you and the horse. You can either move the mounting block over to the horse, or you can lead your horse over to the mounting block.

Once you're in the saddle, muscle memory may kick in, and the horse might decide to start walking on his own. This is the perfect moment to begin establishing a working relationship. The horse needs to understand that he should wait for your cue before moving forward.

Preventing a horse from moving forward before you're ready, requires a combination of body language, rein control, and voice cues: Gently pull back on the reins to apply light pressure, signaling to the horse to stop or stay in place. Keep your hands steady but not rigid. Sit deep in the saddle with your weight centered and relaxed. Avoid leaning forward, which can unintentionally signal the horse to move. Keep your legs still and off the horse's sides, as any squeezing or nudging can cue forward movement. When the horse is standing quietly, release the rein pressure slightly and offer praise with a soft pat to reward the proper response and to reinforce the behavior.

CORRECT POSTURE

Once you are comfortably on the horse, the next step is to adjust yourself and find the correct riding posture. Maintaining the proper riding position is one of the most important fundamentals for any rider, whether you're a beginner or refining your skills. Good posture keeps you balanced, helps you communicate effectively with the horse, and ensures a more comfortable ride for both of you.

The foundation of correct riding posture starts with your seat. When you're in the saddle, you want to sit tall and balanced, but not stiff – upright and aligned. Your spine should be straight, with your shoulders relaxed and square, and your head up, looking in the direction you want to go. Avoid slouching or leaning too far forward or back, as that can throw off your balance and confuse the horse.

Your legs also play a huge role in your posture. They should hang naturally down the horse's sides, with a slight bend in the knee. Your heels should be down, your toes pointing forward or just slightly out, and the balls of your feet resting lightly in the stirrups. This position helps anchor you in the saddle and gives you a stable base from which to cue the horse with subtle leg pressure.

Your arms should form a soft, bent line from your elbows to the horse's mouth via the reins. Elbows should rest close to your sides, not flared out, and your hands should be steady, but gentle, keeping light contact with the horse's mouth through the bit. Think of holding the reins as if you're holding a small bird; firm enough so it doesn't fly away, but gentle enough not to hurt it. Breathing also plays a role. Riders often tense up without realizing it, especially when they're learning. Keeping your breath smooth and steady helps your body stay relaxed and balanced, which your horse can sense and respond to.

Overall, the correct riding posture is about being aligned, balanced, and relaxed. It creates a conversation between you and the horse through your seat, legs, and hands. It takes time to build muscle memory, but once it clicks, everything starts to feel more natural, and your horse will thank you for it.

THE CORRECT WAY TO HOLD THE REINS

The proper way to hold the reins depends on the style you're riding – English or Western – but the goal is the same: clear, gentle communication with your horse.

If you're riding English, you'll hold a rein in each hand, just like you're holding two ice cream cones – your thumbs should be on top, pointing upward, and the reins should come up through the bottom of your fists and out near your thumbs. Your hands should be about a fist's width apart, and you want them to hover just above and in front of the saddle, not way up high or down by the horse's neck. Keep your wrists straight, your elbows relaxed by your sides, and aim for a light, steady contact – you're not pulling or hanging on the reins, just staying in soft touch with the horse's mouth.

If you're riding Western, it's usually one-handed, with both reins in your non-dominant hand; typically, most riders use their left. You hold the reins low and in front of the saddle horn, and the reins come out of the bottom of your hand, between your pinky and ring finger. Your hand should stay relaxed, and you'll guide the horse mainly through neck reining - so instead of pulling directly on the reins, you're gently laying the rein against the horse's neck to signal turns.

Either way, the key is to stay relaxed, use your fingers more than your arms, and keep an even feel. No tugging, no bracing; just subtle gestures that speak to the horse in a way it can understand.

The Basics of Horseback Riding

Once you're securely in the saddle, this is it - it's time to move. Using a combination of the movements of your hands on the reins and the movement of your legs, you'll begin to communicate your commands to the horse.

FORWARD MOVEMENT

To make the horse go, use your legs. Squeeze gently, or bump your heels, to ask the horse to move forward, and as soon as the horse responds and starts forward, stop kicking and remain conscious of your leg movement. Stay aware of what your legs are doing, because your legs are continually communicating messages to the horse. An inexperienced rider might kick the horse once, sending the horse into a trot, and then the rider will just start bouncing along, not realizing that the legs are constantly hitting the horse and telling the horse to go faster. (Yeah, I've done this before.) One gentle kick is enough, and once the horse responds and moves forward, keep your legs steady until you're ready to pick up speed.

In addition, don't tighten your legs around the horse in an effort to stay in place; you remain in the correct position by keeping your weight centered in the saddle and using your balance. Trying to wrap your legs tightly around the horse will send mixed signals and risk making him uncomfortable - and you don't want to be sitting on top of an uncomfortable horse.

CONTROLLING DIRECTION

To move in the direction you want to go; pull the reins to the left to tell the horse to go left, and you pull the reins to the right to tell the horse to go right. You also use the reins to stop the horse by simply pulling the reins towards you. You don't need to apply much pressure. The correct way to hold the reins is to grab them from the outside, so that you can see the top of your hands. The reins are going from the outside of your hands, from your pinkie area, toward the mouth of the horse, and you hold them where you can take up the slack.

When your forearms are rested in your lap, the slack that goes from your hands to the horse's mouth should be taught. A simple dip in your hand gesture will apply a moderately gentle pressure on the horse's mouth, signaling your command to the horse to go either right or left. You shouldn't need to pull with your arms at all; just this slight change in pressure with the flick of a wrist should be all the horse needs to understand your command.

The same goes for stopping a horse. Applying pressure with both wrists will signal to the horse that it's time to stop. Gentle pressure with a backwards motion with your hands is all you need. Hold that pressure until the horse has obeyed your command, and has come to a complete stop. You should do this in a motion that is gentle but firm.

CONTROLLING SPEED

As we mentioned earlier, you use your legs to achieve forward movement. Bumping your heels or squeezing with your calves gently will communicate to the horse the command to move forward. Once the horse responds and begins to move, you will keep your legs steady until you're ready to pick up speed. As we said; beware of sending mixed signals.

When you're ready for your horse to pick up the pace – whether moving from a walk to a trot, or trot to a canter – the process is all about clear communication with your horse using your body, legs, and maybe your voice.

First, get your body ready. Sit up tall, relaxed but alert, with your shoulders back and your eyes looking where you want to go. You don't want to lean forward dramatically, but allow your posture to tell the horse, *"Hey, we're about to do something."* Next comes your leg cue. Gently squeeze with your calves; not a hard kick, just a firm squeeze. That's your main "go" button. If your horse doesn't respond right away, you can give a little nudge or bump with your heels. Some horses also respond well to a soft kissing sound or a 'click' with your mouth, or even a word like "trot" or "canter" as some horses are trained to respond to voice cues.

Your seat plays a role, too. Let your hips move more actively with the horse's motion, kind of like you're riding the rhythm forward. This tells the horse you're ready for more motion and more energy. At the same time, give the horse just a little more slack on the rein – not dropping the contact entirely, but easing off a bit so they don't feel restricted when they start moving faster.

Once the horse picks up speed, stay balanced, keep your hands steady, and keep riding forward. Don't drop your energy just because the horse has responded; you're still part of the conversation.

Understanding Gaits

If you remember earlier, we used the word '**gait**.' The gait refers to the way a horse moves its legs when it travels, specifically the speed and movement of the animal's feet. Each gait has its own rhythm, speed, and pattern of footfalls, and typically fall into four categories:

The slowest gait is the **walk**. Simply, it's the horse's version of strolling. The walk is a slow, steady, four-beat lateral gait. Four beats implies that all four of the horse's feet move off the ground separately. When one foot is lifted the other three feet are still touching the ground. The horse's front foot will start to move forward, followed by the opposite hind foot, then the other hind foot, and then the other front foot.

The next gait is a little quicker, more brisk, and a little 'bouncier.' The **trot** is a two-beat gait where the diagonal pairs of legs move at the same time. The right front and rear left leg move forward at the same time, and then the front left and the rear right move forward together, and then both the front left leg and the back right leg also move forward together. When you listen to a horse trot you will hear that familiar "clop clop" sound, which indicates two beats. English riders often 'post the trot,' rising up and down with the rhythm to make it more comfortable. *(More on 'posting' shortly.)*

Faster than a trot, but not as fast as a gallop, the **canter** is an asymmetrical three beat gait. If you listen to a horse canter, it sounds as if there are only three hooves hitting the ground. The hind foot hits the ground first, followed by the other hind foot and its opposite front foot together, then the final front foot hits the ground, and then there is an audible pause when all four legs are in the air before the next stride begins.

Finally, the **gallop** is the horse's full-on sprint. It's a four-beat gait and the fastest one, used in racing and when horses are running at top speed. From the saddle, the gallop feels like a stretched-out, more intense version of the canter. Your seat will naturally lift slightly out of the saddle, and your body will lean forward a bit – not in a crouch like a jockey, unless you're actually racing – but enough to go with the horse's motion. You don't want to be bouncing or holding back; your goal is to move fluidly with the horse. It's not a gait you use casually – galloping is usually saved for open fields, cross-country courses, or when you're letting your horse stretch out. Most trail horses or school horses won't go into a gallop unless you really ask for it.

WHAT DO THESE DIFFERENT GAITS MEAN TO THE RIDER?

Depending on how fast – or which gait – the horse is moving, your posture and movements should correspond correctly. The simplest of the gaits is the walk. Good things to keep in mind when you are riding a walk; try not to be stiff and inflexible in the saddle, move your hips back and forwards with the horse's movements, and stay light in your seat. It's at this stage where you want to get comfortable on the horse, learn balance, and practice communicating your commands to the horse.

As a beginner, you should feel confident at the walk before moving on to the trot. Take a moment to evaluate your riding: Are your hips moving with the horse's rhythm? Is your upper body steady but relaxed? Are your arms and legs quiet? Staying relaxed is key, but it's also important to maintain control – your legs shouldn't be bumping the horse unintentionally, and you don't want to pull on the reins unless you mean to. Once you're comfortable with these basic skills, you'll be ready to step up to the trot.

You'll hear the term "posting" when you attempt the trot. **Posting** refers to the action of rising slightly out of the saddle in rhythm with the horse's movement. How high you rise depends on how fast the horse is trotting, but the goal is always the same: to move smoothly with the gait versus just bouncing around in the saddle. You lift yourself up as one diagonal pair of the horse's legs hits the ground, then gently sit back down as the other pair lands. It's a bit like dancing – there's rhythm and timing involved, so it may feel tricky at first. But with practice and patience, it'll start to click.

When riding the canter, your goal is to move with the horse rather than resist or bounce against the motion. You'll want to sit deep in the saddle while allowing your hips to follow the movement, keeping your upper body tall and relaxed. Your legs should stay steady, gently supporting the horse's sides without gripping tightly, and your hands should maintain a soft connection with the reins, following the motion so you don't accidentally pull. Be careful not to tense up when you start to canter. Tensing up or holding your breath could bounce you right out of the saddle. Also, stiffening up could cause you to lean forward, which will signal to most horses to pick up their speed. Remember, the canter doesn't have to be lightning fast; it can be done at a very moderate pace.

When riding the gallop, you'll want to come up into a light, forward position – often called a "half-seat" or "two-point" – where your seat is just out of the saddle and your weight is supported by your legs and stirrups. This helps you stay balanced while allowing the horse's back to move freely. Your upper body should lean slightly forward, but stay relaxed and athletic, not stiff or hunched. Keep your legs steady and gently hugging the horse's sides, and your hands soft but secure – holding the reins with enough contact for control, while allowing the horse to stretch its head and neck to balance. Look ahead to where you're going, not down, and stay calm and balanced as the horse moves beneath you. If the gallop feels too fast, don't panic; use your seat and reins gradually. Over time and with patience you will begin to feel comfortable with all three gaits and you will be well on your way to becoming an experienced rider.

Stopping the Horse

Of course, if you're about to unleash the full power of a horse, allowing it to race at a full-blown gallop, you'd better be sure you know how to 'rein it in' and stop when the time comes.

As we said earlier, gentle pressure applied to the reins will signal to the horse to stop. Be sure to let go of the reins as soon as the horse comes to a stop, as continuing to apply pressure after the horse has stopped sends a mixed message. You will learn over time that you can use your body to communicate these commands to the horse as well. For example, as you are riding you will try to be light in the saddle, but when you want to come to a complete stop, just sit heavy in the saddle and the horse will generally understand what this means. With enough experience, over time you will eventually be using your entire body to communicate your wishes to the horse.

The Dismount

First, make sure your horse is standing still and calm. Bring them to a complete stop, either at the mounting block or another safe area. Give them a moment to settle if needed – no one wants to dismount a fidgety horse.

Take both feet out of the stirrups. This is important – trying to dismount with a foot still in a stirrup is how people end up tangled or dragged if the horse moves unexpectedly. Hold both reins in one hand (the hand closest to the horse's neck) with just enough contact to keep control – don't yank or pull, but be ready in case the horse decides to move. Some riders also grab a bit of mane or rest their hand on the pommel for balance. Take your other hand and place it on the back of the saddle (the cantle).

Then swing your right leg up and over the horse's back in one smooth motion. Be careful not to kick the horse's rump – just lift high and clear. Once both legs are on the same side, gently hop down and land with your knees slightly bent to absorb the impact, landing softly and staying balanced. Still holding the reins, step slightly away from the horse's side to give them space. Then give your horse a pat and say 'thank you.'

With that, you have just completed your first riding lesson. With a little bit of time and experience you will be able to ride a horse any time and in any part of the world.

Building Your Confidence

As with any other Bond-related activity, you're bound to feel like a novice in the beginning, and your nerves may get the better of you. This is particularly true with an activity like horseback riding, which brings the potential for injury. Working on your confidence is a crucial part of the journey, and honestly, every rider – no matter how experienced – deals with confidence ups and downs at some point. Here are a few points to help you stay comfortable and self-assured.

OVERCOMING FEARS AND NERVES

It's totally normal to feel nervous, especially in the beginning. Horses are big, powerful animals, and riding asks a lot of your body and your focus. The key is not to ignore your fears, but to acknowledge them and work with them, one step at a time. Start small; get comfortable just being around horses, then gradually move into grooming, leading, and eventually riding. Celebrate little wins. Every step you take with calmness and intention builds trust with the horse – and with yourself.

PRACTICING GROUNDWORK AND BONDING

Before you even get in the saddle, spending time on the ground with your horse can do wonders for your confidence. Grooming, walking, or simply hanging out with your horse builds a connection. Horses are incredibly intuitive – they pick up on your energy – so if you're calm and kind, they'll respond to that. Groundwork exercises like leading, stopping, turning, and yielding to pressure help establish respect and communication, and it gives you a sense of control and partnership.

This is huge. Don't rush your progress just to "keep up." Go at a pace that feels right for you, even if that means repeating the basics. A solid foundation makes everything else easier and safer. Some days will feel amazing; other days might shake your confidence, and that's okay. Keep showing up, stay curious, and lean on instructors or fellow riders who support and encourage you. Over time, you'll realize you're not just riding a horse – you're growing braver and more capable in the process.

Safety and Etiquette

When it comes to horseback riding, safety always comes first for both the rider and the horse. Let's recap: wearing a properly fitted helmet is non-negotiable, regardless of your experience level. Sturdy boots with a small heel help keep your feet from slipping through the stirrups, and gloves can offer extra grip and protect your hands. Before mounting, always double-check your tack (the saddle, girth, and bridle) to make sure everything is secure and in good condition. Stay alert to your surroundings, especially in busy arenas or on trails, and remember: horses are animals with their own thoughts and reactions. Staying calm, balanced, and attentive goes a long way toward avoiding accidents.

Riding etiquette is about respect for both for other riders and for the horses. In group settings, like riding arenas, it's important to follow basic right-of-way rules. Typically, riders going in opposite directions pass left shoulder to left shoulder, and those riding faster gaits stay to the outside track. Always announce your intentions clearly and politely if you're passing another rider or changing direction. (Your instructor will go over all of this.) Keep a safe distance between horses, as some can be reactive or nervous when another horse crowds their space. And when you're not riding, don't walk too closely behind a horse, as they can kick if startled.

Above all, good etiquette means being a thoughtful partner to your horse. Approach them calmly, speak softly, and move with purpose. Don't yank on the reins or use your legs too harshly. Communication with a horse should always be about guidance, not force. Reward them with gentle praise and pats when they respond well, and always end your ride on a positive note, even if it's something as simple as a smooth halt. A respectful, safety-conscious rider helps build trust and ensures that every ride – no matter how casual or challenging – is a positive experience for everyone involved.

Where to Learn

Whew! With all that under your belt, the next thing to do is find a stable that offers riding lessons, which is a pretty simple process.

Start by searching for riding schools, stables, or equestrian centers in your area. Check Google or even local Facebook groups to see what's nearby. Look for places with good reviews, a professional-looking website, and clear information about the types of lessons they offer. Many will offer beginner programs, and some may specialize in English or Western styles of riding. It's also worth checking if they're affiliated with any national riding organizations, like the United States Pony Clubs (USPC) or Certified Horsemanship Association (CHA), which can be a sign of quality instruction.

Once you have a few options, reach out to schedule a visit. A good barn will be happy to show you around, introduce you to an instructor, and answer your questions. Pay attention to the condition of the horses and facilities, the vibe of the place, and whether the instructors seem patient, knowledgeable, and enthusiastic. Ask about group versus private lessons, what kind of gear you'll need, and how they match students with horses. Trust your instincts—if the place feels safe, welcoming, and well-run, you're likely in good hands.

Further Reading

The resources I used for this chapter are *"The Complete Idiot's Guide to Horseback Riding"* by Jessica Jahiel PhD, also *"The Everything Horseback Riding"* book by Cheryl Kimble and *"Illustrated Horseback Riding for Beginners"* by Jeanne Mellin. Last but not least, I couldn't have put this together without a lot of help and guidance from Sandy Shepherd, lifestyle trainer and author of *"Fempowerment: Unleashing Your Inner Bond Girl,"* as well as a skilled equestrian.

So whether you're calmly learning to post the trot, or thundering across open ground in a full gallop, remember that every skill you build in the saddle brings you closer to mastery – not just of horseback riding, but of yourself. The journey takes patience, practice, and a bit of humility, but the rewards are as great as the adventures that await you. After all, whether you're chasing down that steeplechase rival, or catching the eye of a mysterious beauty riding along the surf, you'll want to ride with skill, confidence, and style. This is more than a hobby – it's part of the life you were meant to lead. So tighten your girth, square your shoulders, and ride on.

Good luck and happy trails.

CONCLUSION

So where do we go from here?

Hopefully, by this point, you have been given plenty to keep you engaged. If **Being James Bond** can convince you of anything, it's that nothing we've explored here – nothing James Bond can do – is beyond your reach.

Begin by taking one topic from this book, really get into it, and make it your own. Get into a poker game, make yourself a proper martini, get ready for ski season, or look into taking a flying lesson. Then be sure to subscribe to the **Being James Bond** podcast, and head over to **being-jamesbond.com** to stay up to date on what's new and exciting. And be sure to check us out on social media: Facebook, Instagram, LinkedIn, etc.

A few more thoughts before I leave you. I'm a big fan of *"The 4-Hour Workweek"* by Tim Ferriss. If you haven't already read it, I highly recommend it. In the book, Tim Ferris suggests that most adults are suffering from a different type of ADD; Adult-onset Adventure Deficit. And I couldn't agree more!

He goes on to say – it's not enough to strive to be happy; in fact, he can make you rethink the very concept of happiness. He says that sadness is not the opposite of happiness, in the same way that hate is not the opposite of love (the true opposite of love is indifference) – instead, happiness and sadness are simply two sides of the same coin.

Ferriss takes this concept one step further. He suggests that the true polar opposite of happiness is boredom.

For me, James Bond was never about imitation (although imitation can be a lot of fun), but rather, James Bond is about inspiration. A fascination with the James Bond films is more than just an escape from the everyday; it's a calling to experience as much as you can out of life.

Life is serious enough. It's more important than ever to hold on to a sense of wonder and a thirst for adventure. The older I get, the more convinced I am that you owe it to yourself and the people you love to live your most authentic self.

I thank you for joining me. Congratulations on accepting this mission, and making the adventure a part of your life. I think you will find that the world is truly not enough.

Being James Bond will return.

Afterward to
the Second Edition

What a difference fifteen years makes!

In the original edition of this book, I concluded by directing read-ers over to the Being James Bond website, and to the forum section, which at the time had exploded into a great place for like-minded people to share their passions, ask questions, and discuss their plans for the future. A few of my favorite threads were '*What have you done Bond today?*,' '*The Essence of Bond,*' '*Wine Pairings Made Easy,*' '*The Perfect Shave,*' and '*The Cocktails of Bond.*'

Each of the various sections was represented on the message boards; *Bond the Sportsman, Gambling, The Good Life, etc.,* so folks could discuss any James Bond-related topic, including the topics we cov-ered in *Volume One.* To just chat about your favorite Bond films and books, there were the *Cinematic James Bond* and *Literary James Bond* forums, or you might just head over to *The Martini Lounge* if you wanted to meet and greet with your fellow 'Bonds-in-training' about any subject, Bond-related or otherwise.

At that time, the message boards were robust, boasting hundreds of members, and tens of thousands of posts.

Then, social media came along, and everything started to change. People had moved over to Facebook, and then YouTube, and then Instagram. Soon, there was the emergence of the term *"influencer."*

We're now flooded with familiar faces, all discussing the different aspects of James Bond, from the broadest subjects to the tiniest of niches. It's easier than ever to get involved with the larger discussion, and to chat with like-minded people.

So today, how do you up your game? Go to a 'Gatherall.'

I really have to hand it to David Zaritsky. Not only did he become the powerhouse among James Bond influencers in a relatively short time, but he's also done something that I think is his true opus; he's created regular in-person events for Bond fans to meet and greet and socialize. They started out much more modest – they weren't exactly 'official' events; it was more like, *"Hey, a few of us will be at this bar at this date and time, so please feel free to join us."* Since then, they've exploded and become the hottest ticket in town, attracting hundreds of attendees, and from all around the world. Not only has David really made these events special by finding interesting venues and throwing in different contests and challenges, but he's also managed to attract brand ambassadors, and even Bond actresses to attend these gatherings. They've truly become the stuff of legend.

When you're ready to move even further, and truly walk in the footsteps of Bond, I highly recommend some world travel. Martijn Mulder, the author of *'On the Tracks of 007'* which I recommended multiple times in this book, puts together amazing trips to places that James Bond has been to. If you read my section on Piz Gloria in the Skiing chapter, highlighting the various spots we visited in Switzerland, then you know how strongly I feel that Martijn does an amazing job with his trips. You get to travel the world, see some of the iconic locations that helped make you a fan, and probably meet people involved with the films along the way.

Regardless of what our next step looks like: start slow. Pick one of the topics in this book, make that skill your own, and get into the conversation. You'll find that the people in the James Bond Community are some of the nicest you'll ever meet. Don't be shy. I talk to people who are considering attending a Gatherall for the first time, but they're a little nervous that they don't know anyone. I always say the same thing, "Just get in the door." By the time you leave, you'll have a laundry list of new friends! Thank you for making this community, and this experience, one of the most wonderful parts of my life!

And thank you again for purchasing and reading *'Being James Bond: Volume One - Second Edition.'* This new edition has been a joy to revisit and expand. I hope it speaks to you, inspires you, and brings a bit of Bond-like confidence to your own adventures. Enjoy the journey.

Once again, *'Being James Bond, Volume Two'* is just around the corner.

Joseph W. Darlington